Twice Shy

By
Joel Orff

ALTERNATIVE COMICS

D1309707

Twice Shy

Published by Alternative Comics

Cupertino, CA 95014

website: www.indyworld.com

This book is a work of fiction. The characters,
incidents and dialogue are drawn from the
author's imagination and are not to be
construed as real. Any resemblance to actual
events or person, living or dead, is entirely
coincidental.

Published in 2019

ISBN 978168148606 2

Digital edition
ISBN 978168148607 9

joelorff@gmail.com www.jorff.com

Also by Joel Orff from Alternative Comics

Strum and Drang #1
Strum and Drang - Great Moments in Rock 'n' Roll
Waterwise
Thunderhead Underground Falls

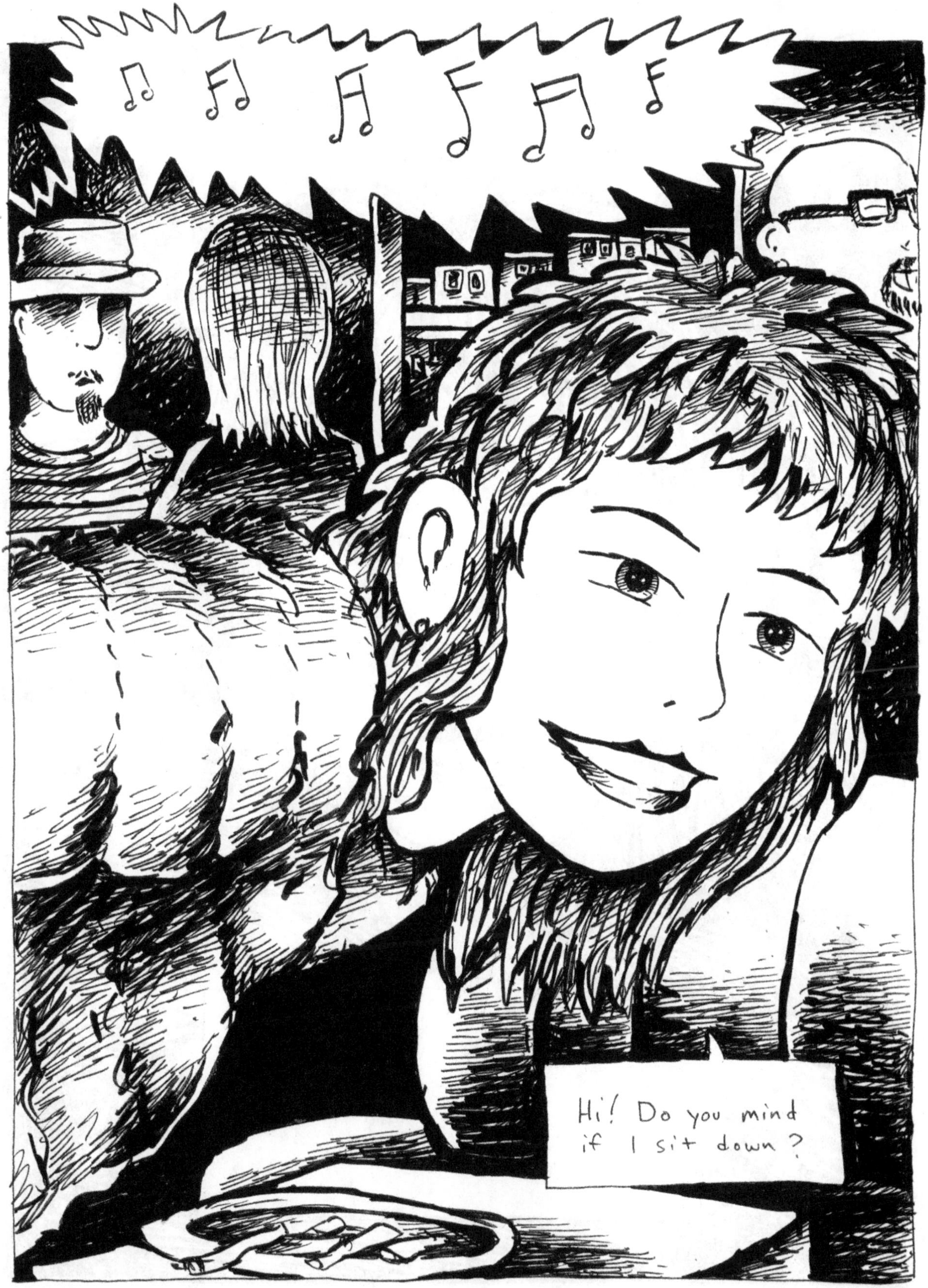
Hi! Do you mind if I sit down?

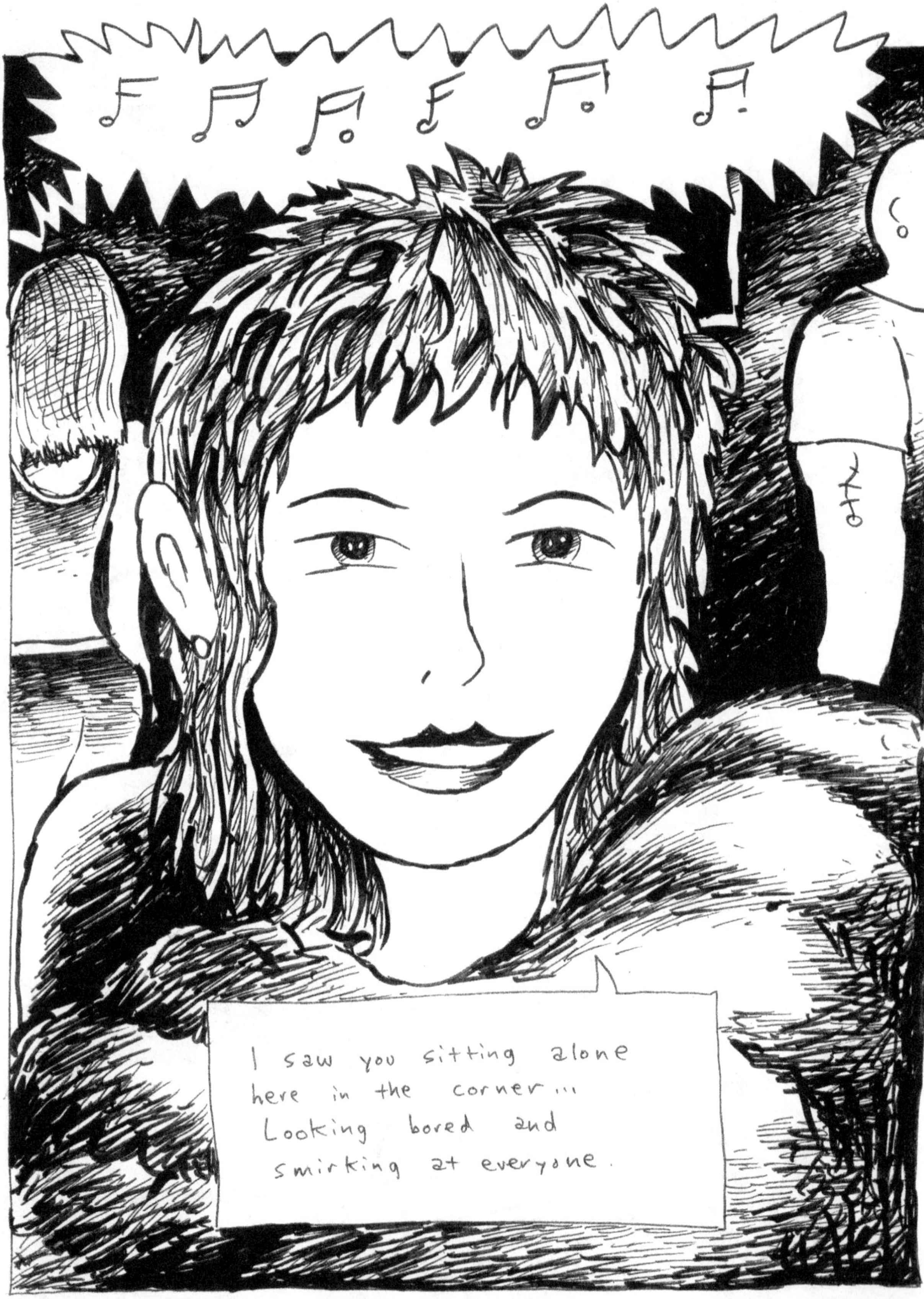
I saw you sitting alone here in the corner... Looking bored and smirking at everyone.

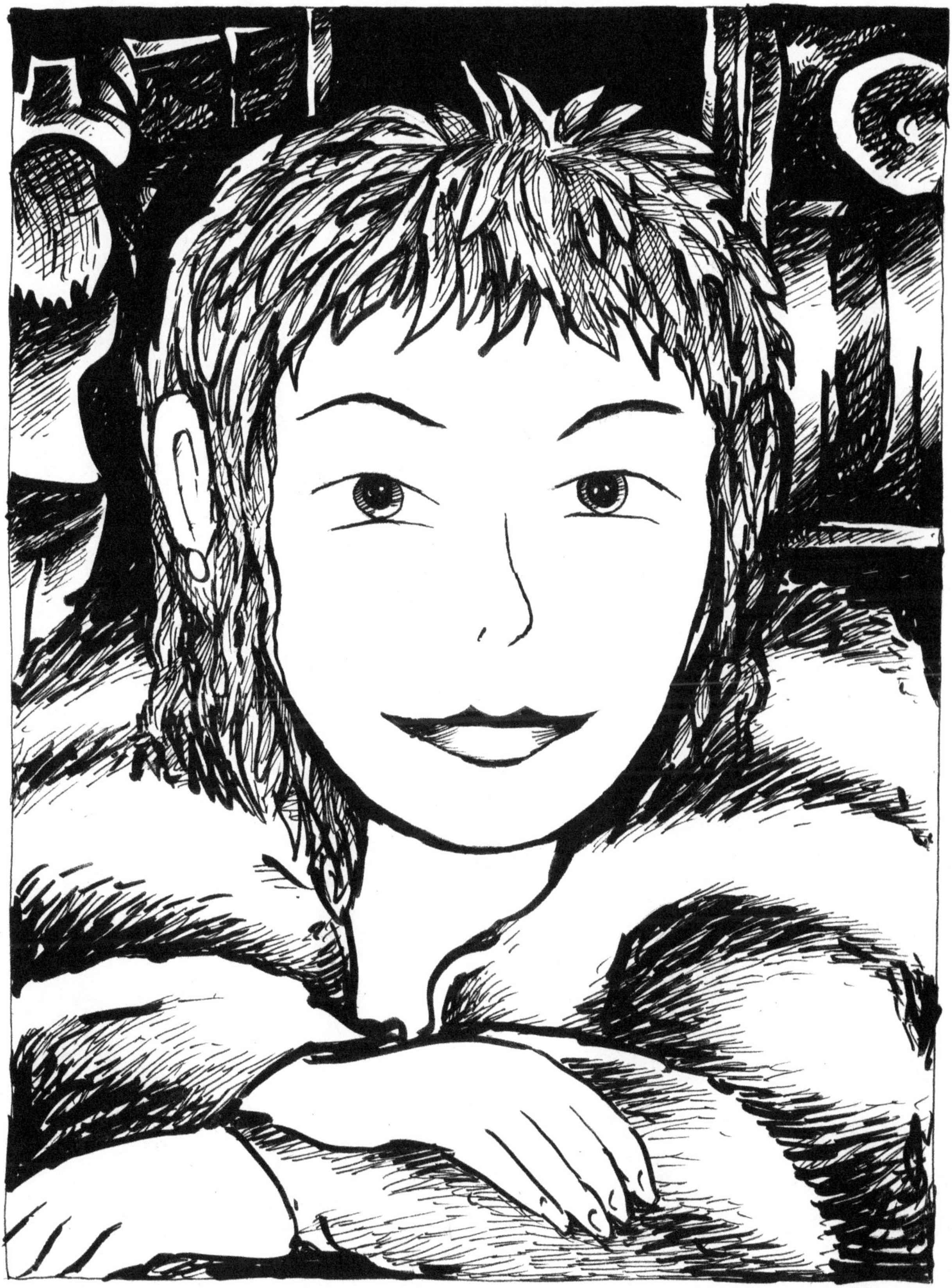

Many years later

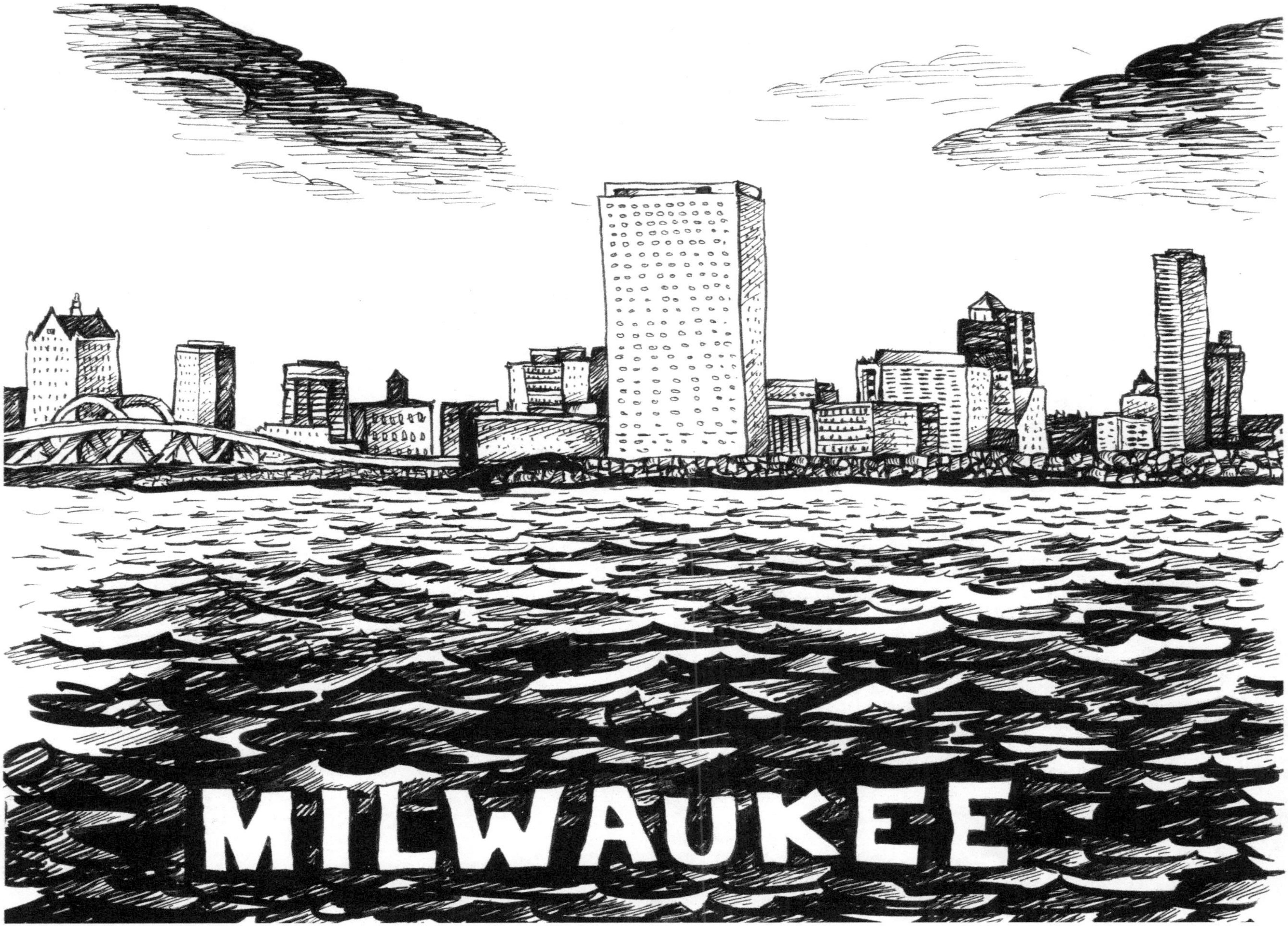
MILWAUKEE

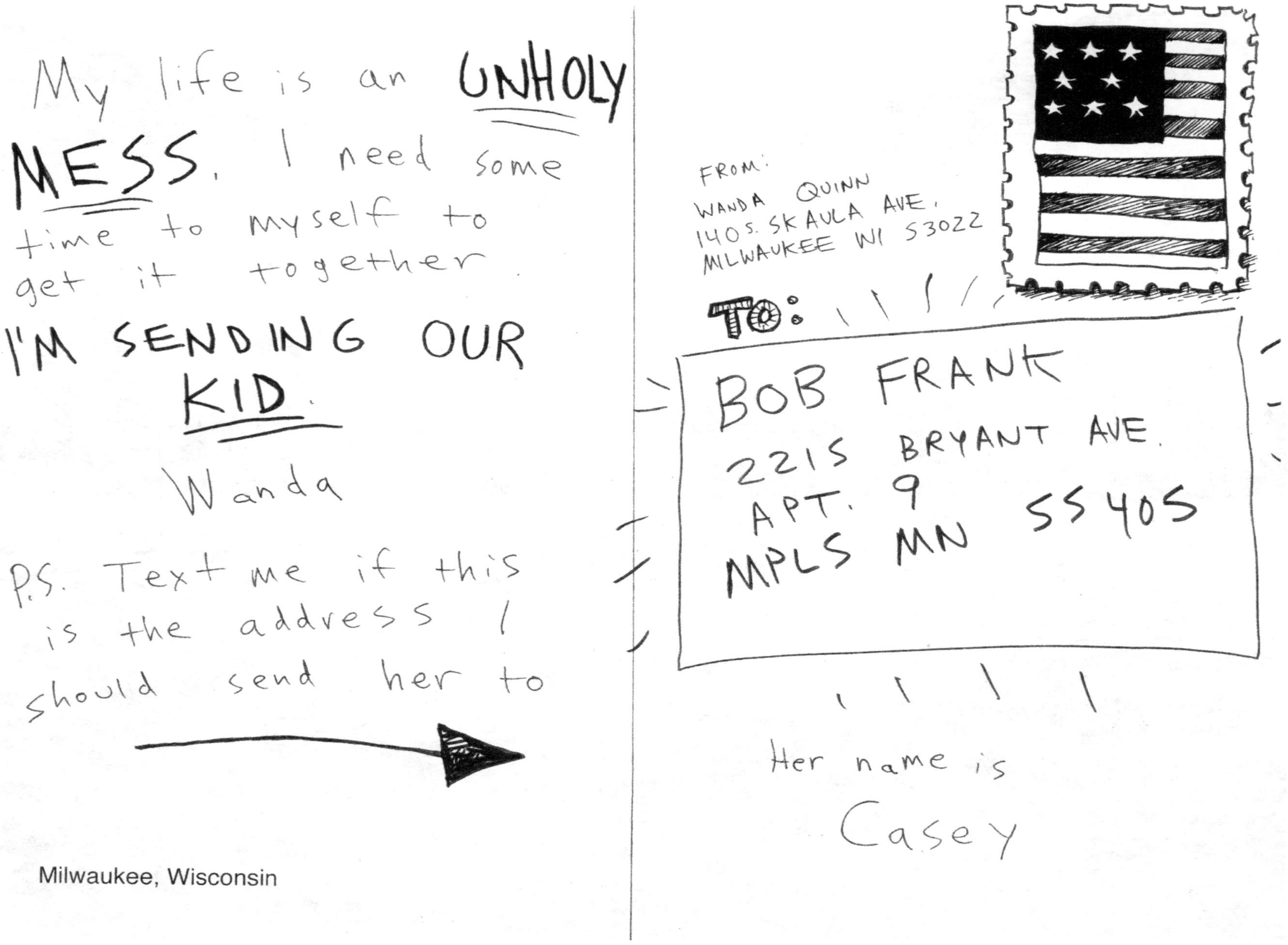
My life is an UNHOLY MESS. I need some time to myself to get it together.
I'M SENDING OUR KID.
Wanda
P.S. Text me if this is the address I should send her to
Milwaukee, Wisconsin
FROM:
WANDA QUINN
140 S. SKAULA AVE.
MILWAUKEE WI 53022
TO:
BOB FRANK
2215 BRYANT AVE.
APT. 9
MPLS MN 55405
Her name is Casey

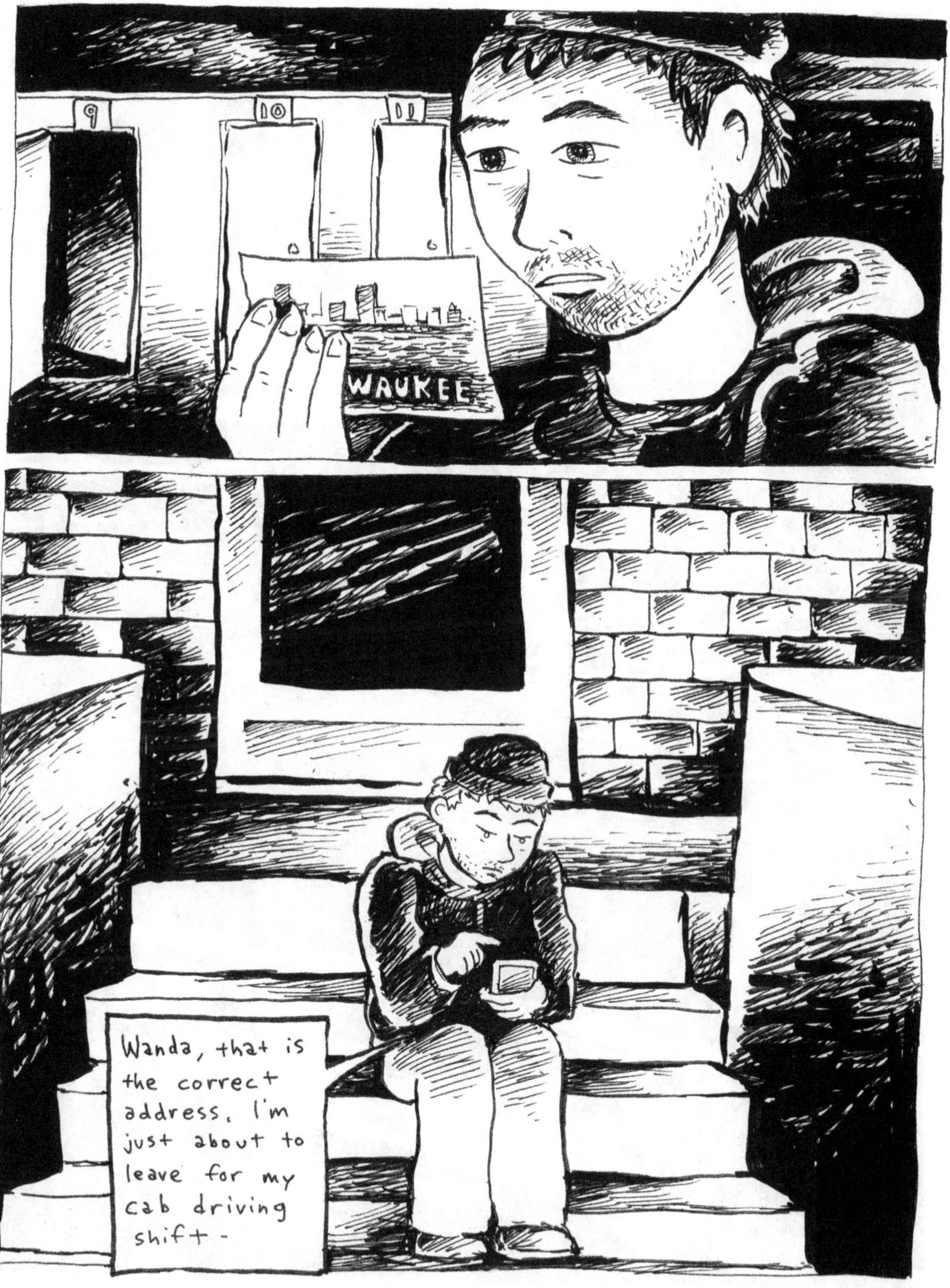
WAUKEE
Wanda, that is the correct address, I'm just about to leave for my cab driving shift -

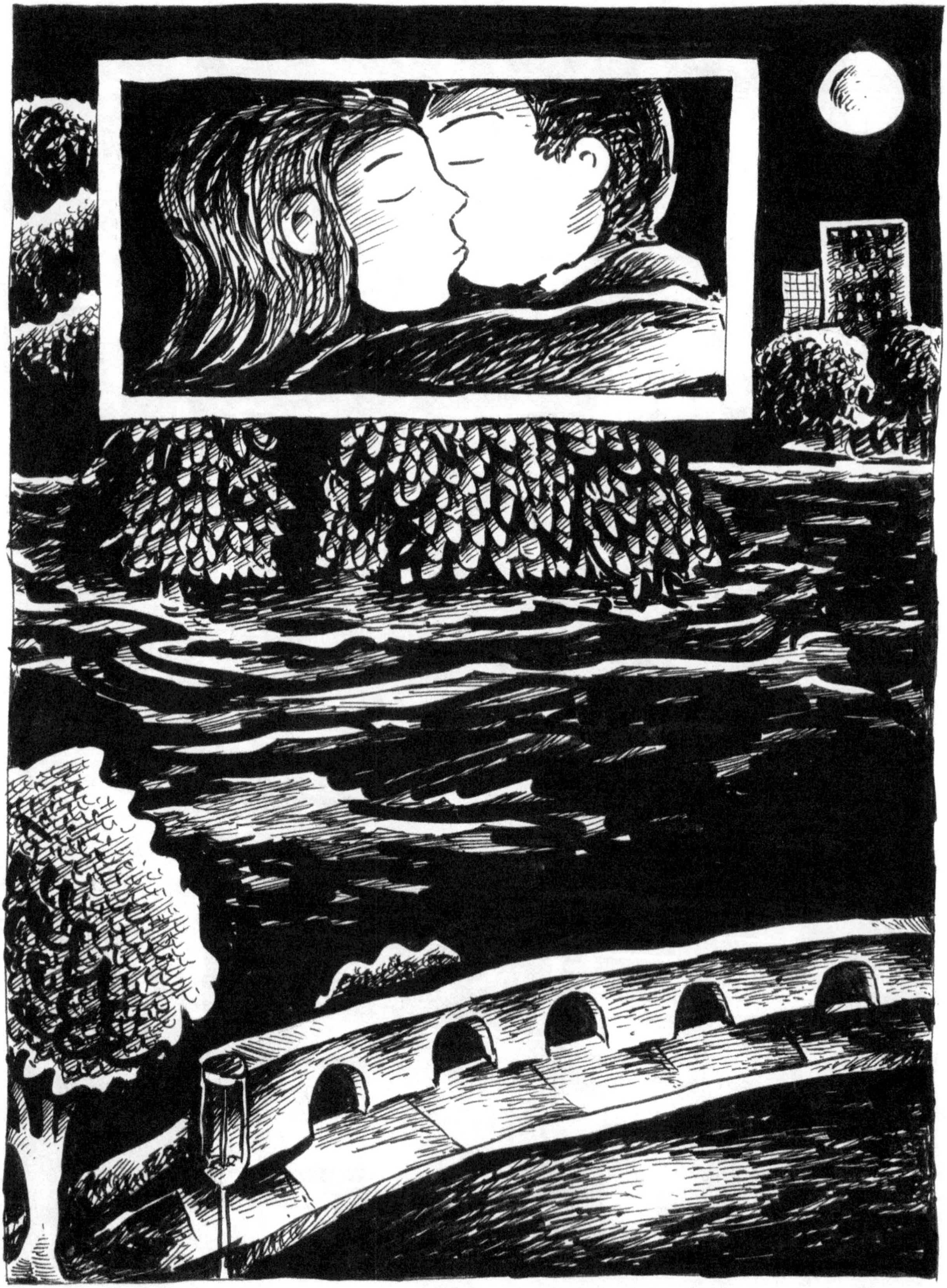

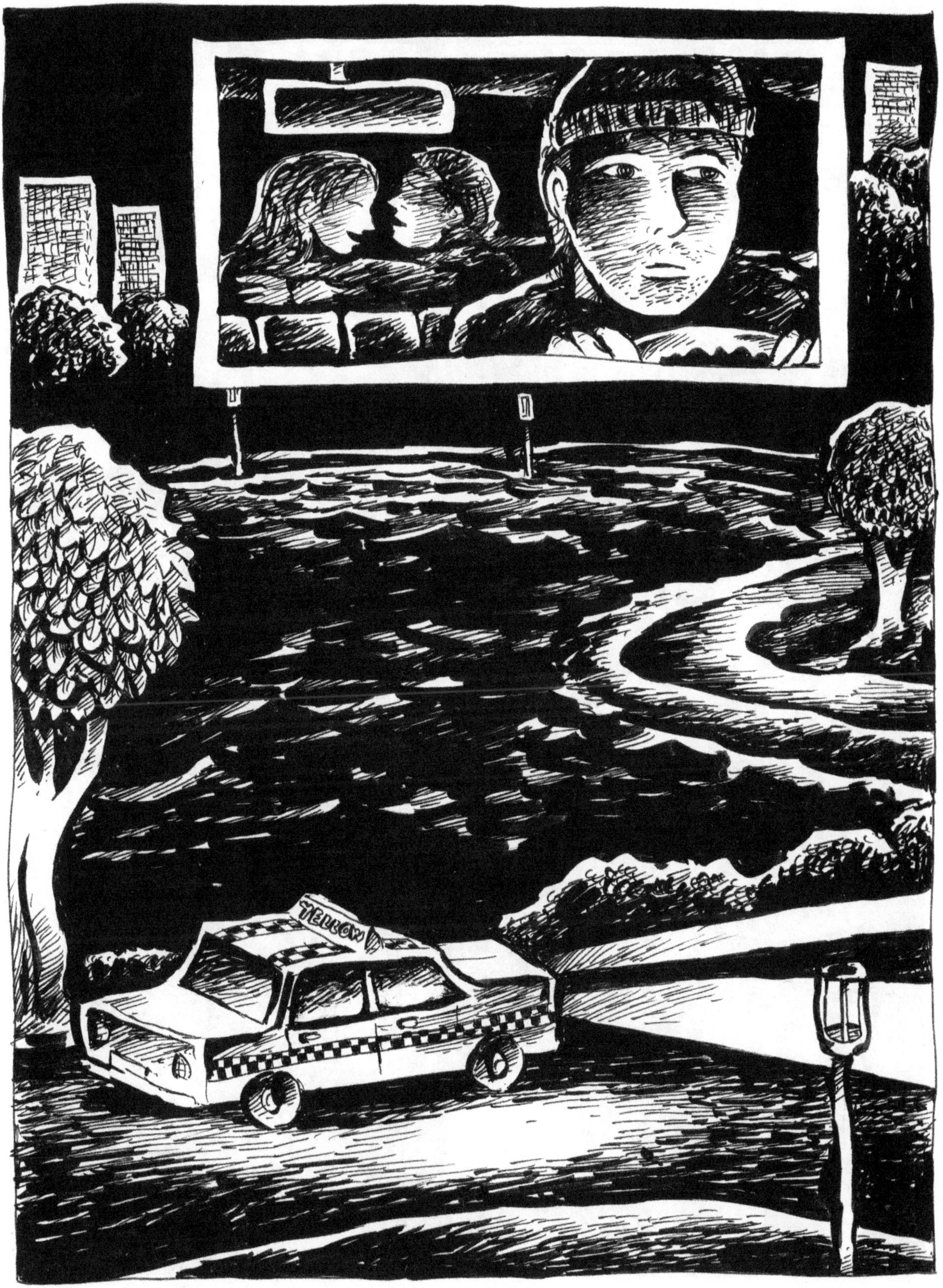
YELLOW

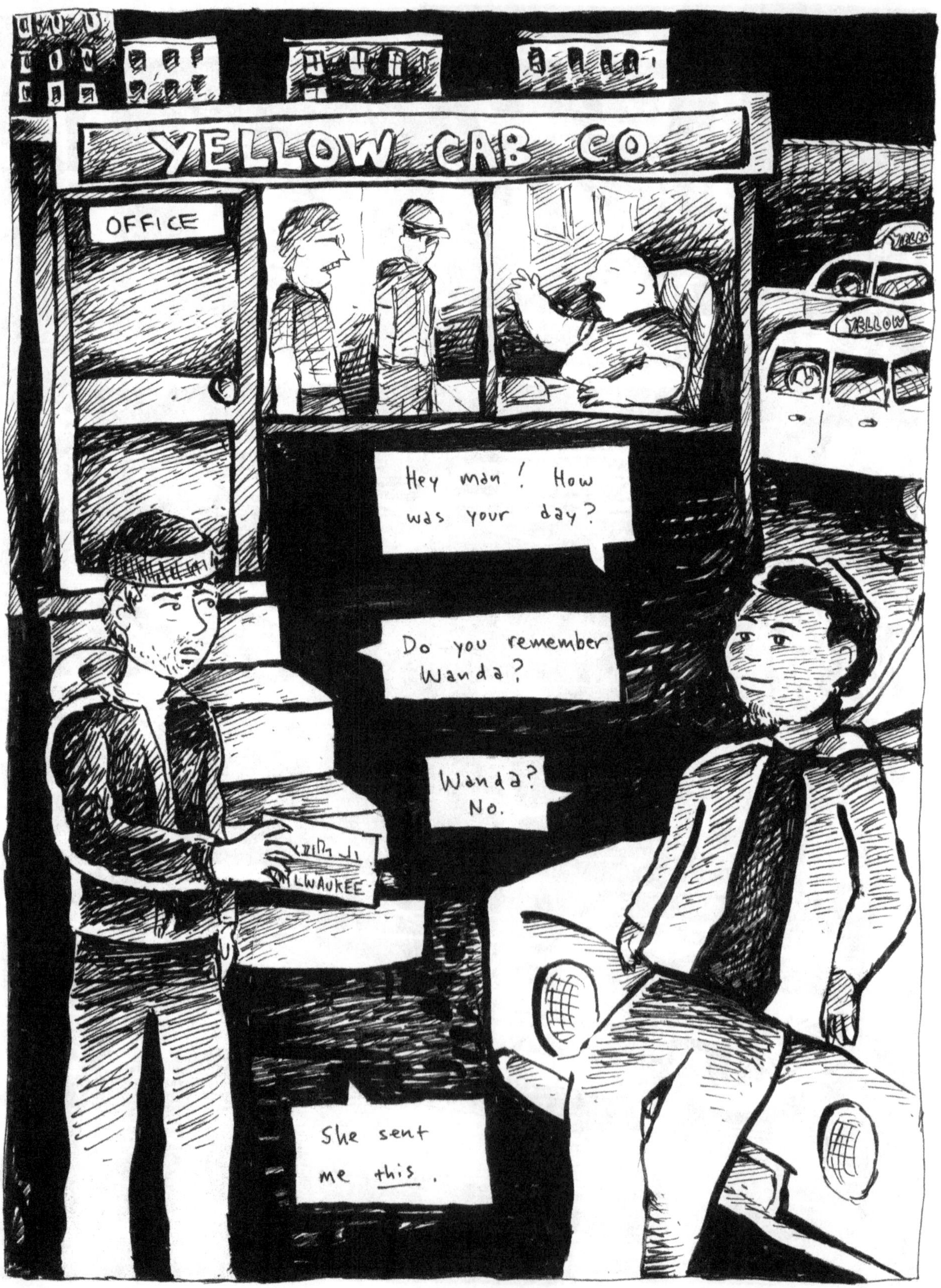
YELLOW CAB CO.
OFFICE
YELLOW
Hey man! How was your day?
Do you remember Wanda?
Wanda? No.
She sent me this.
MILWAUKEE

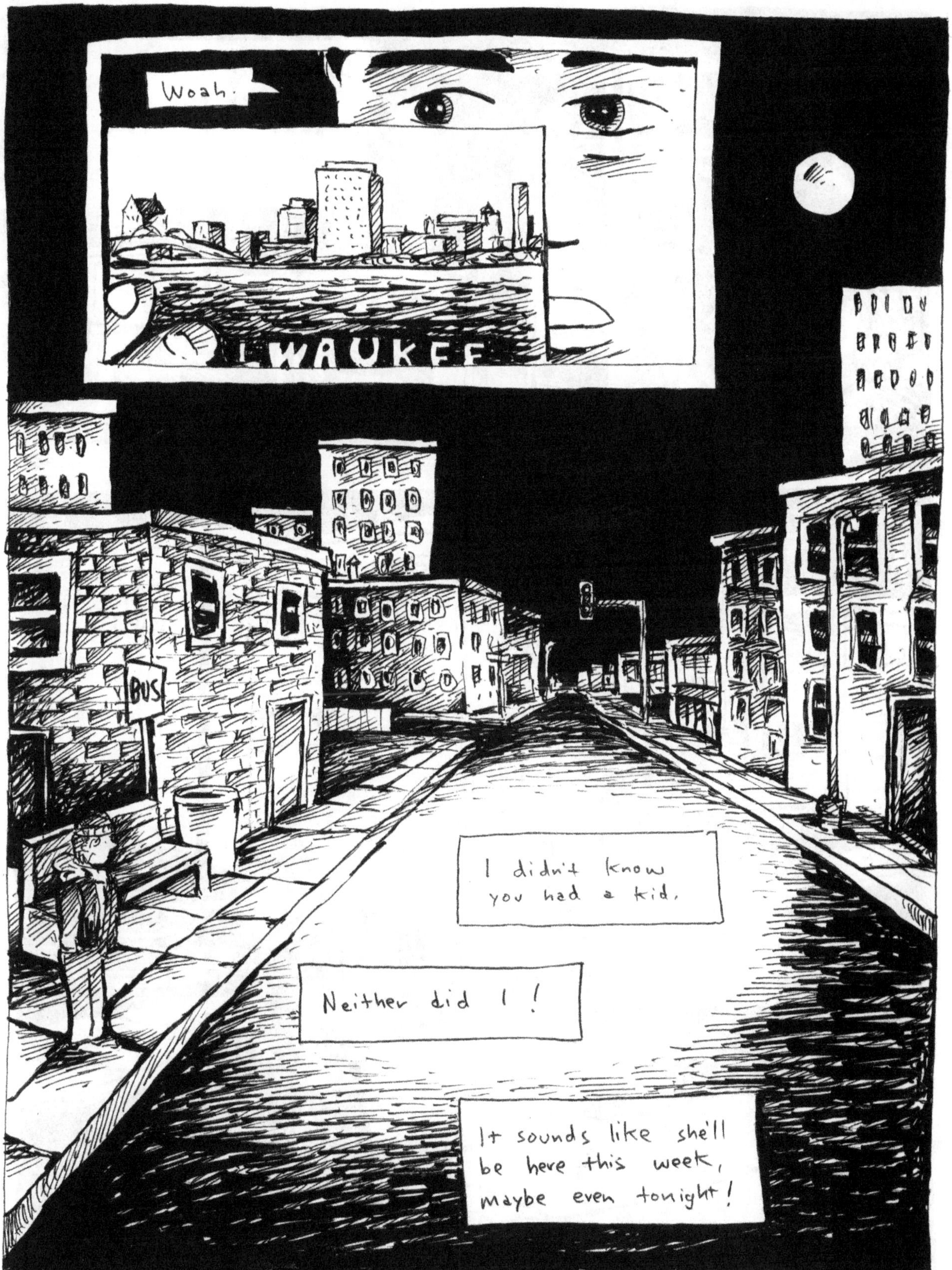
Woah.
LWAUKEE
BUS
I didn't know you had a kid.
Neither did I!
It sounds like she'll be here this week, maybe even tonight!

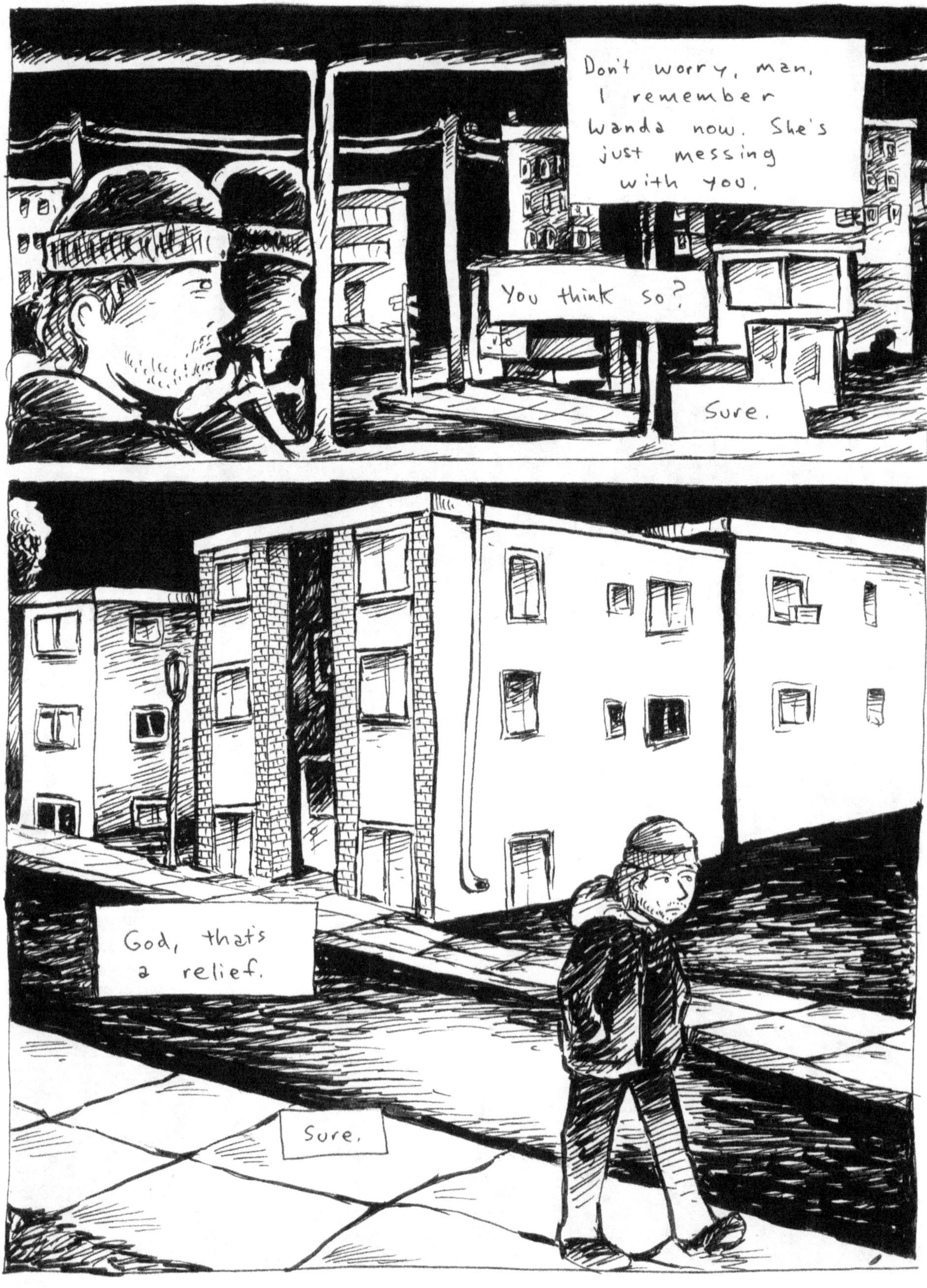
Don't worry, man. I remember Wanda now. She's just messing with you.
You think so?
Sure.
God, that's a relief.
Sure.

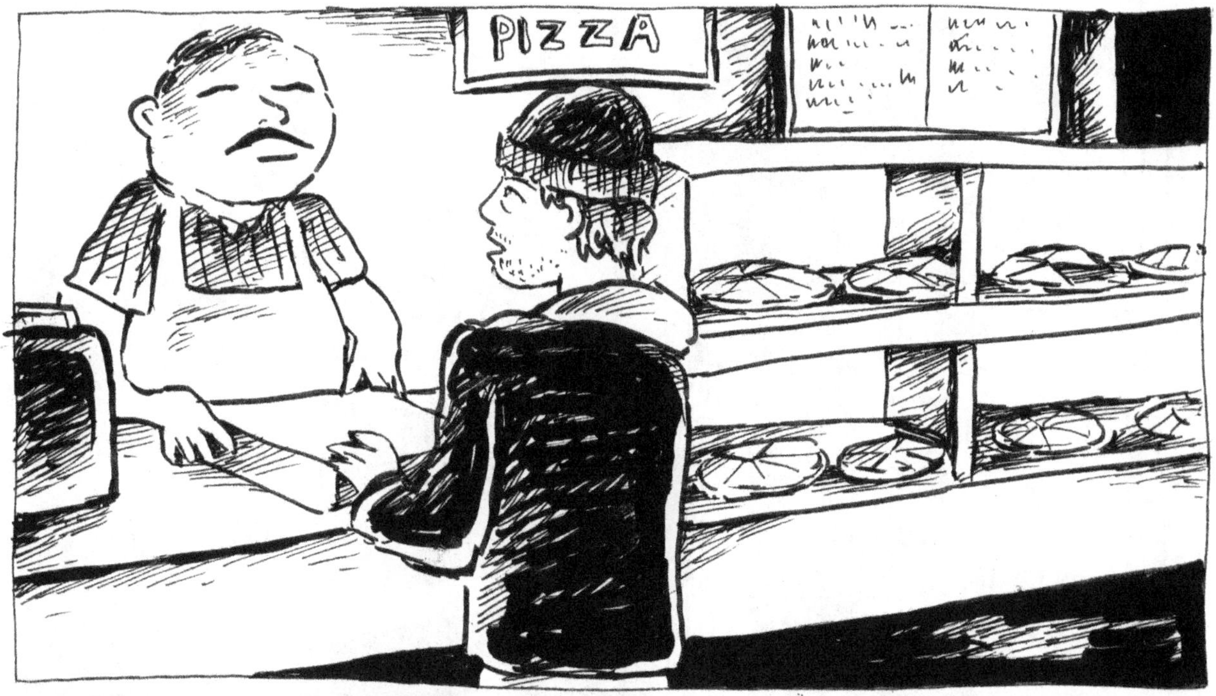
PIZZA

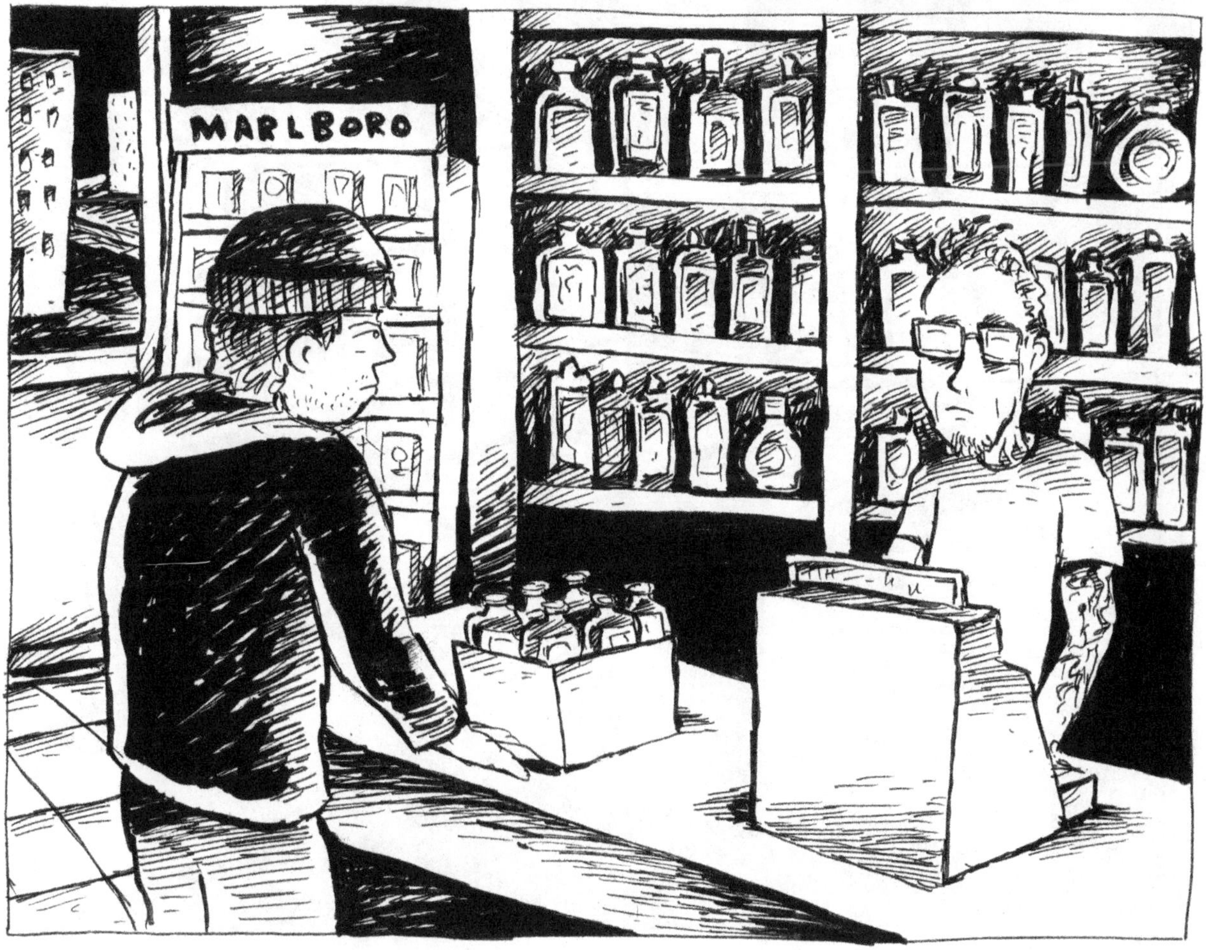
MARLBORO

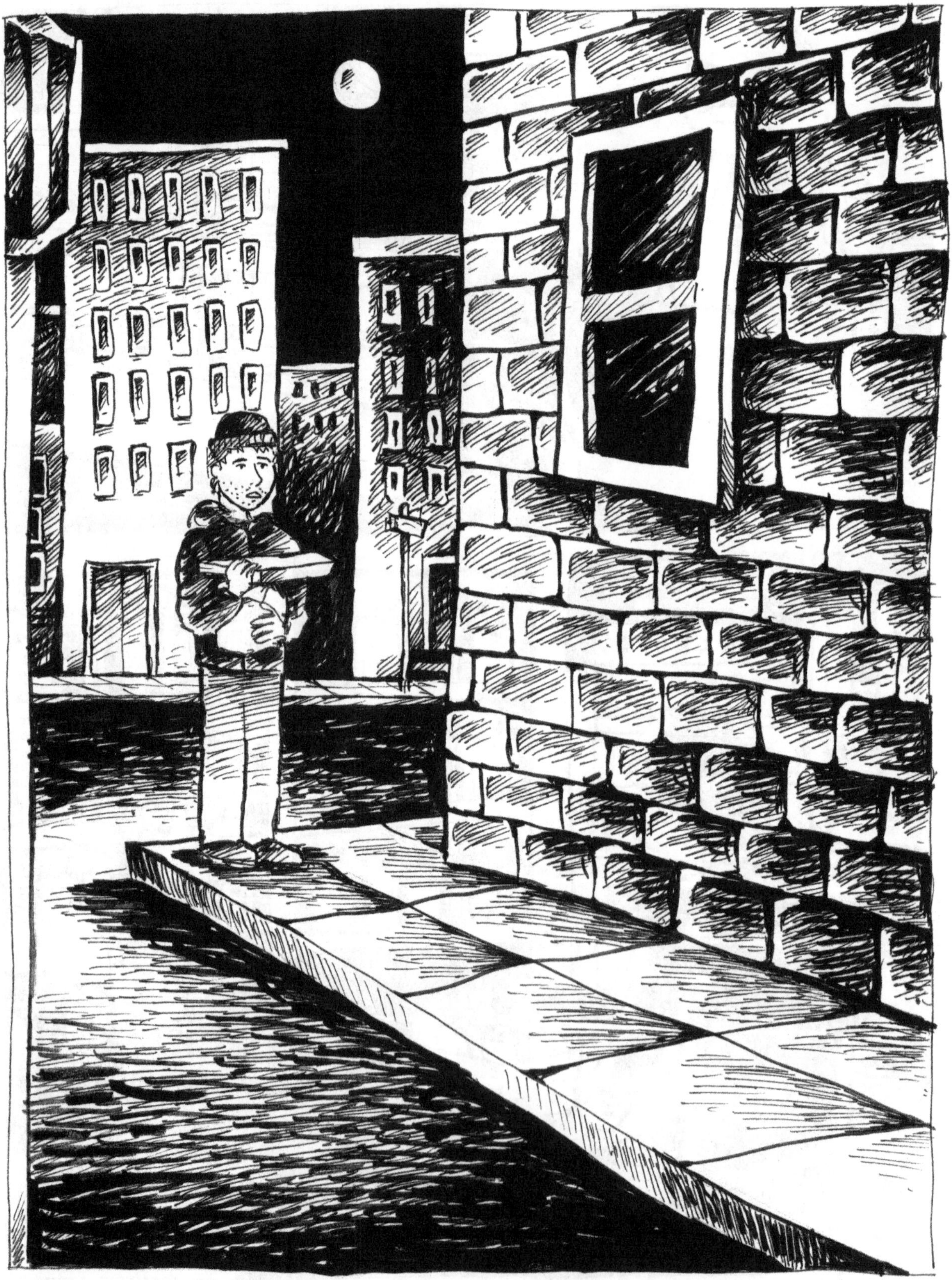

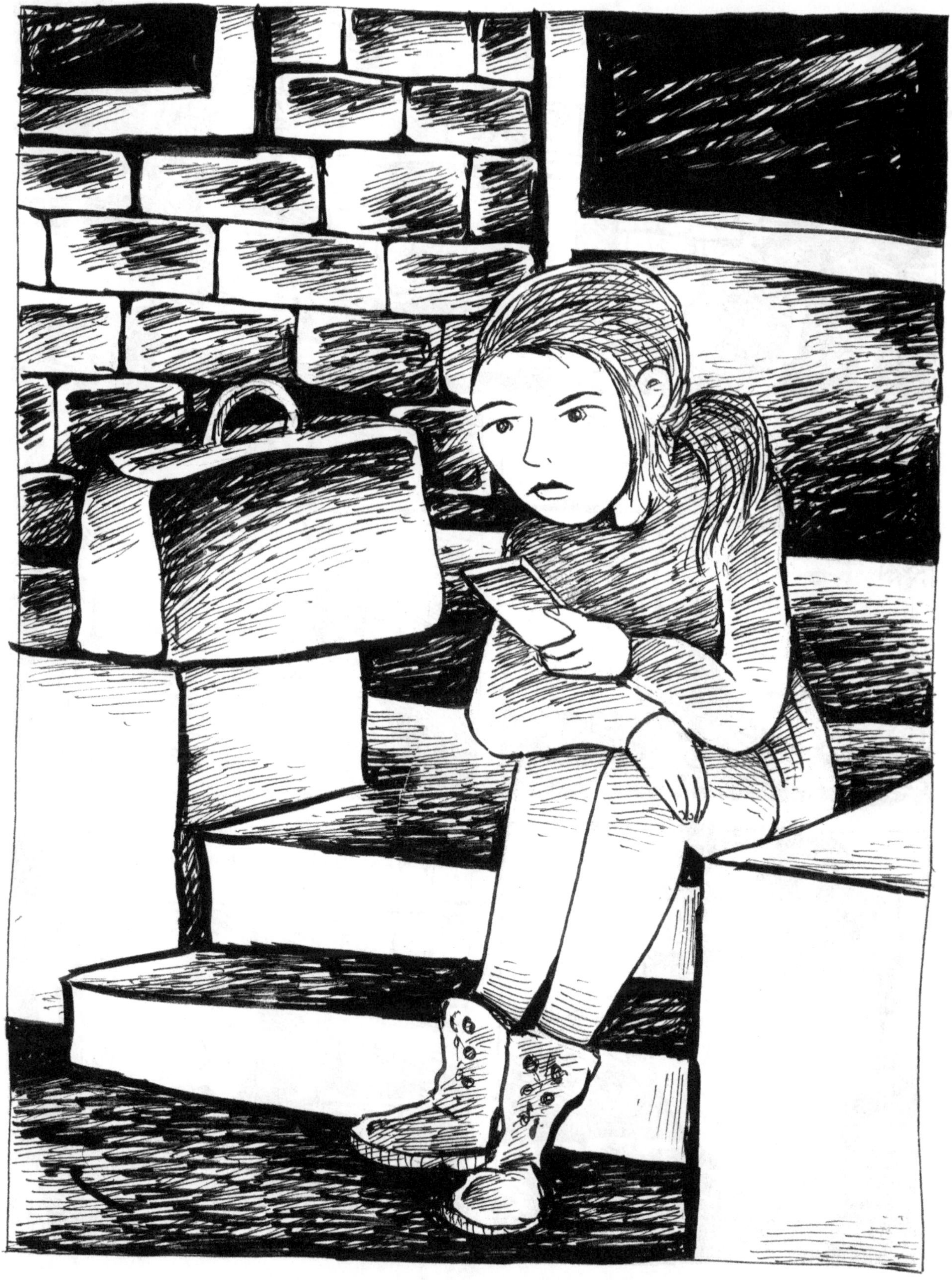

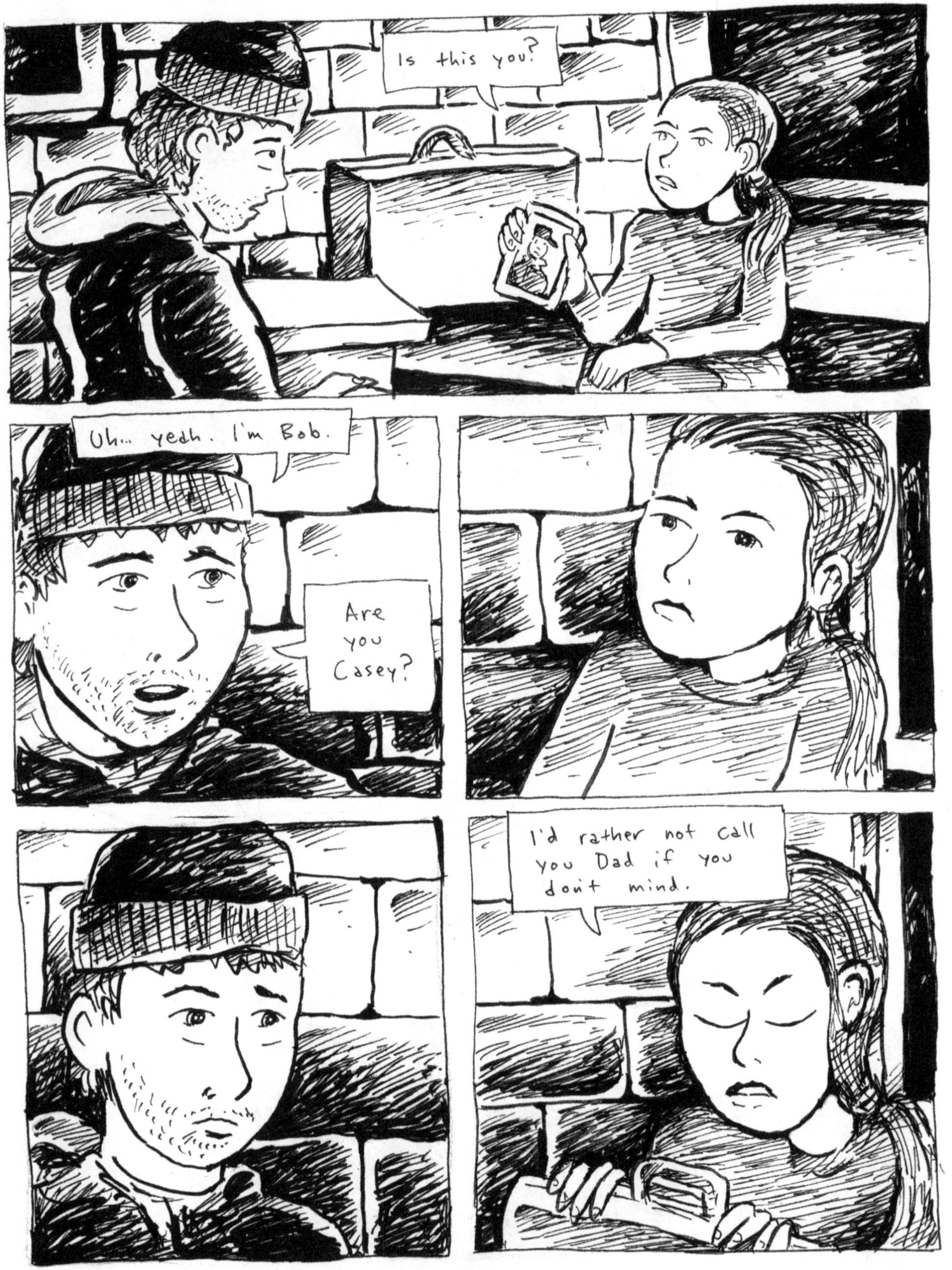
Is this you?
Uh... yeah. I'm Bob.
Are you Casey?
I'd rather not call you Dad if you don't mind.

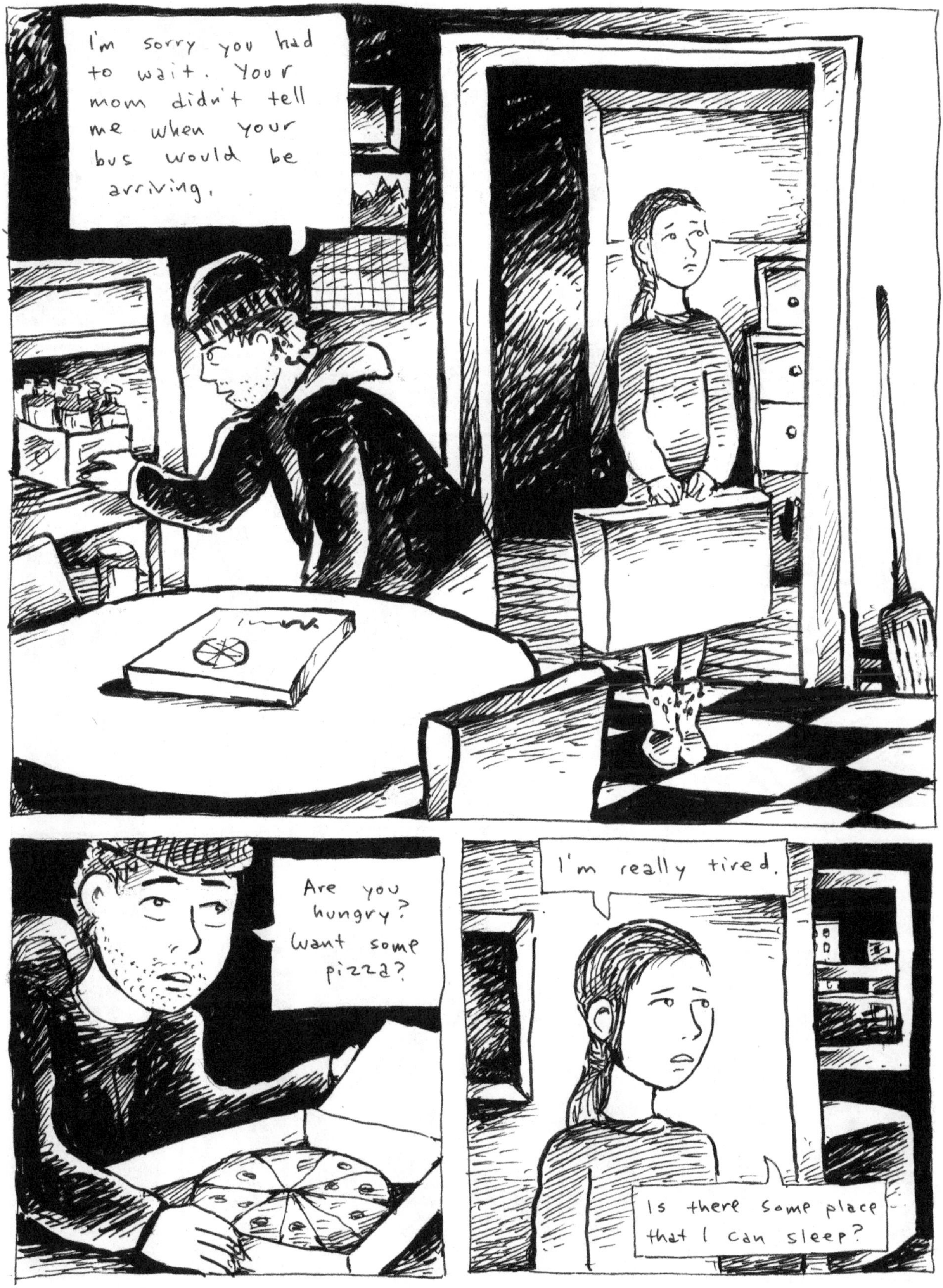
I'm sorry you had to wait. Your mom didn't tell me when your bus would be arriving.
Are you hungry? Want some pizza?
I'm really tired.
Is there some place that I can sleep?

Sure, you can have the bed. I'll crash on the couch.

Okay?

You know... this wasn't my idea. Mom made me do it.

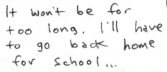

It won't be for too long. I'll have to go back home for school...

Hey...

Don't worry. Stay as long as you like.

I'm really glad to have you here.

Really.

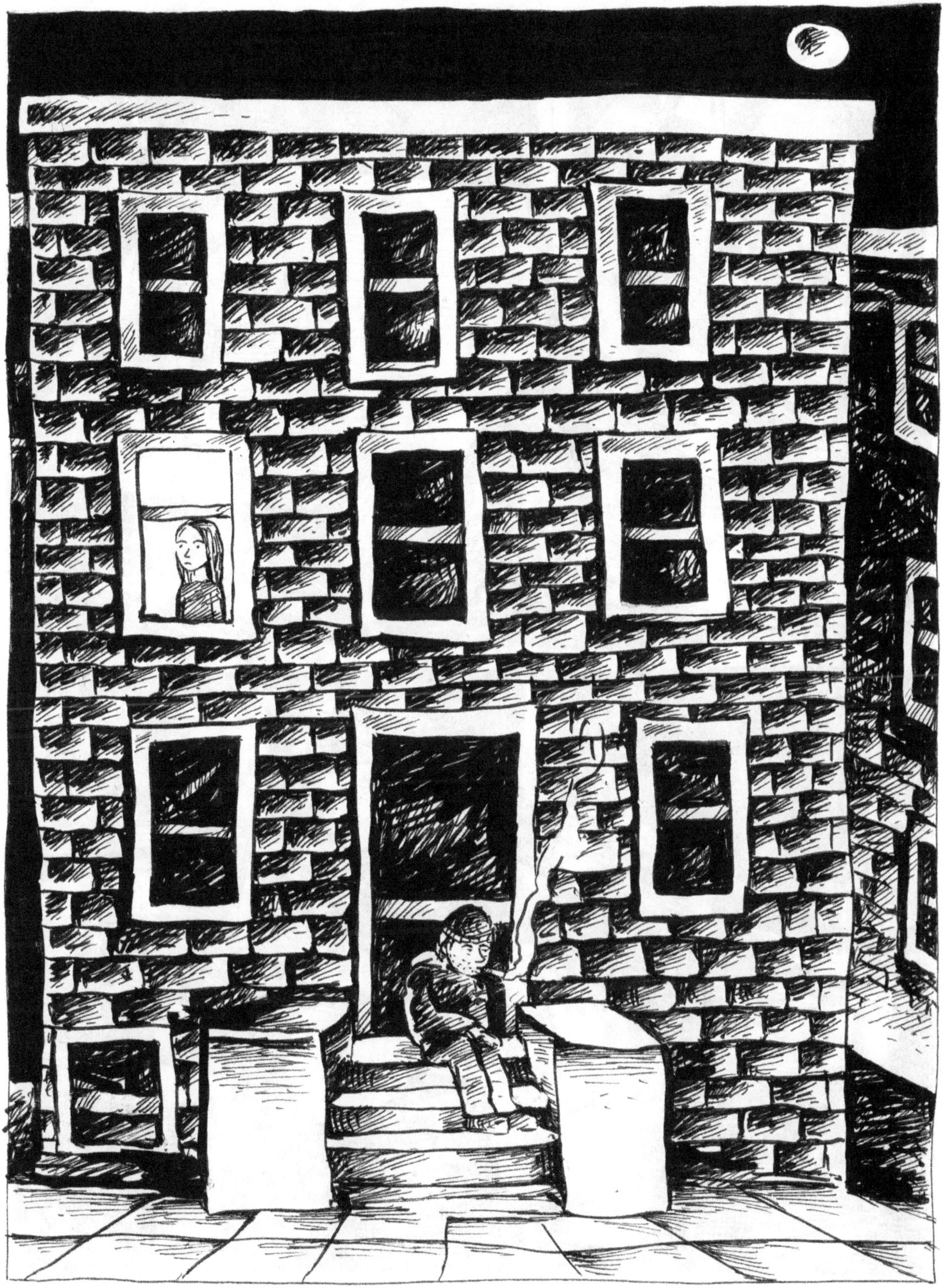

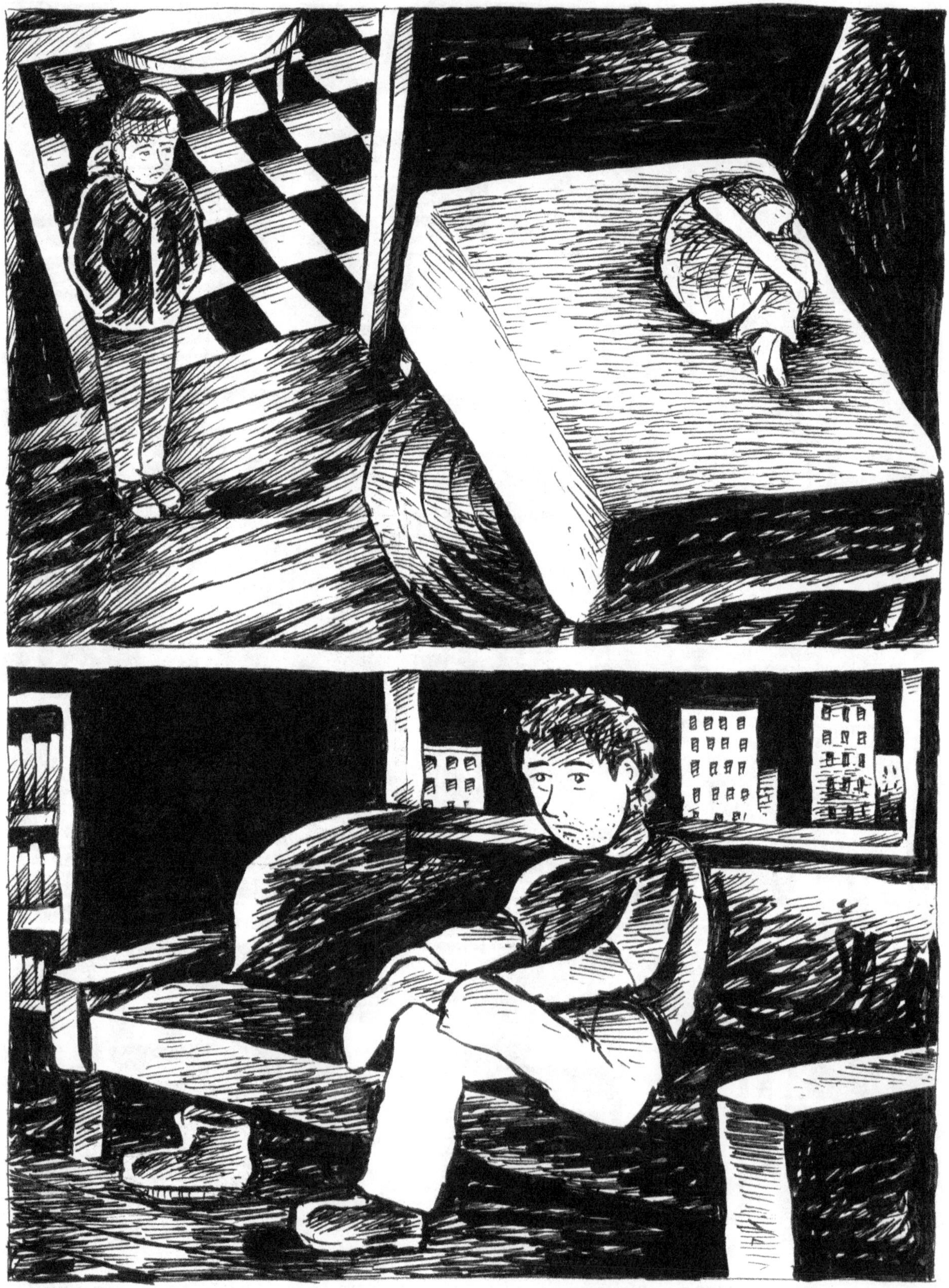

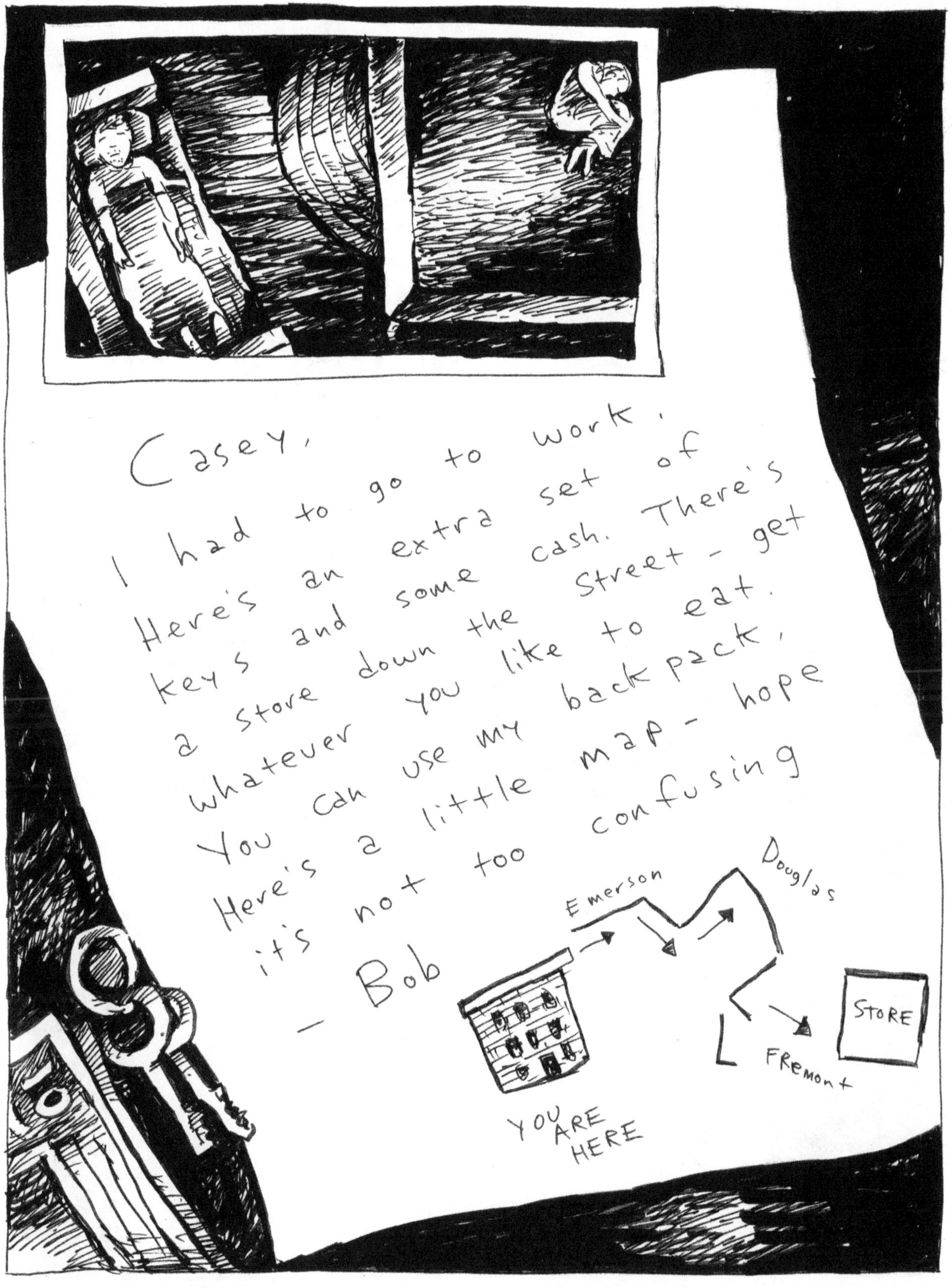
Casey,
I had to go to work.
Here's an extra set of keys and some cash. There's a store down the street - get whatever you like to eat.
You can use my backpack,
Here's a little map - hope it's not too confusing
- Bob
Emerson
Douglas
STORE
FREMONT
YOU ARE HERE

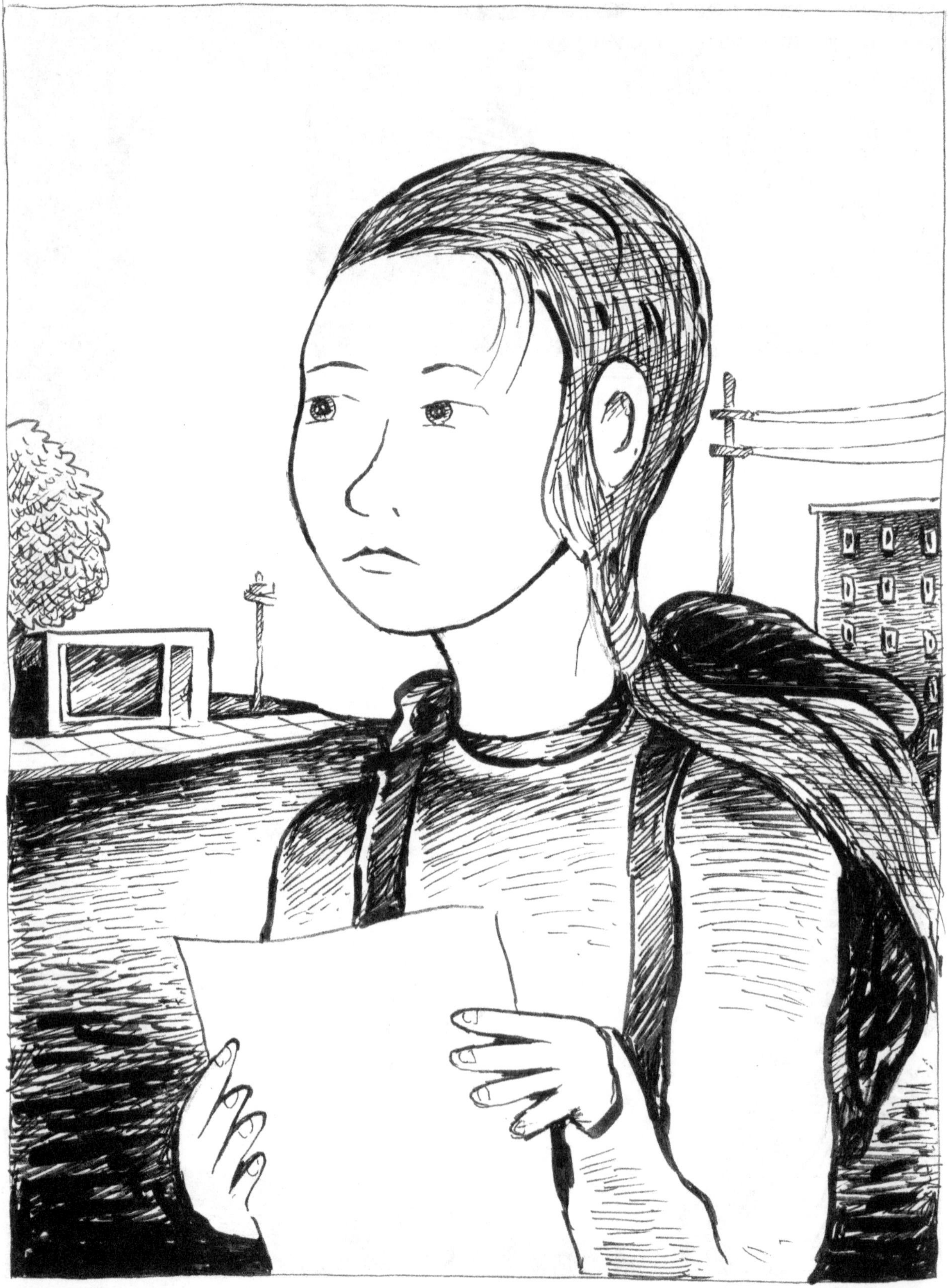

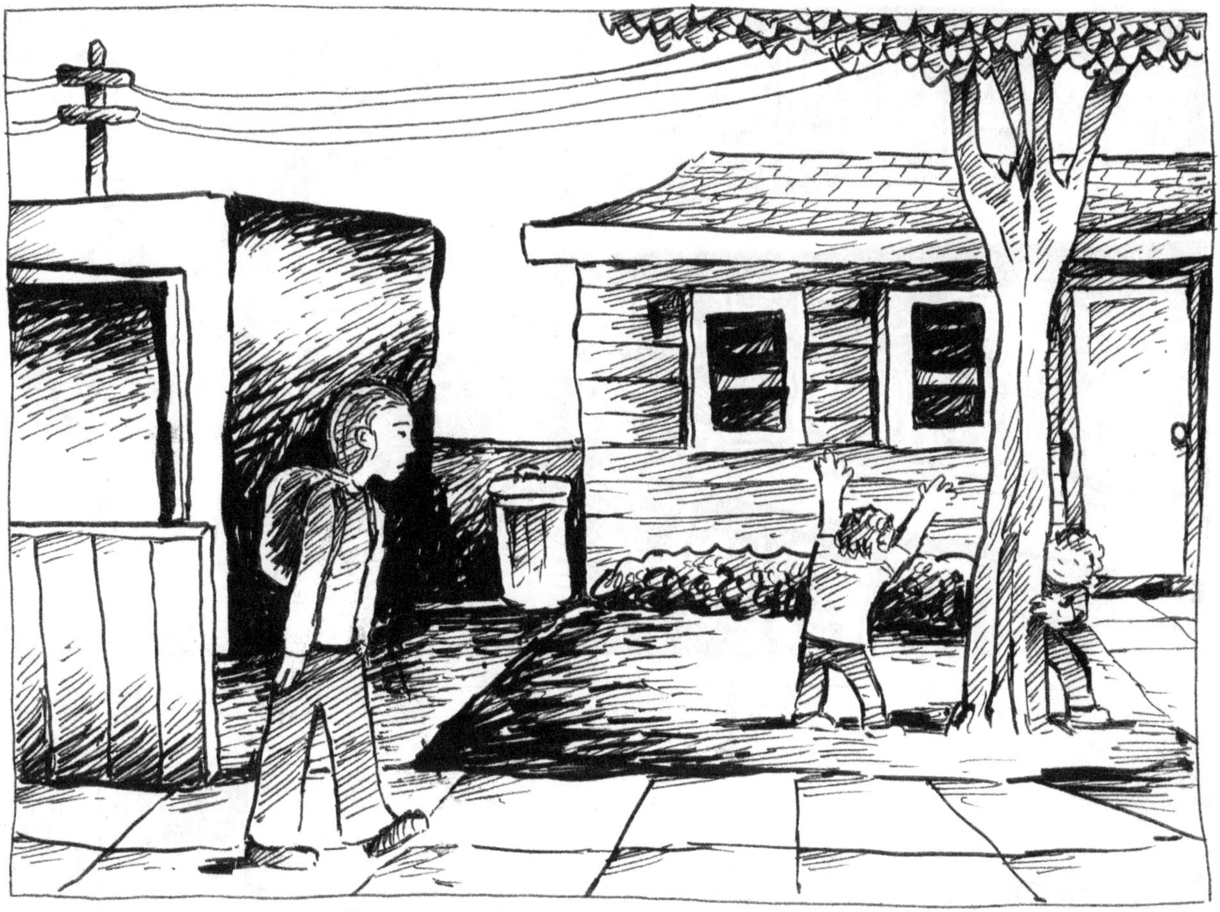

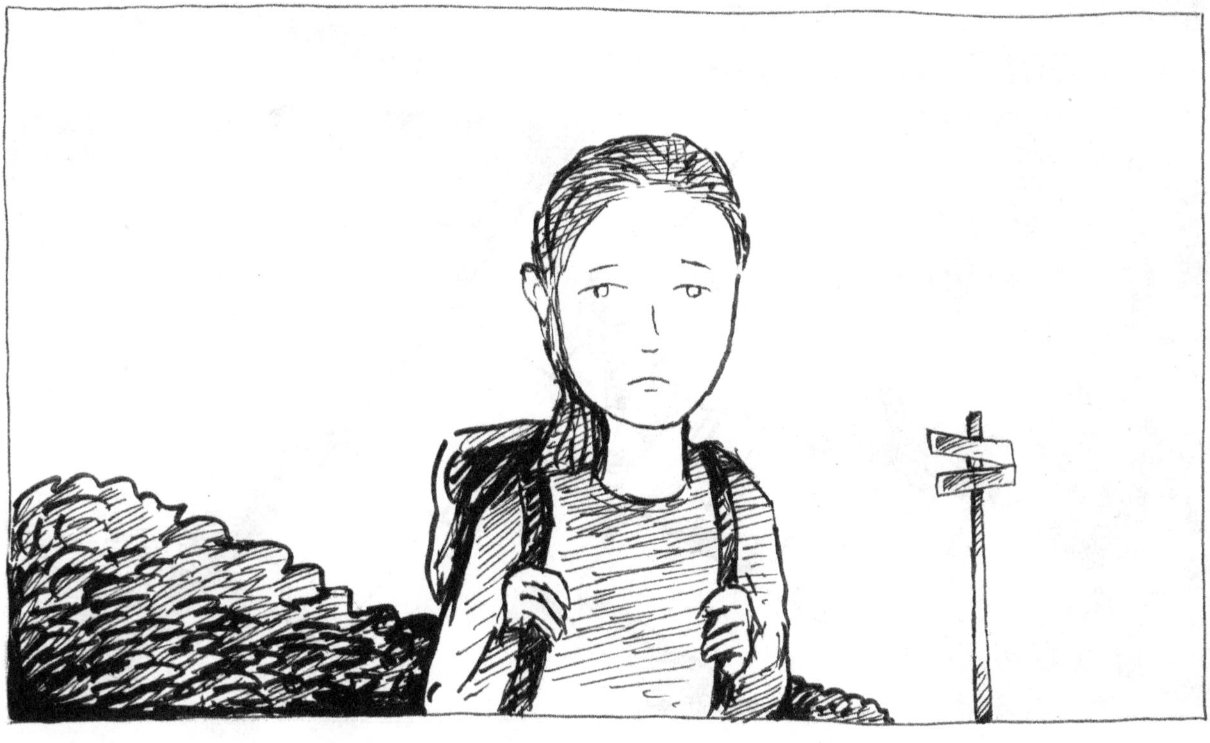

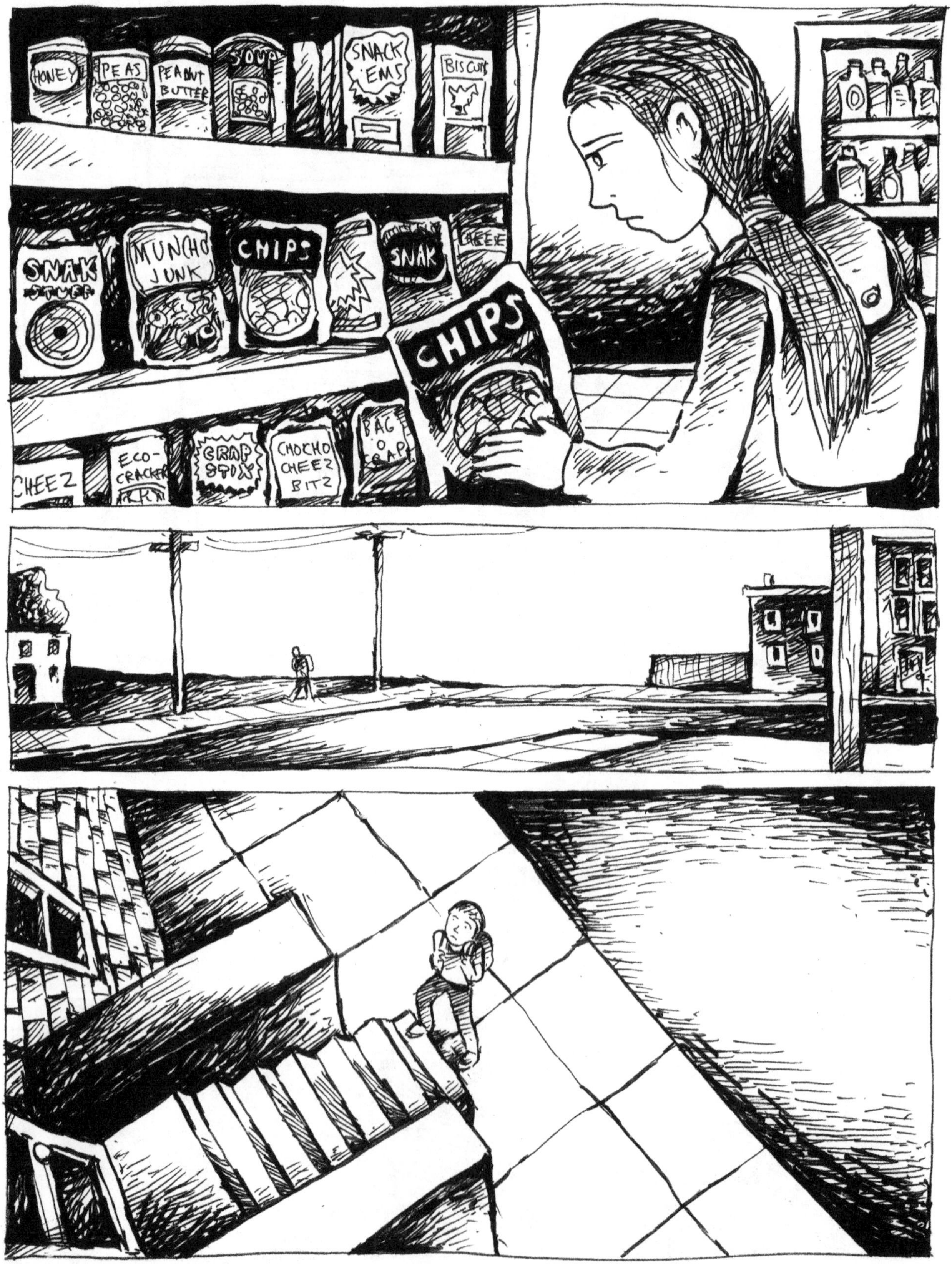
HONEY
PEAS
PEANUT BUTTER
SOUP
SNACK 'EMS
BISCUITS
SNAK STUFF
MUNCHO JUNK
CHIPS
SNAK
CHIPS
CHEEZ
CRAP STIX
CHOCHO CHEEZ BITZ
BAG O CRAP

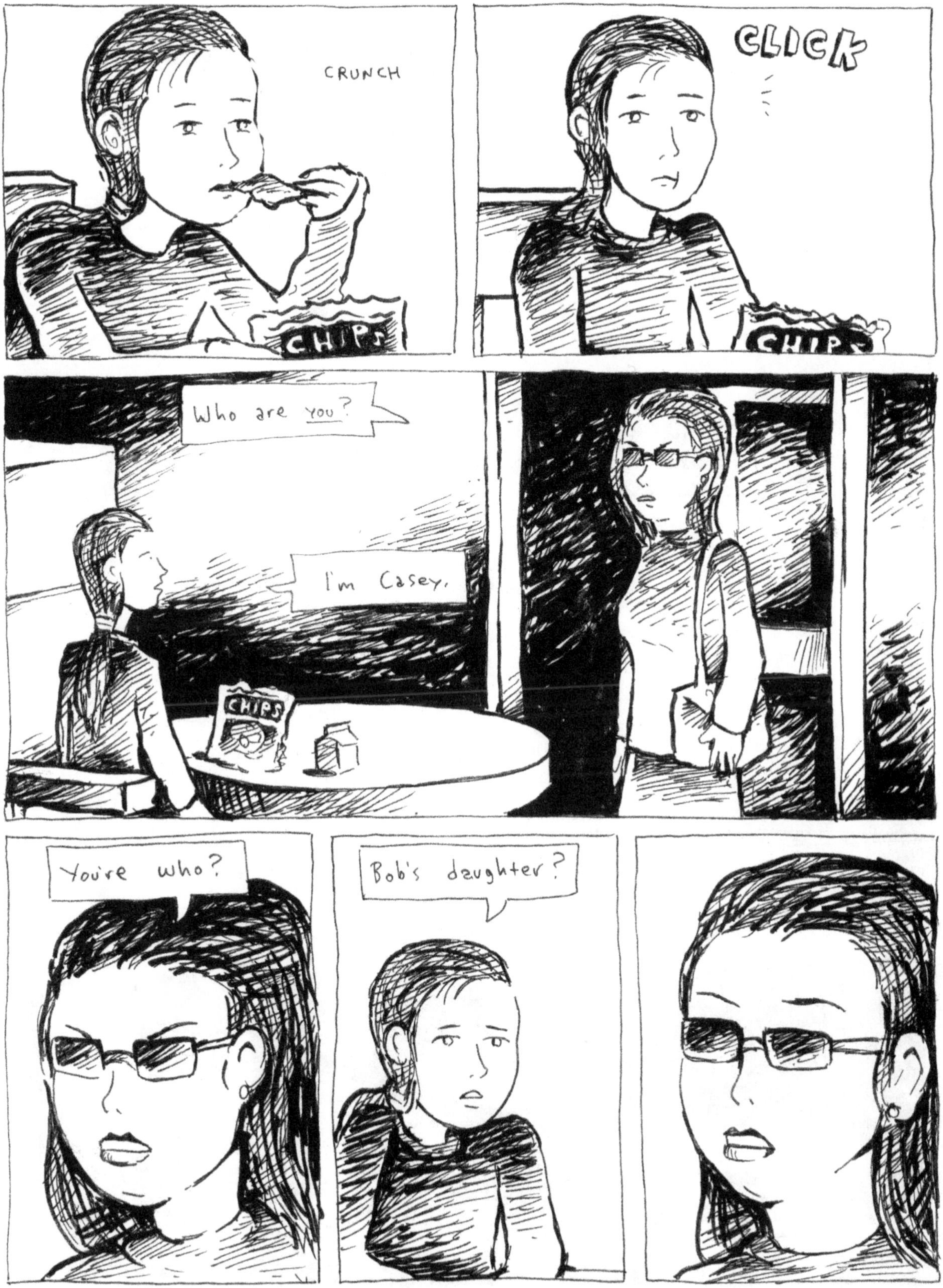
CRUNCH
CLICK
CHIPS
Who are you?
I'm Casey.
CHIPS
You're who?
Bob's daughter?

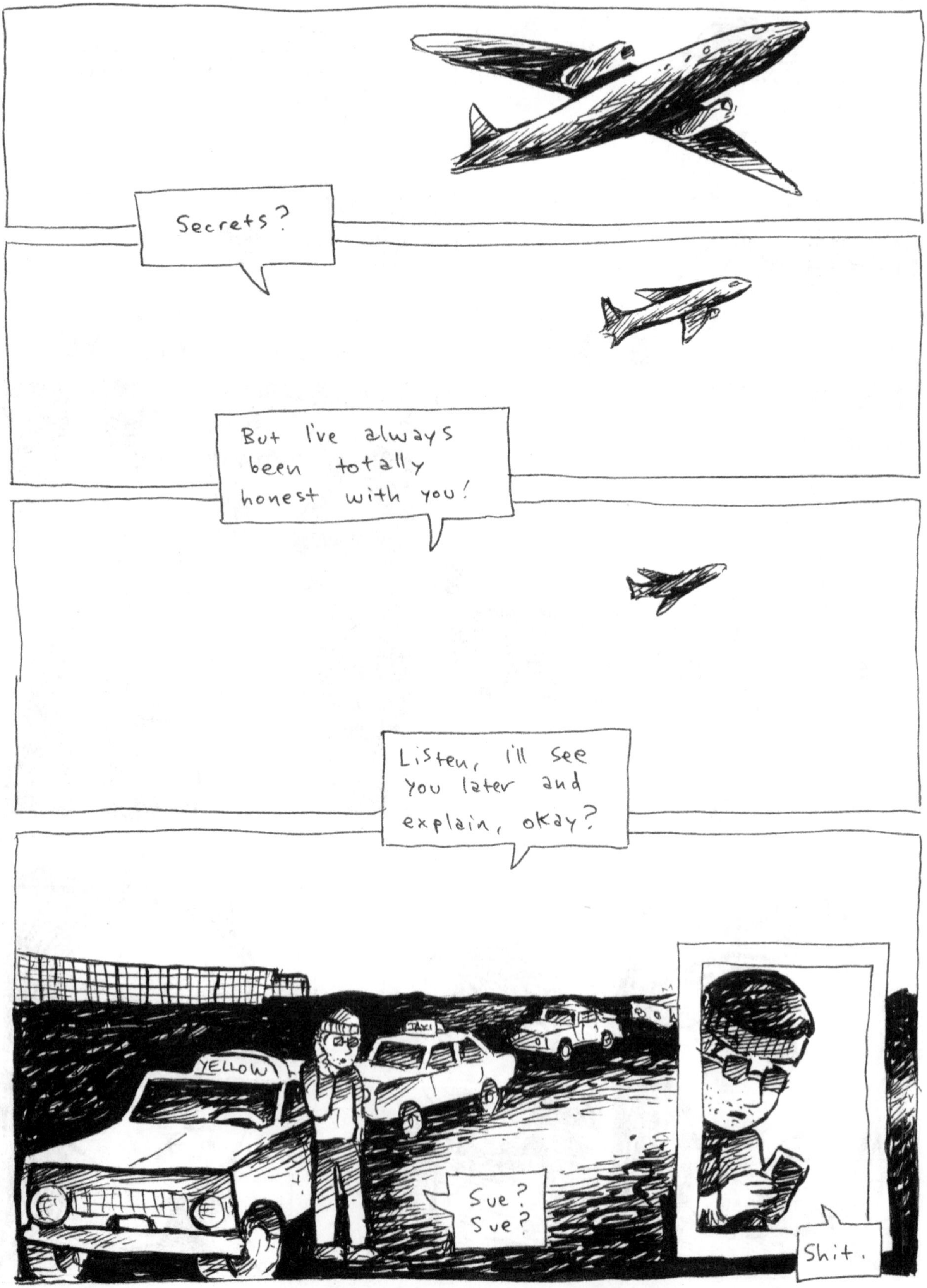
Secrets?
But I've always been totally honest with you!
Listen, I'll see you later and explain, okay?
YELLOW
TAXI
Sue? Sue?
Shit.

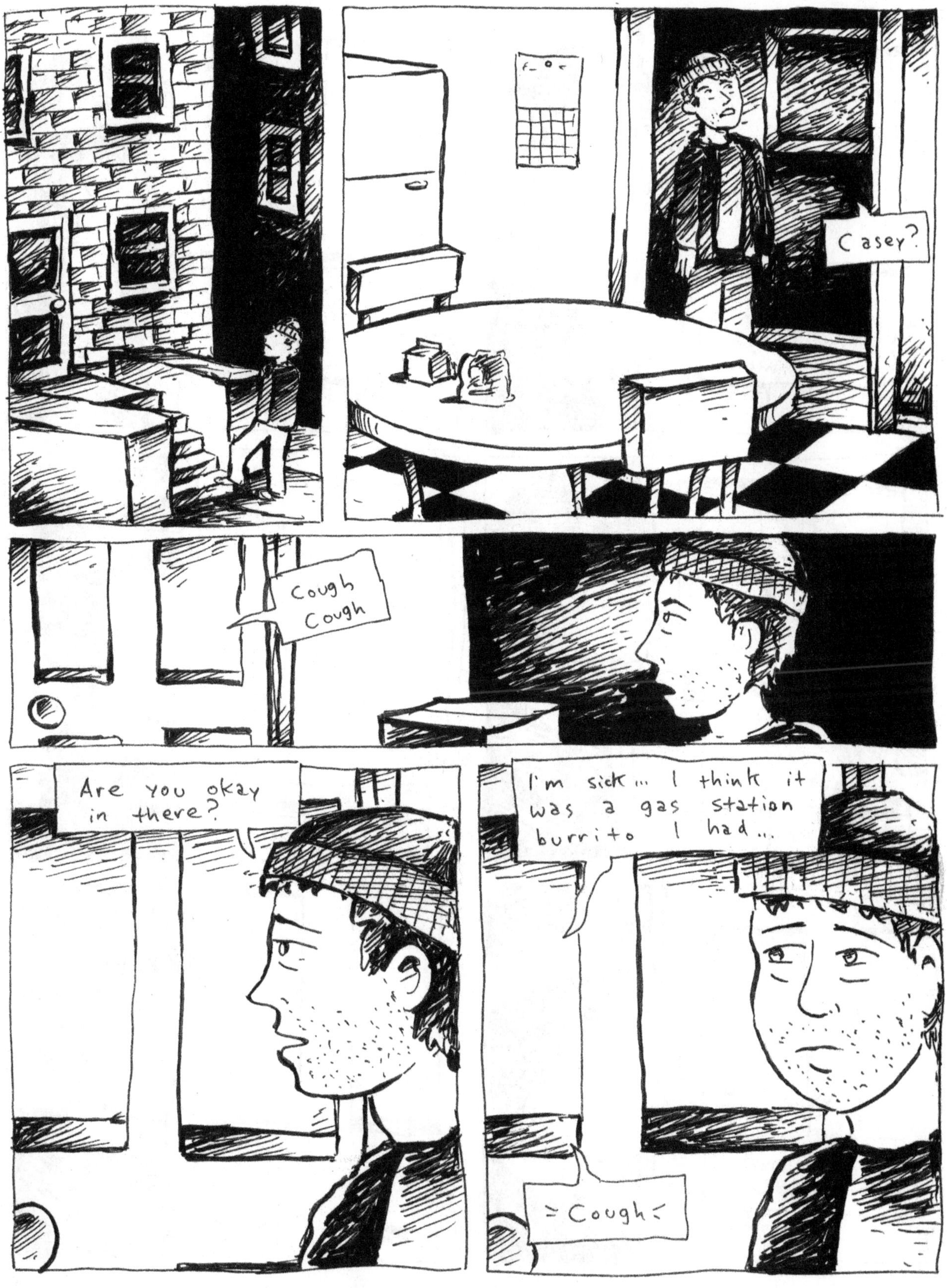
Casey?
Cough Cough
Are you okay in there?
I'm sick... I think it was a gas station burrito I had...
Cough

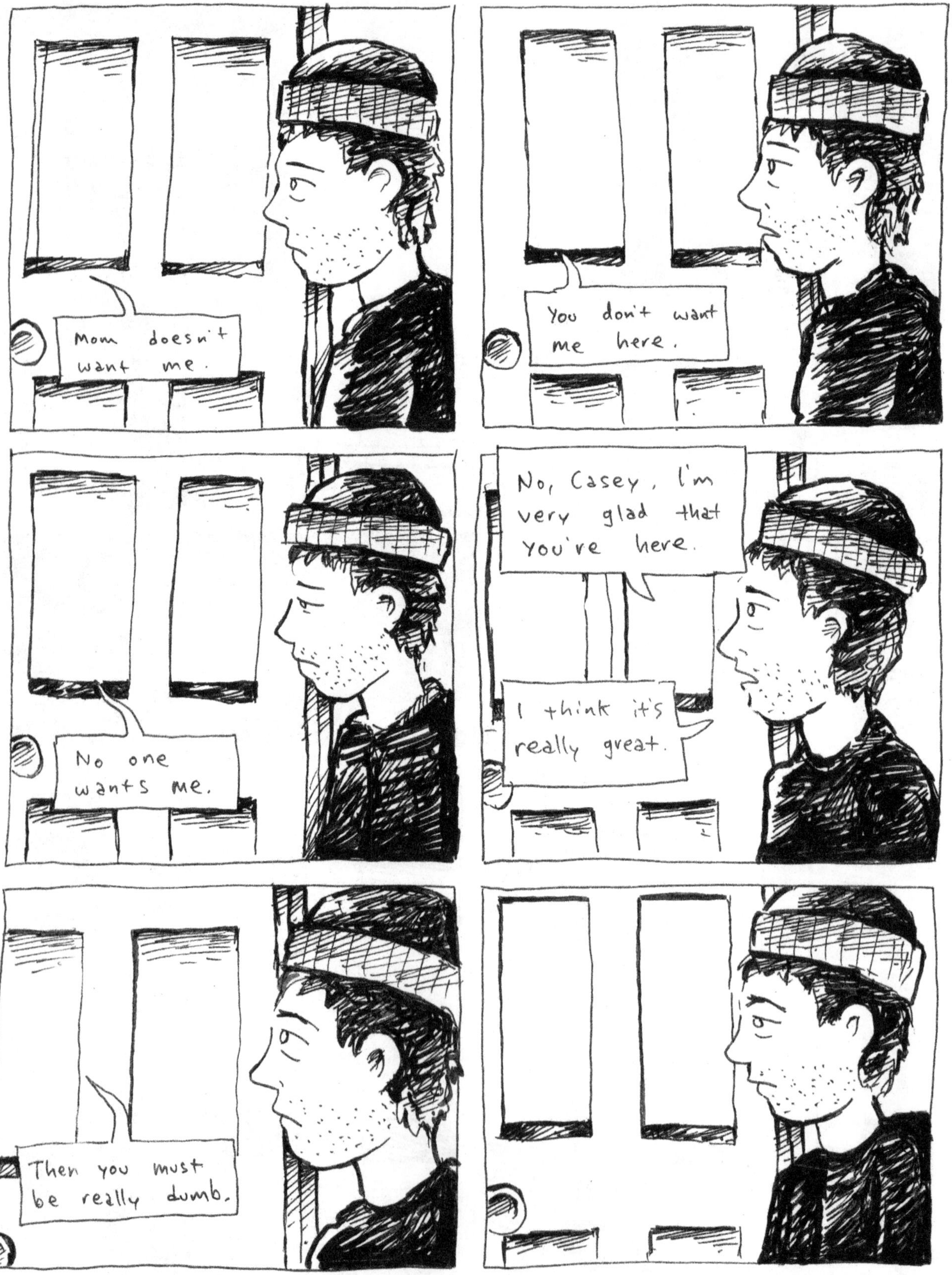
Mom doesn't want me.
You don't want me here.
No one wants me.
No, Casey, I'm very glad that you're here.
I think it's really great.
Then you must be really dumb.

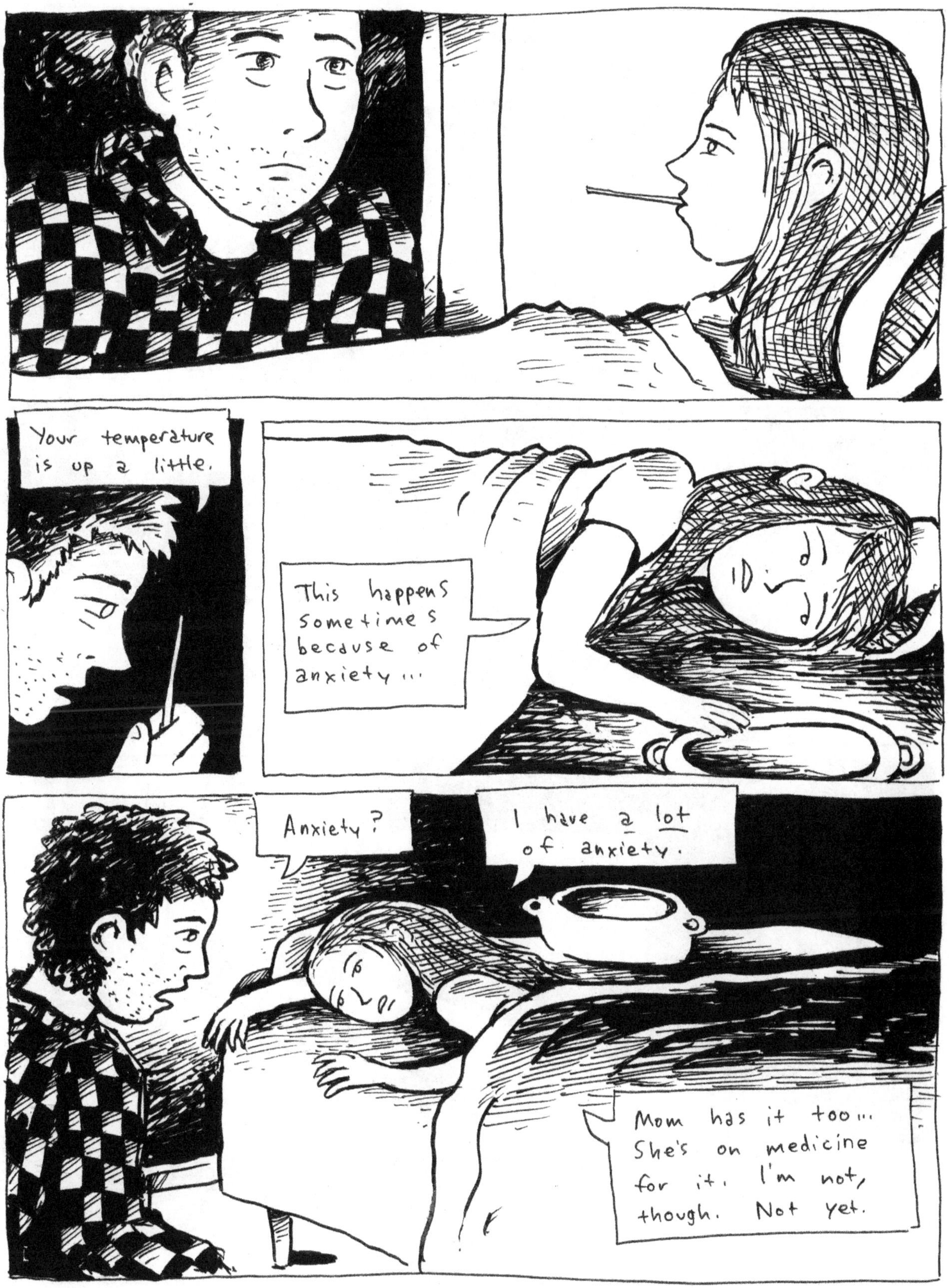

Your temperature is up a little.
This happens sometimes because of anxiety...
Anxiety?
I have a lot of anxiety.
Mom has it too... She's on medicine for it. I'm not, though. Not yet.

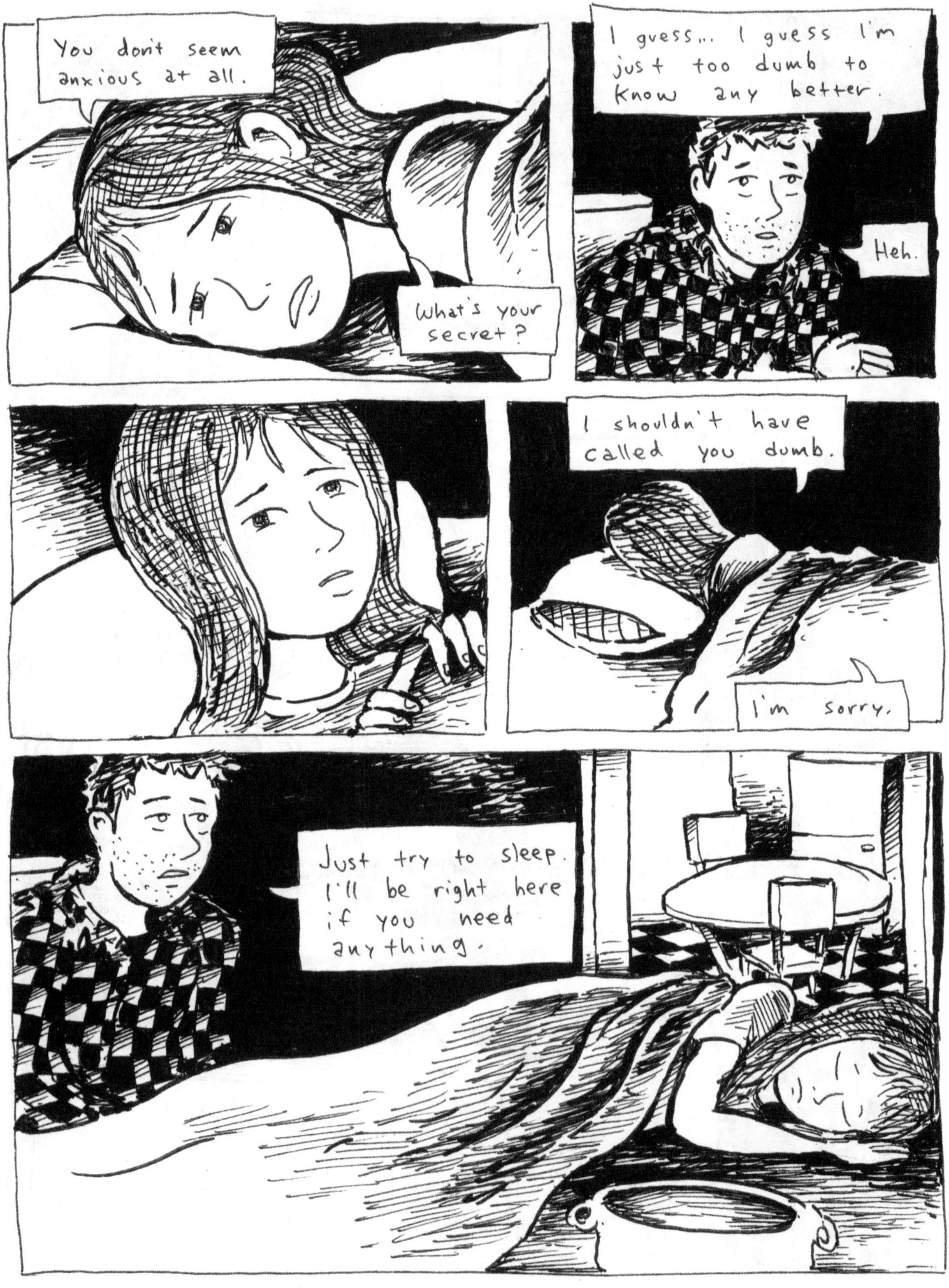
You don't seem anxious at all.
What's your secret?
I guess... I guess I'm just too dumb to know any better.
Heh.
I shouldn't have called you dumb.
I'm sorry.
Just try to sleep. I'll be right here if you need anything.

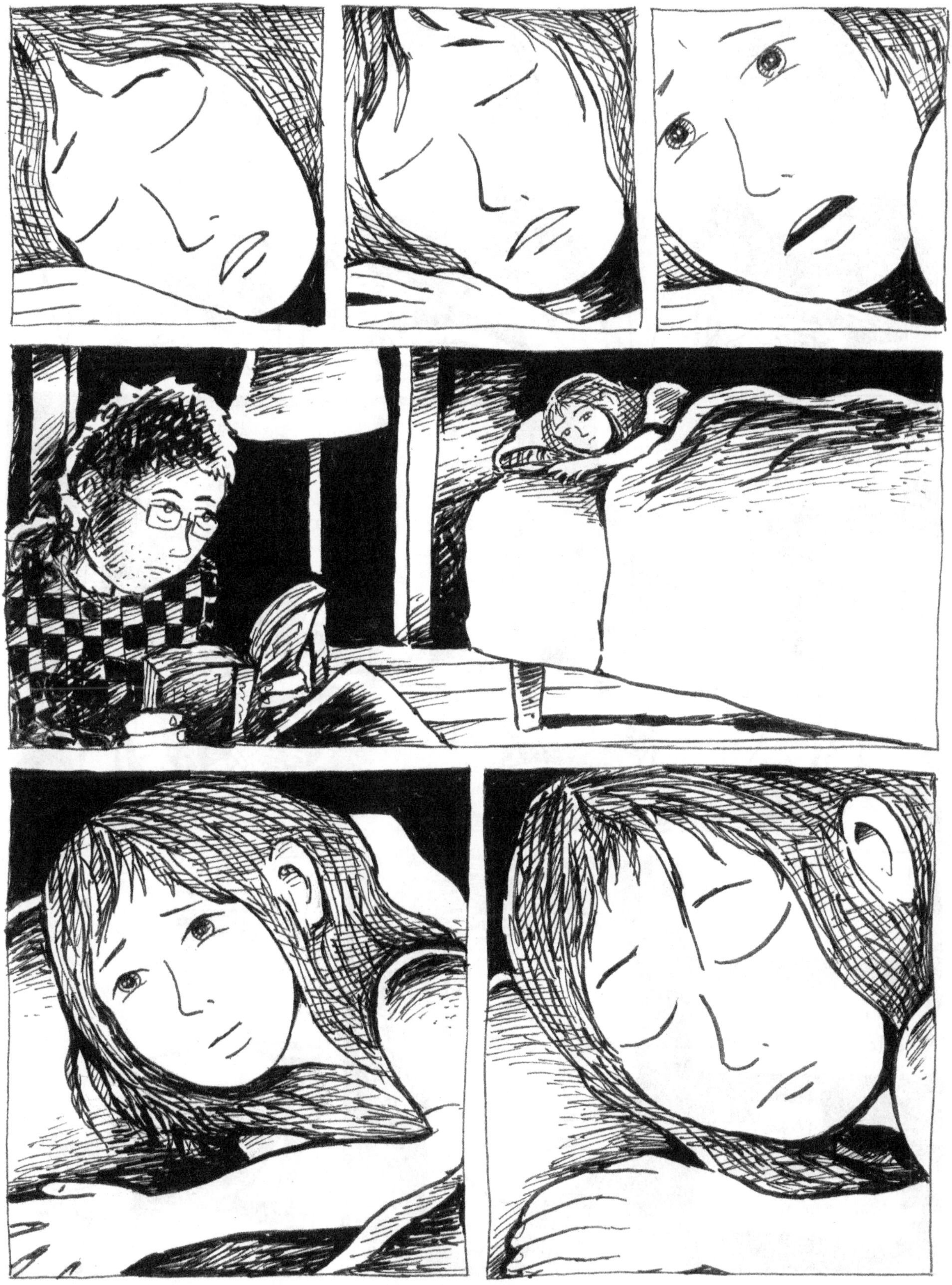

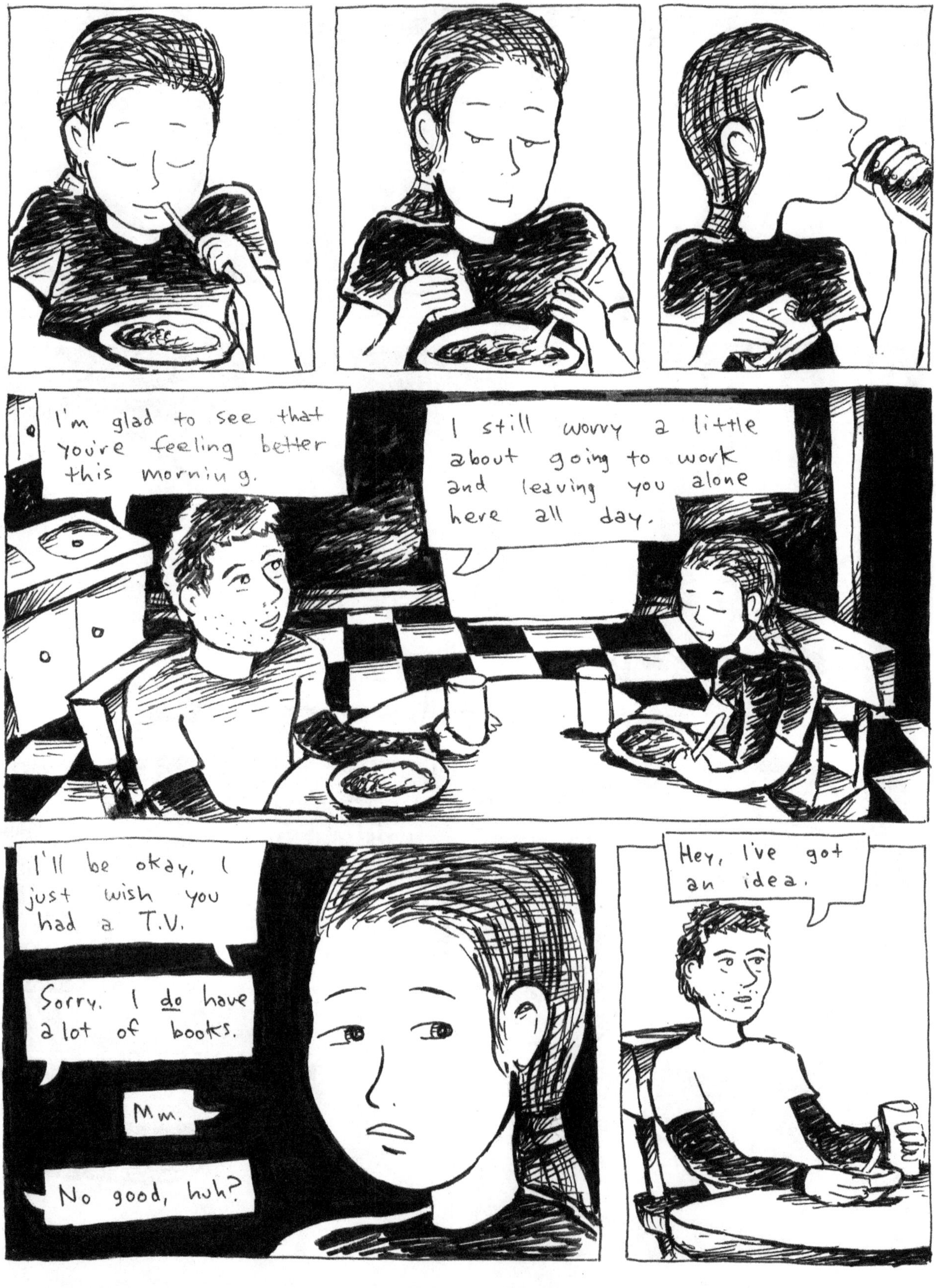
I'm glad to see that you're feeling better this morning.
I still worry a little about going to work and leaving you alone here all day.
I'll be okay. I just wish you had a T.V.
Sorry. I do have a lot of books.
Mm.
No good, huh?
Hey, I've got an idea.

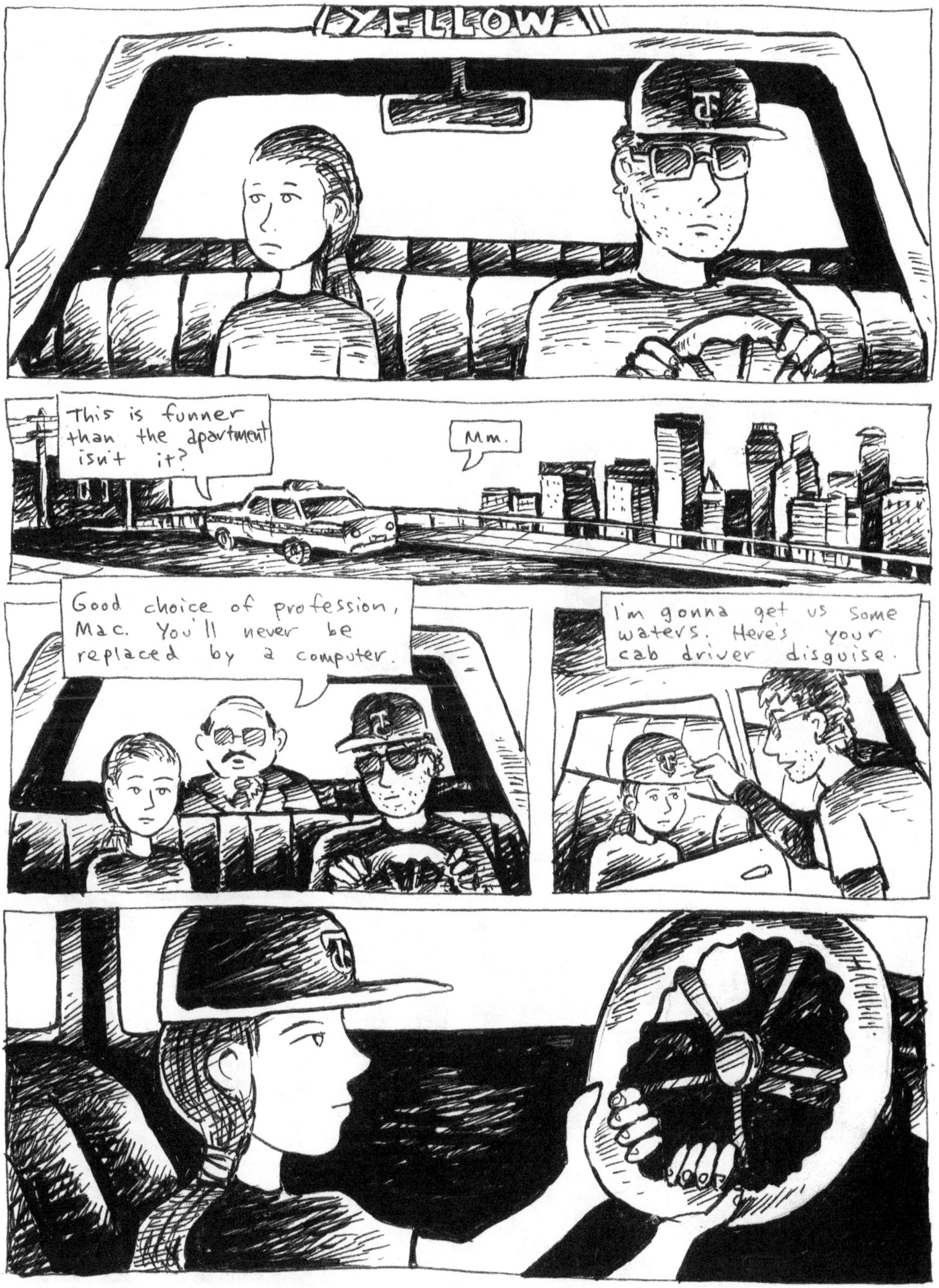
YELLOW
This is funner than the apartment isn't it?
Mm.
Good choice of profession, Mac. You'll never be replaced by a computer.
I'm gonna get us some waters. Here's your cab driver disguise.

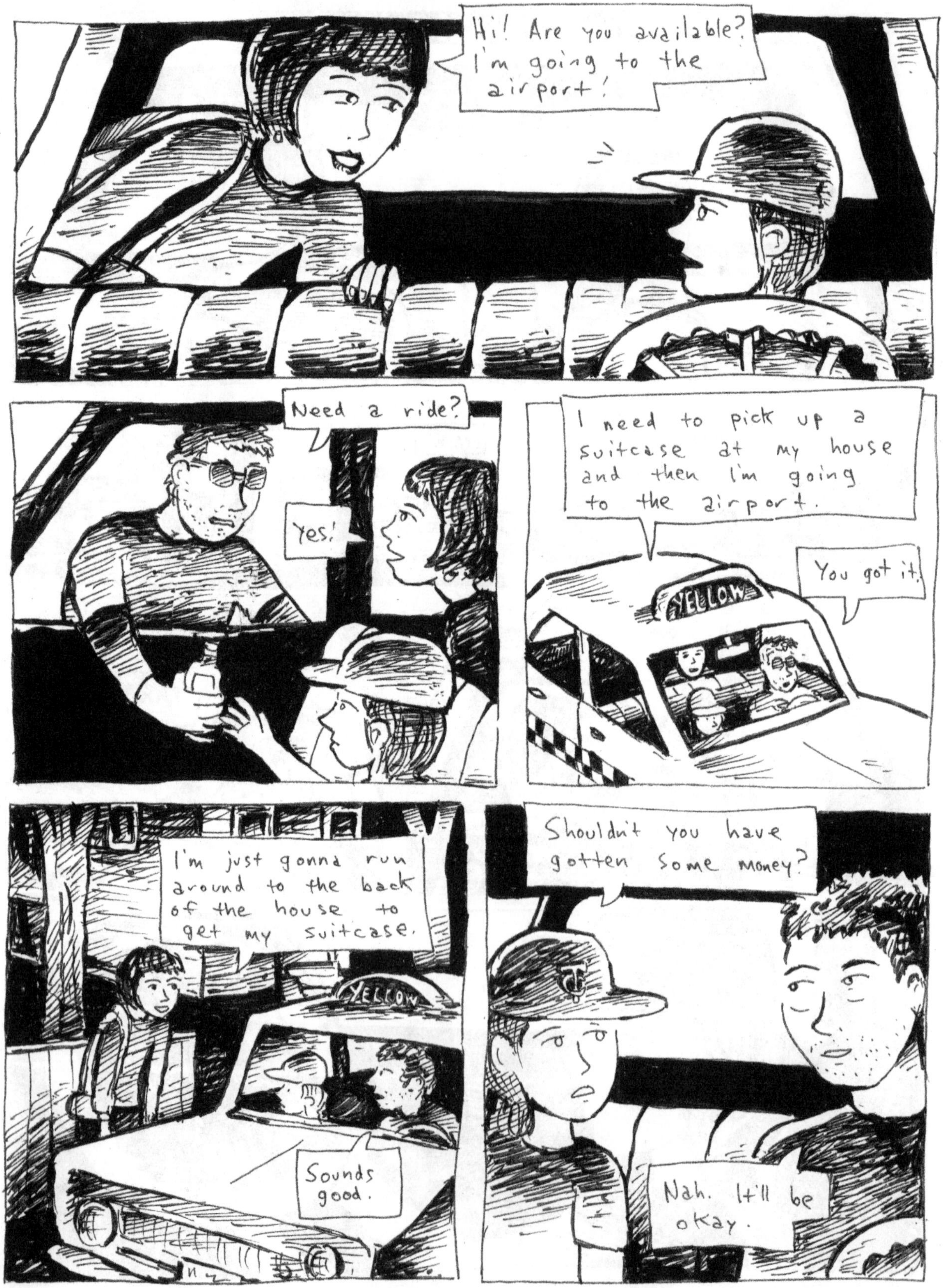
Hi! Are you available? I'm going to the airport!
Need a ride?
Yes!
I need to pick up a suitcase at my house and then I'm going to the airport.
YELLOW
You got it!
I'm just gonna run around to the back of the house to get my suitcase.
YELLOW
Sounds good.
Shouldn't you have gotten some money?
Nah. It'll be okay.

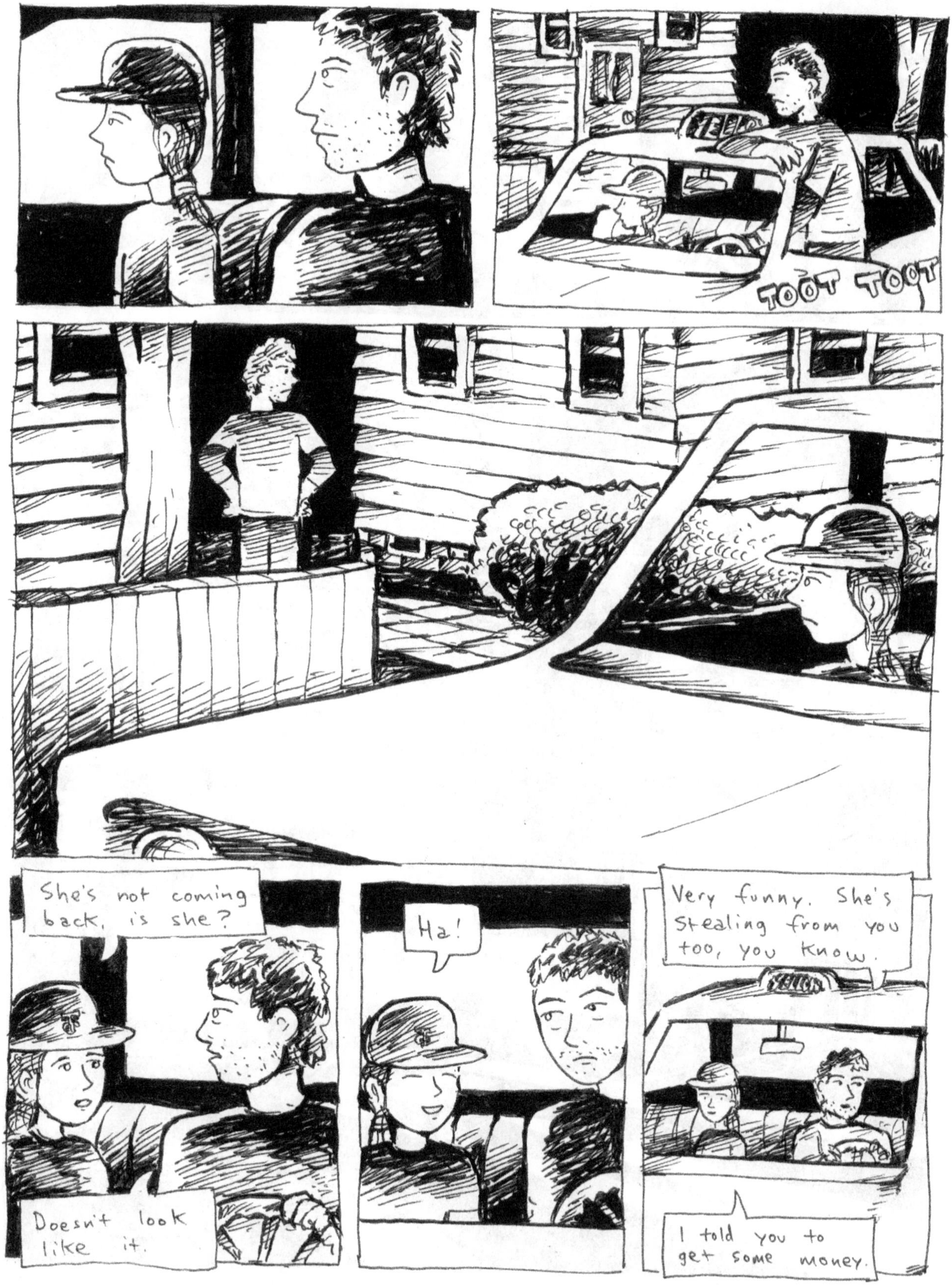
TOOT TOOT
She's not coming back, is she?
Doesn't look like it.
Ha!
Very funny. She's stealing from you too, you know.
I told you to get some money.

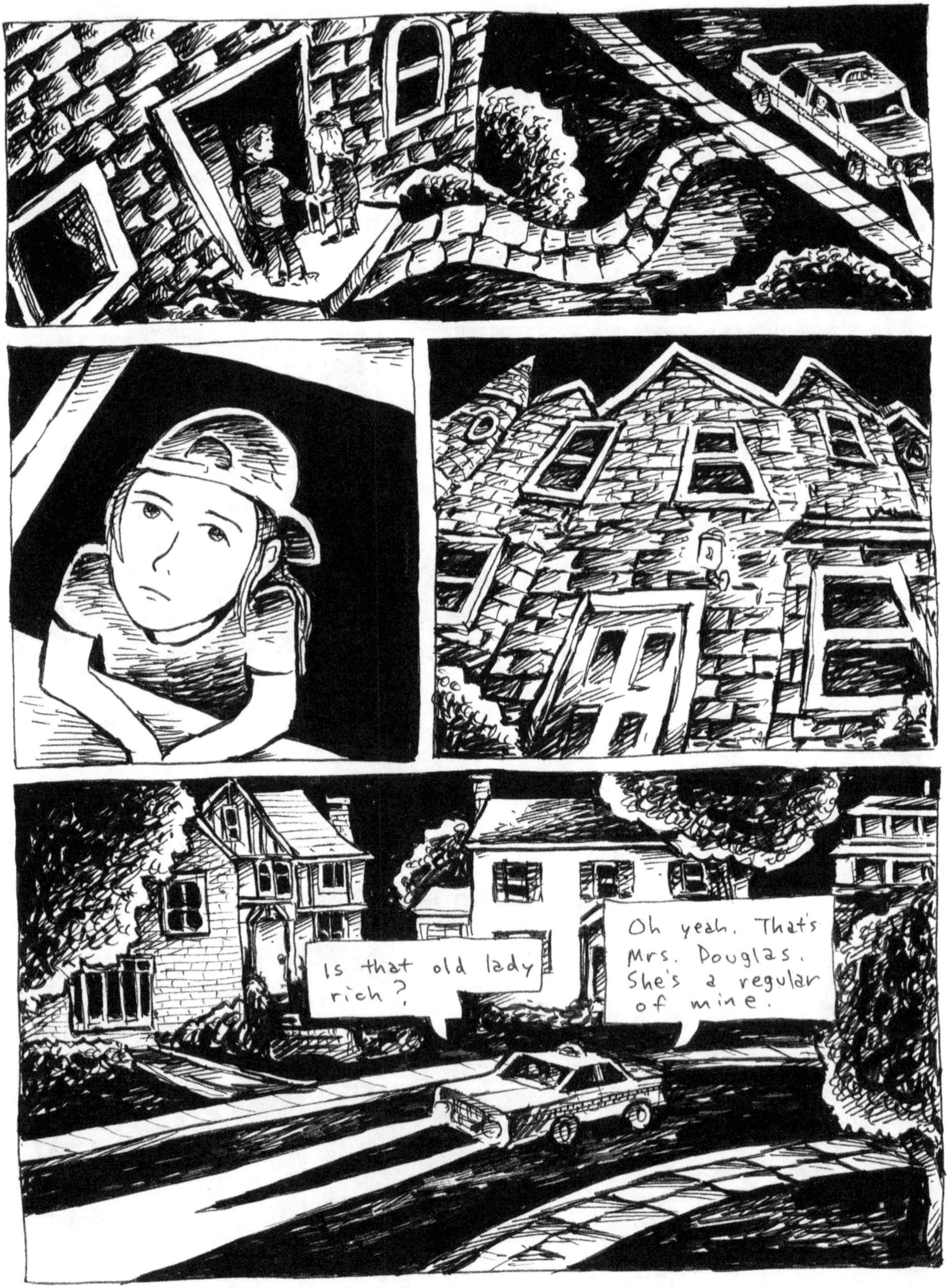
Is that old lady rich?
Oh yeah. That's Mrs. Douglas. She's a regular of mine.

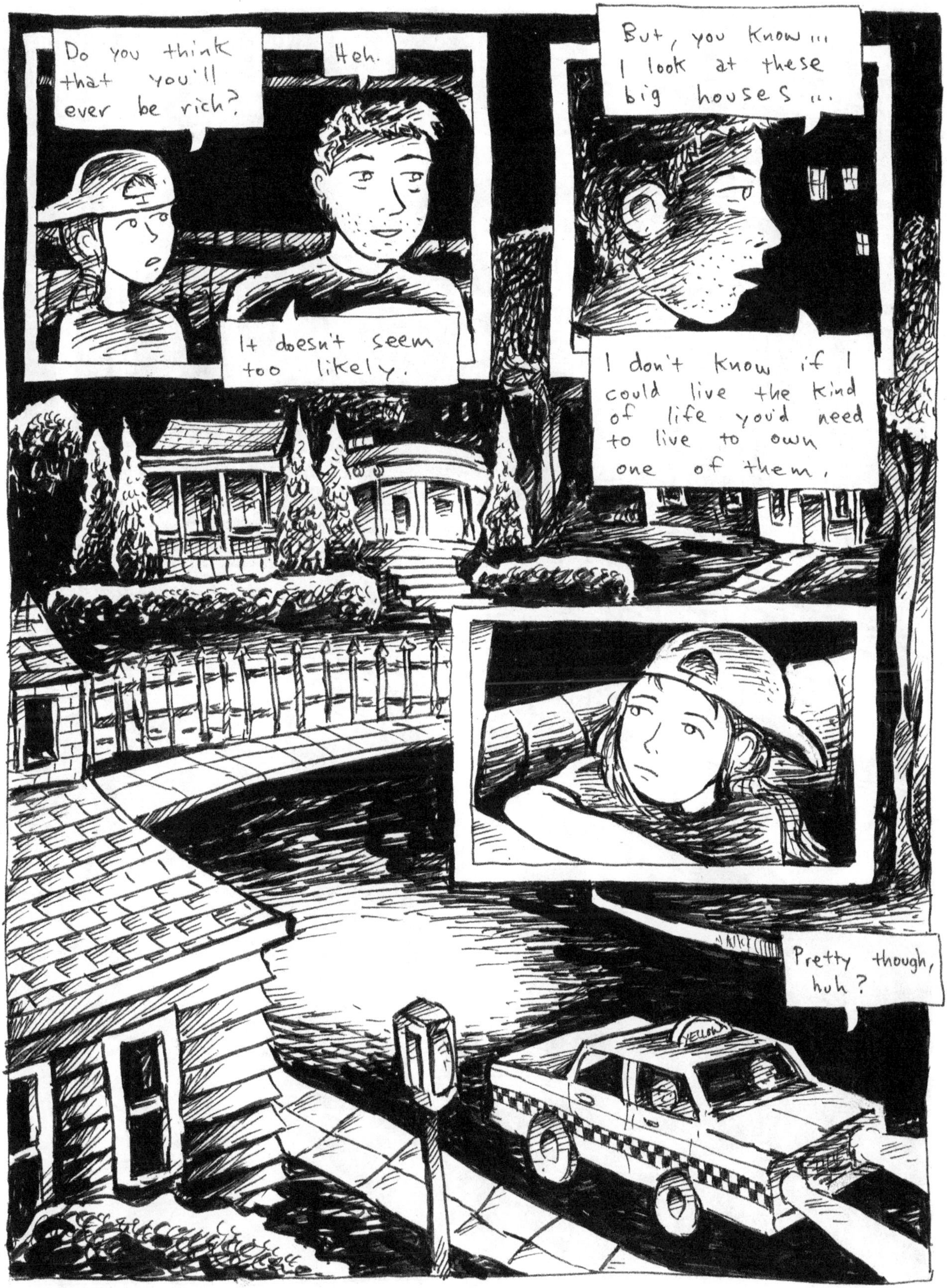
Do you think that you'll ever be rich?
Heh.
It doesn't seem too likely.
But, you know... I look at these big houses...
I don't know if I could live the kind of life you'd need to live to own one of them.
Pretty though, huh?
YELLOW

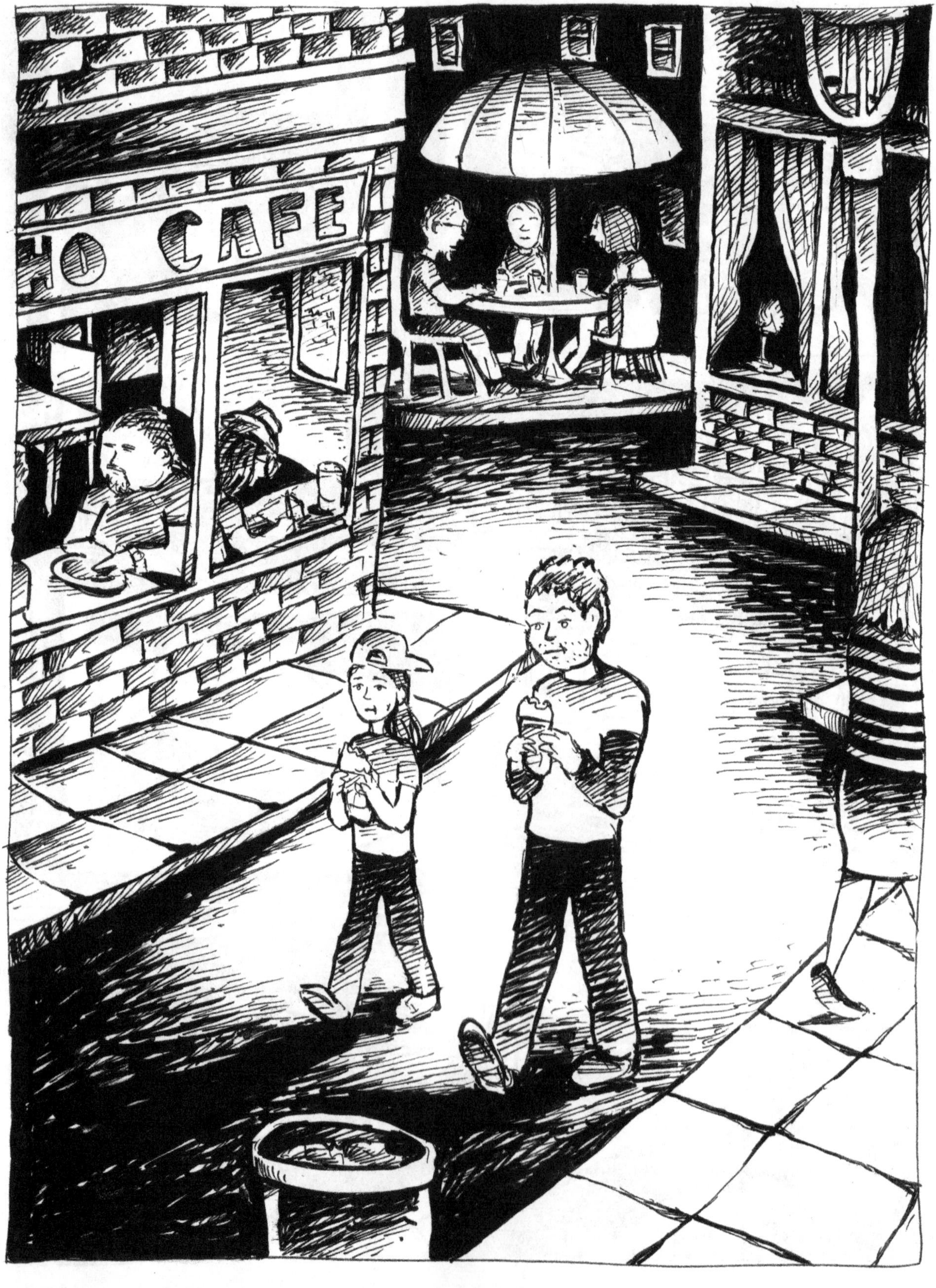
HO CAFE

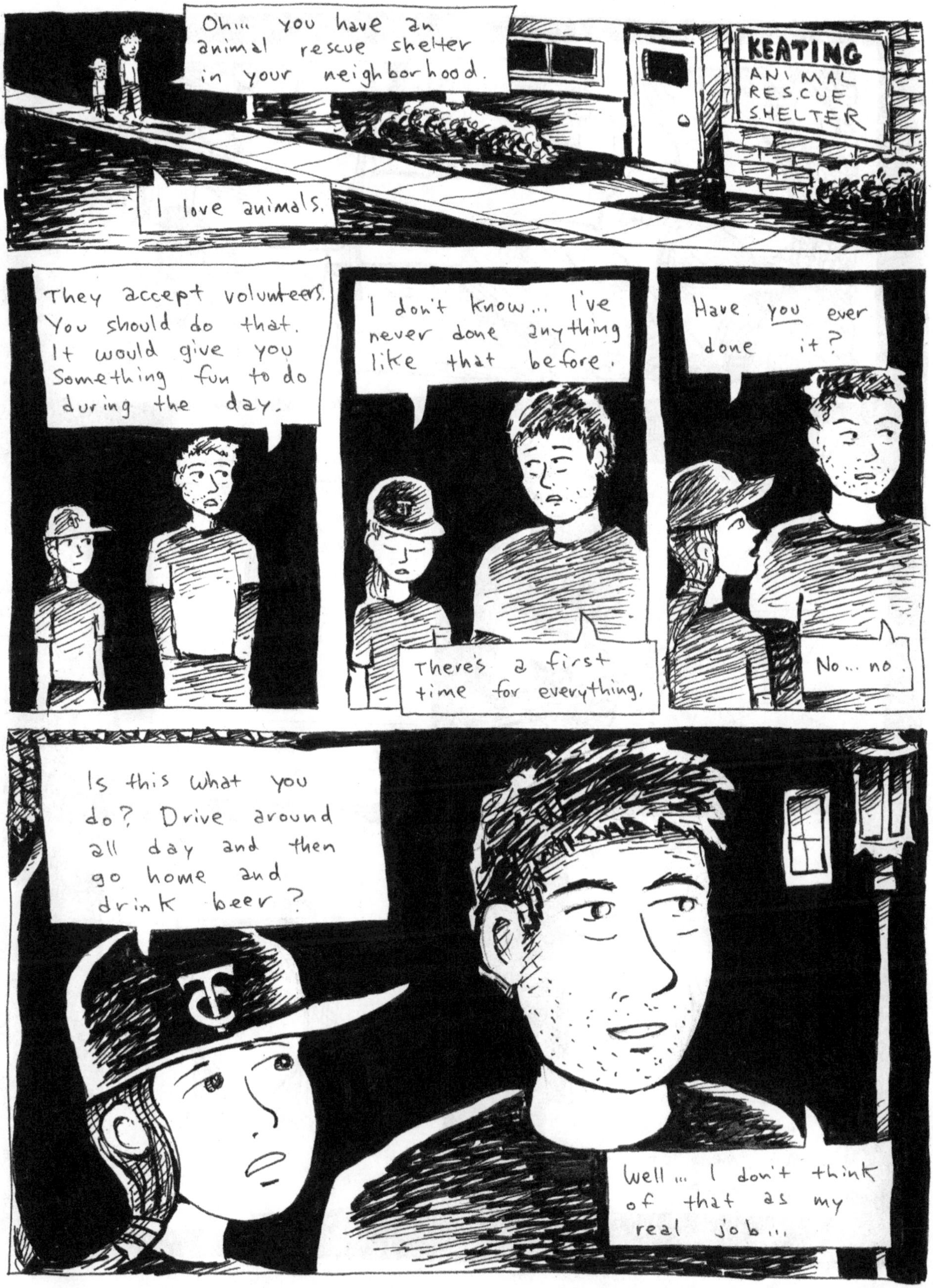
Oh... you have an animal rescue shelter in your neighborhood.
KEATING ANIMAL RESCUE SHELTER
I love animals.
They accept volunteers. You should do that. It would give you something fun to do during the day.
I don't know... I've never done anything like that before.
There's a first time for everything.
Have you ever done it?
No... no.
Is this what you do? Drive around all day and then go home and drink beer?
Well... I don't think of that as my real job...

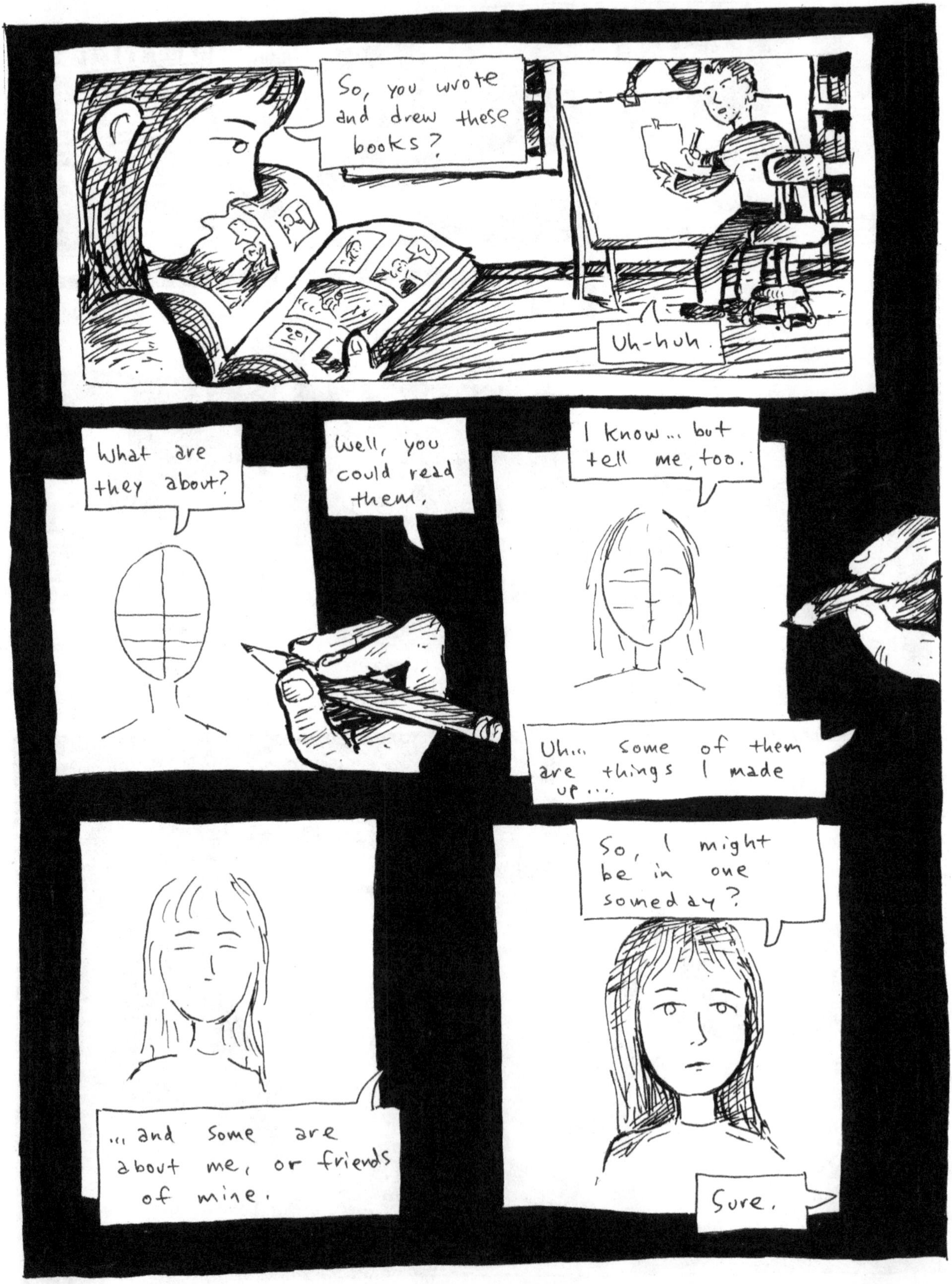
So, you wrote and drew these books?
Uh-huh.
What are they about?
Well, you could read them.
I know... but tell me, too.
Uh... some of them are things I made up...
...and some are about me, or friends of mine.
So, I might be in one someday?
Sure.

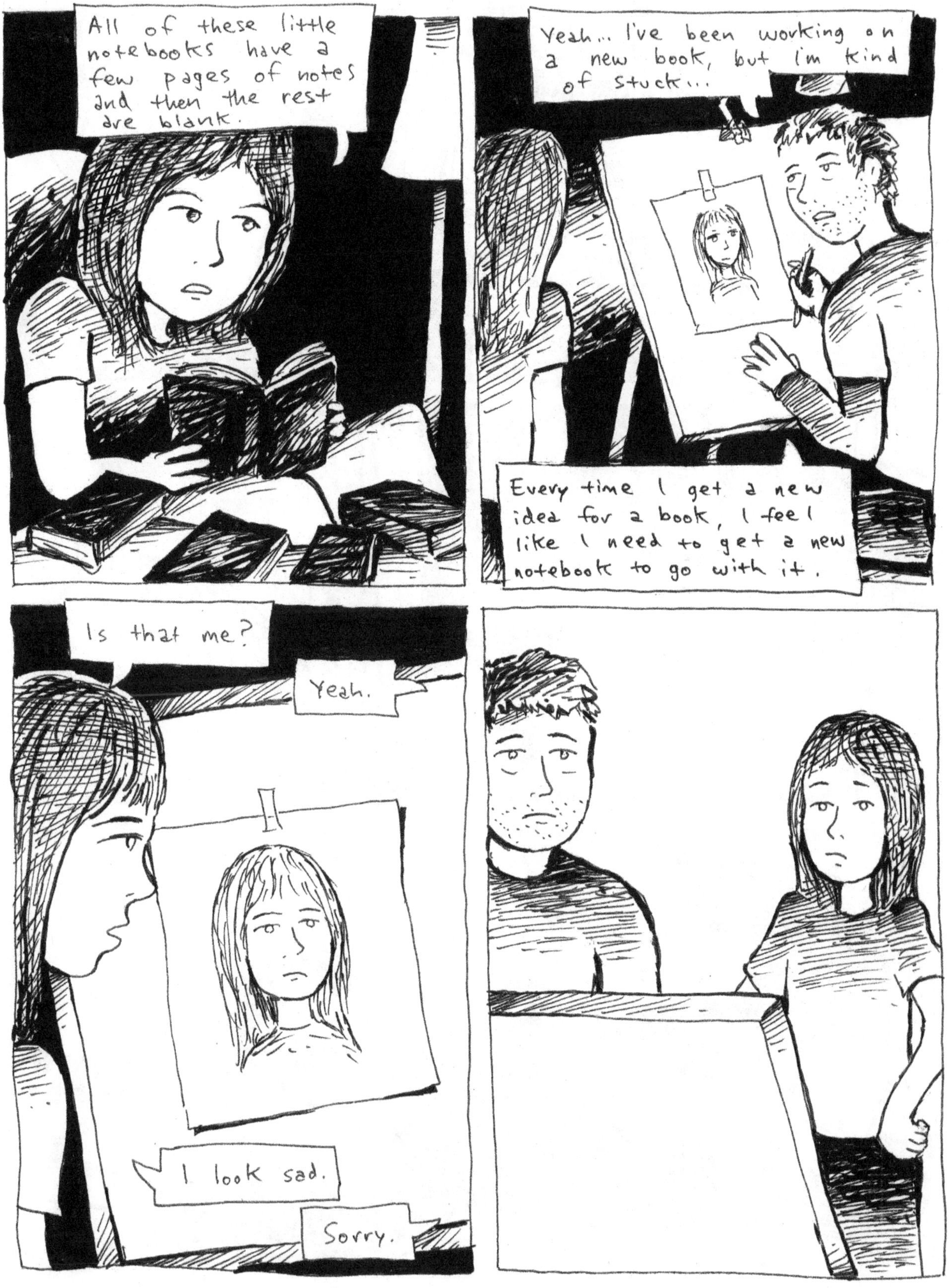
All of these little notebooks have a few pages of notes and then the rest are blank.
Yeah... I've been working on a new book, but I'm kind of stuck...
Every time I get a new idea for a book, I feel like I need to get a new notebook to go with it.
Is that me?
Yeah.
I look sad.
Sorry.

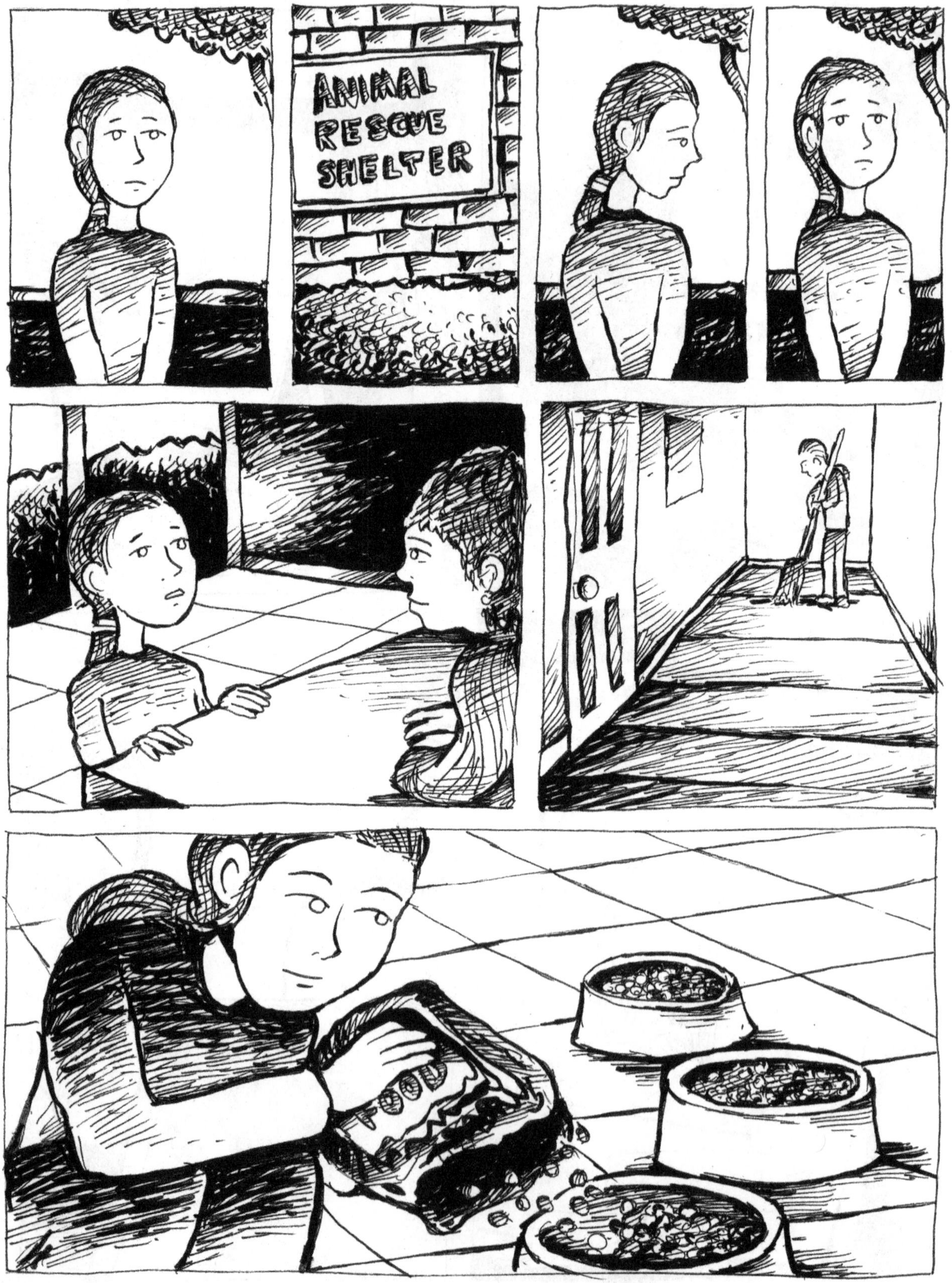
ANIMAL RESCUE SHELTER
FOOD

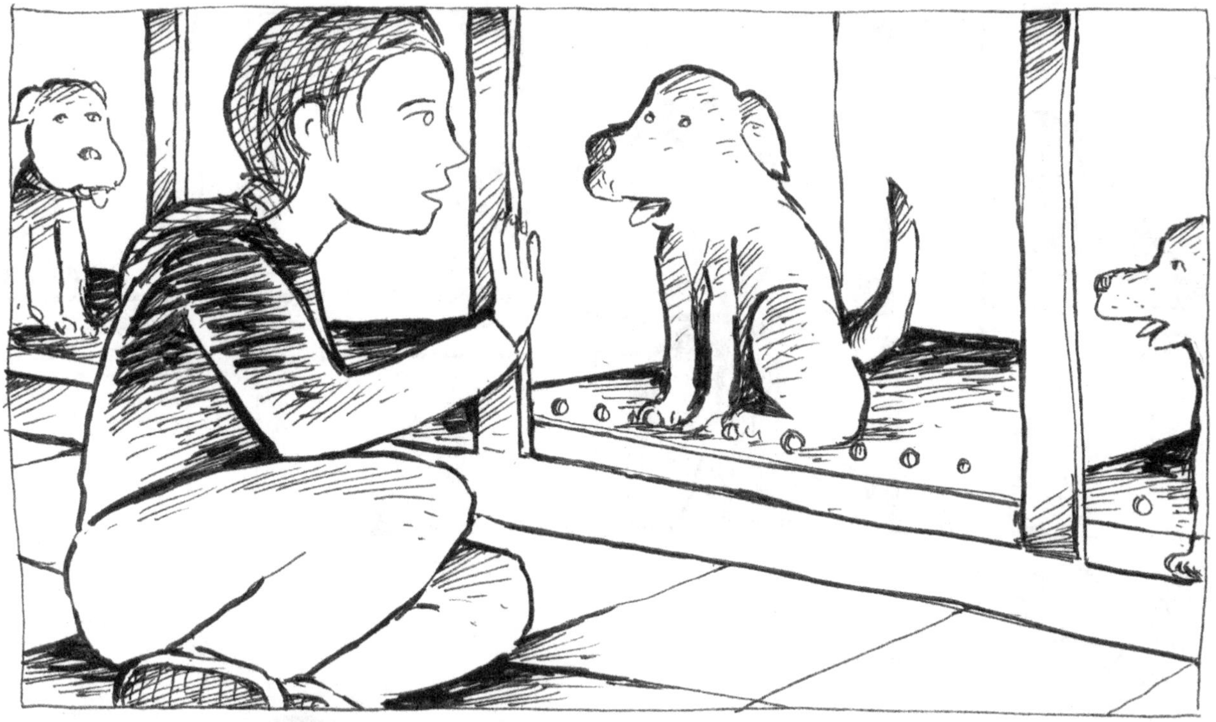
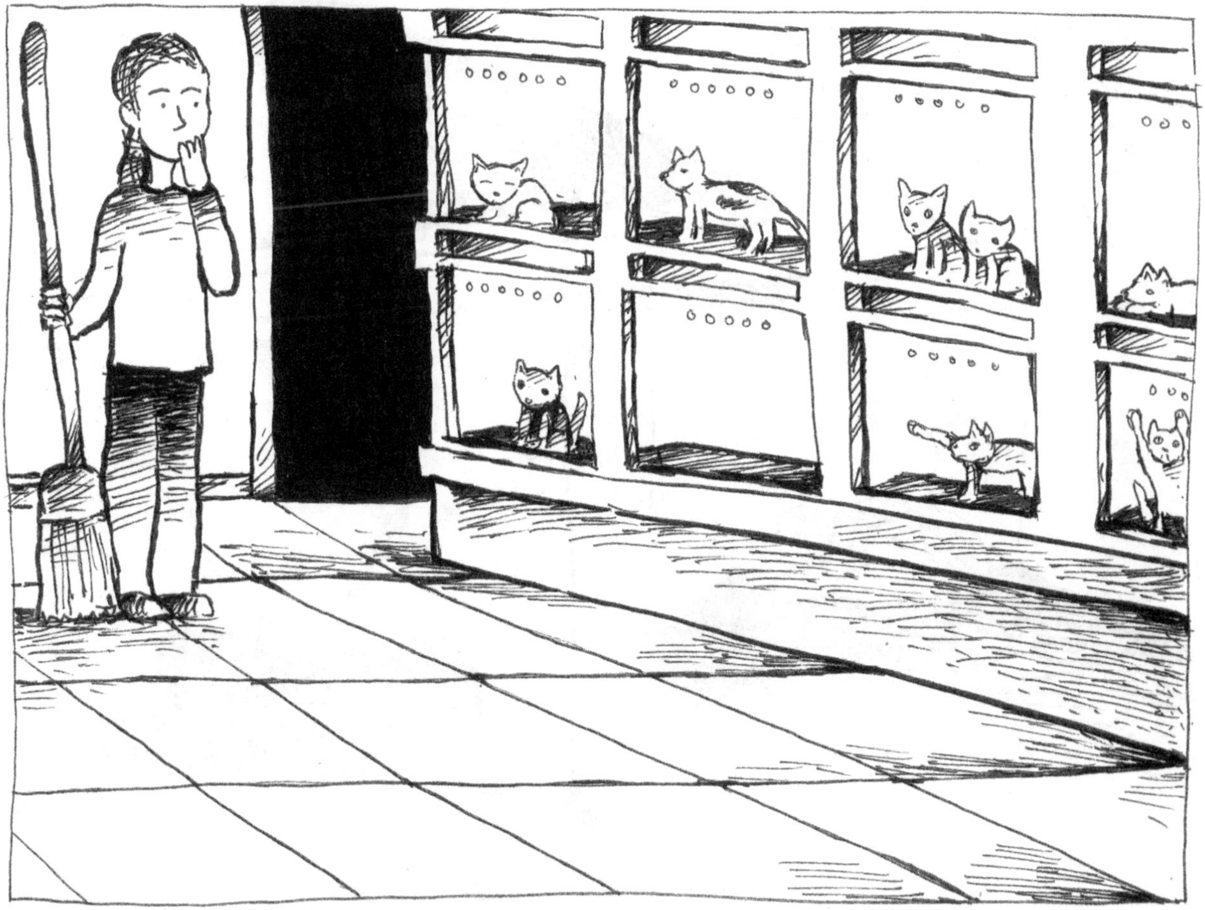

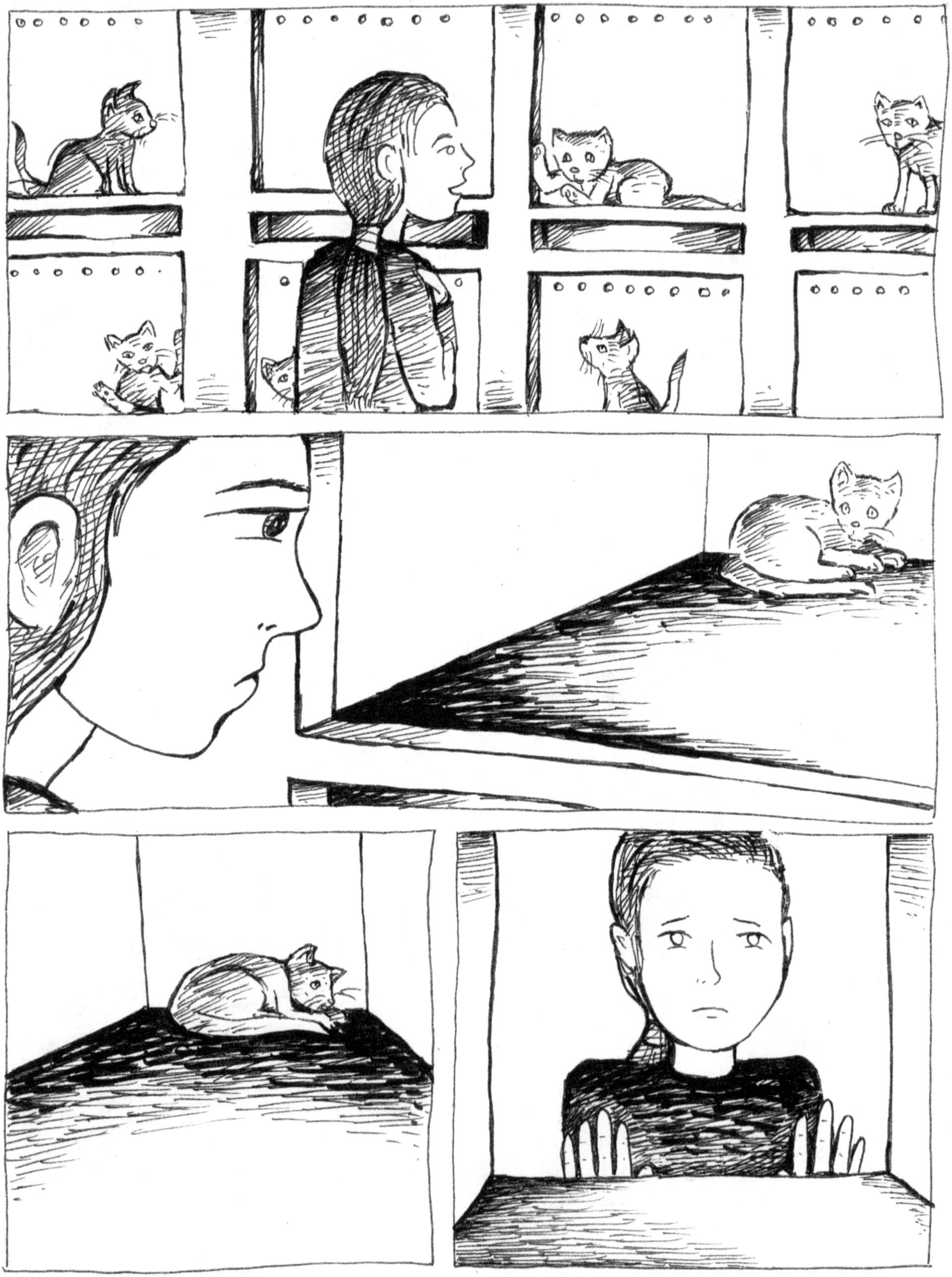

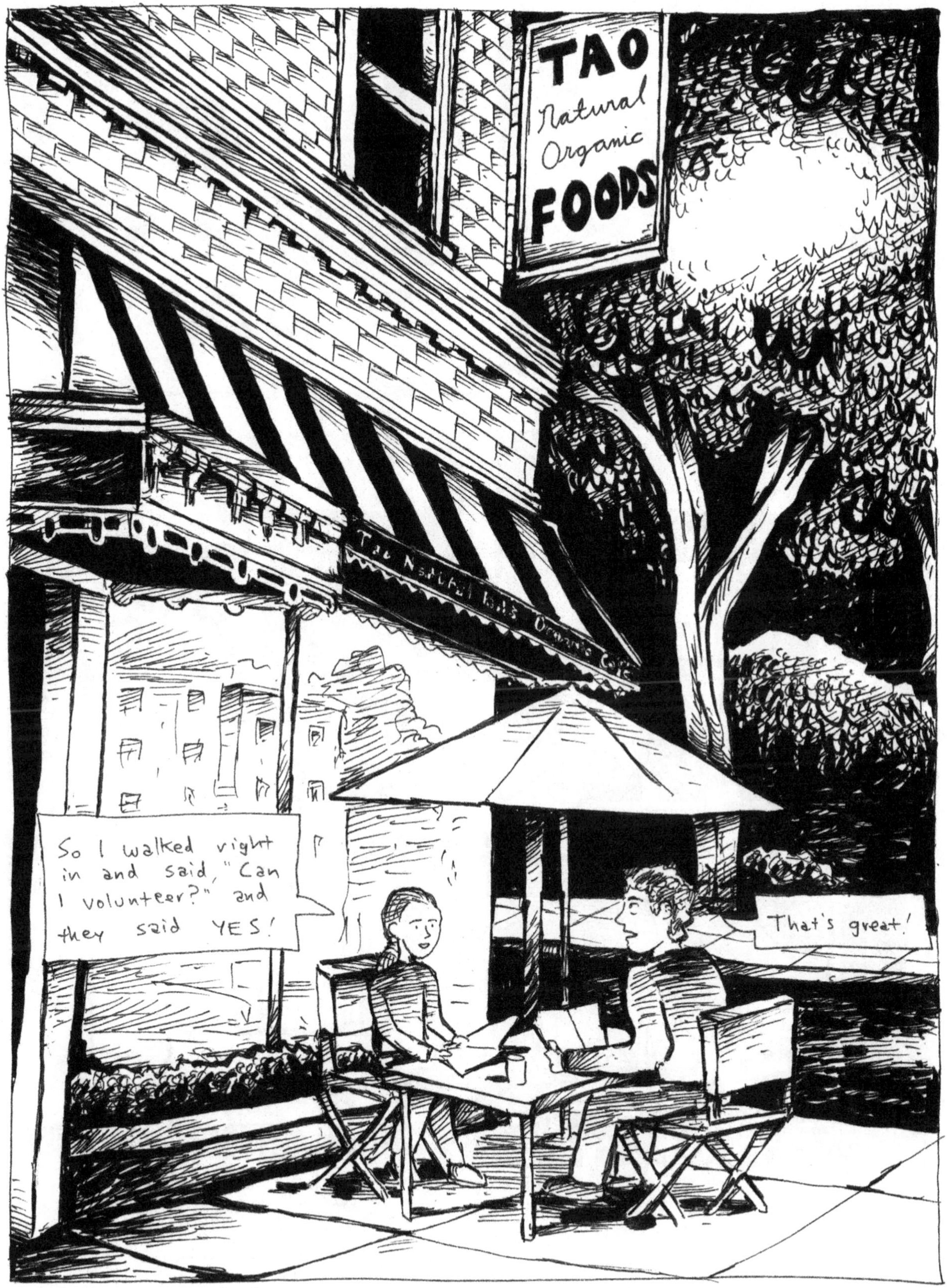
TAO Natural Organic FOODS
So I walked right in and said, "Can I volunteer?" and they said YES!
That's great!

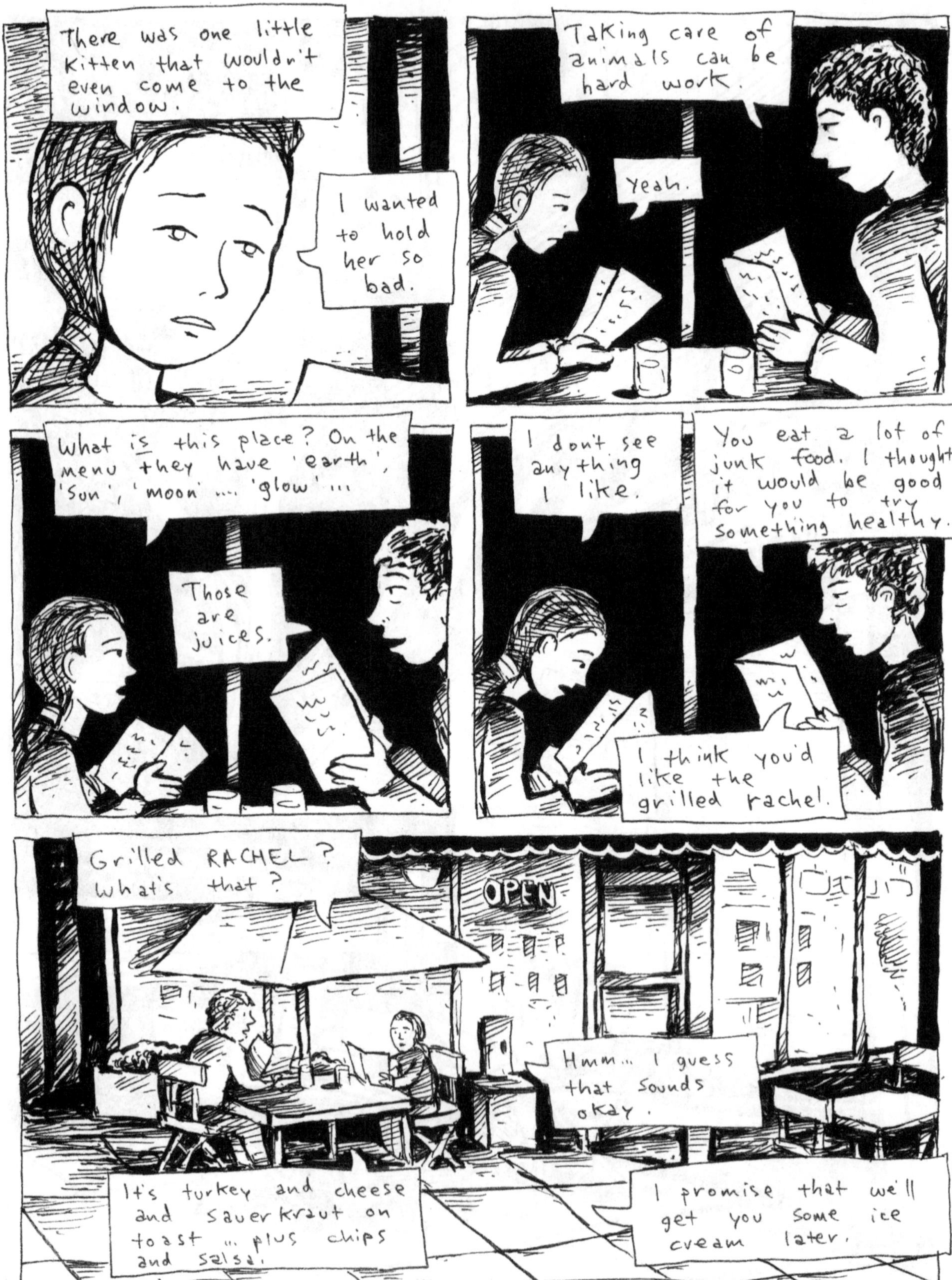
There was one little kitten that wouldn't even come to the window.
I wanted to hold her so bad.
Taking care of animals can be hard work.
Yeah.
What is this place? On the menu they have 'earth', 'sun', 'moon' .... 'glow' ...
Those are juices.
I don't see anything I like.
You eat a lot of junk food. I thought it would be good for you to try something healthy.
I think you'd like the grilled rachel.
Grilled RACHEL? What's that?
OPEN
Hmm... I guess that sounds okay.
It's turkey and cheese and sauerkraut on toast ... plus chips and salsa.
I promise that we'll get you some ice cream later.

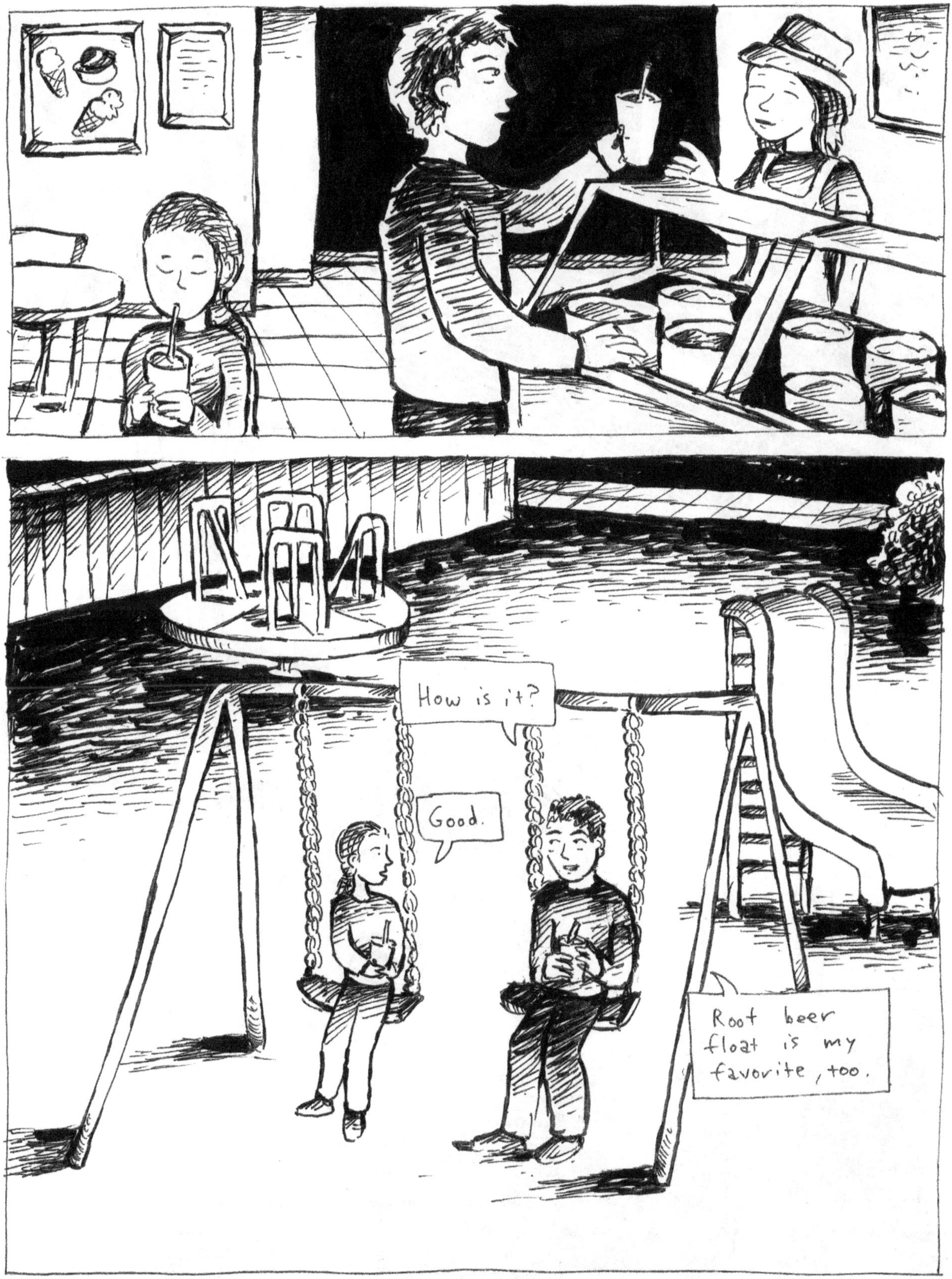
How is it?
Good.
Root beer float is my favorite, too.

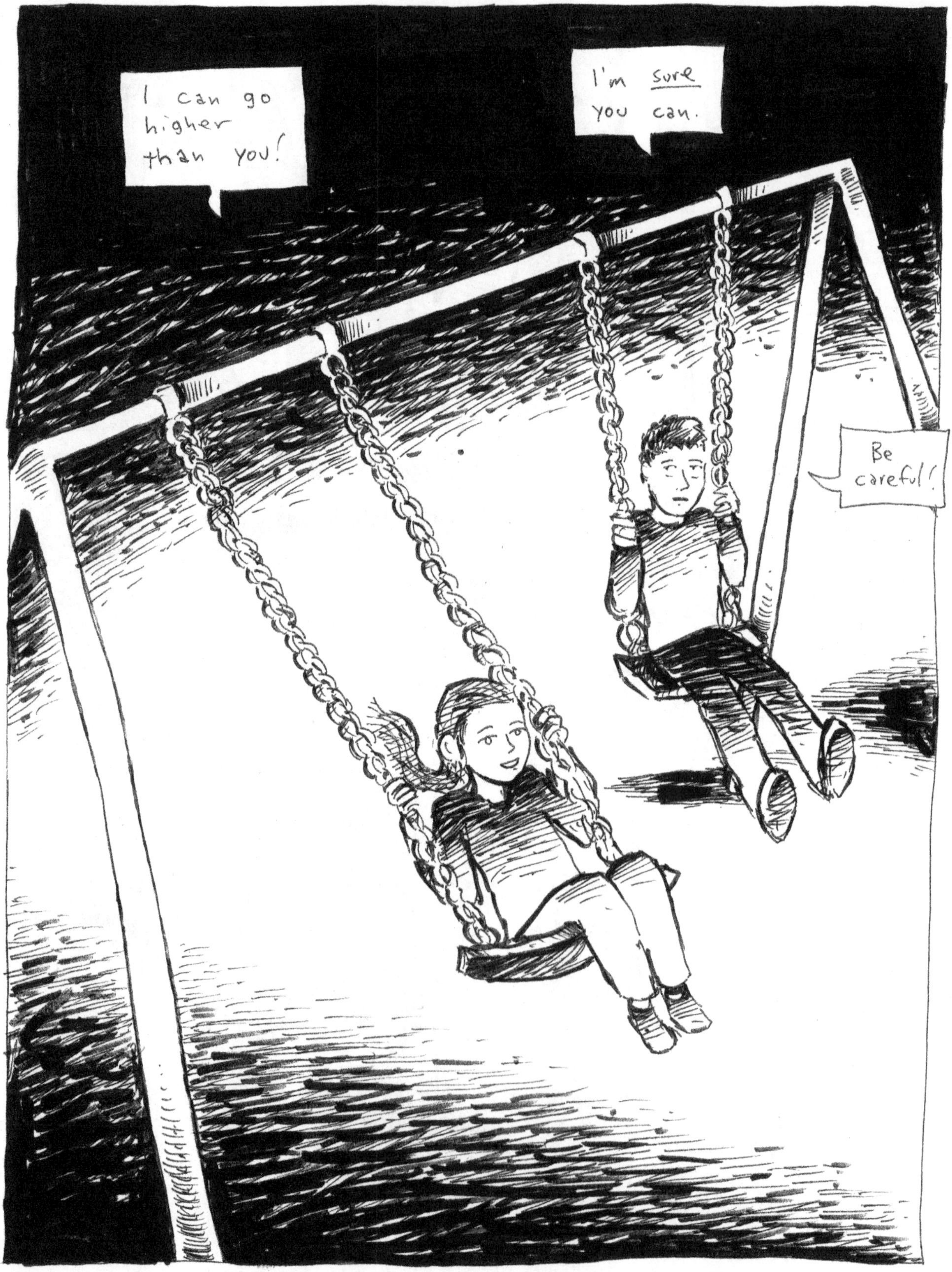
I can go higher than you!
I'm sure you can.
Be careful!

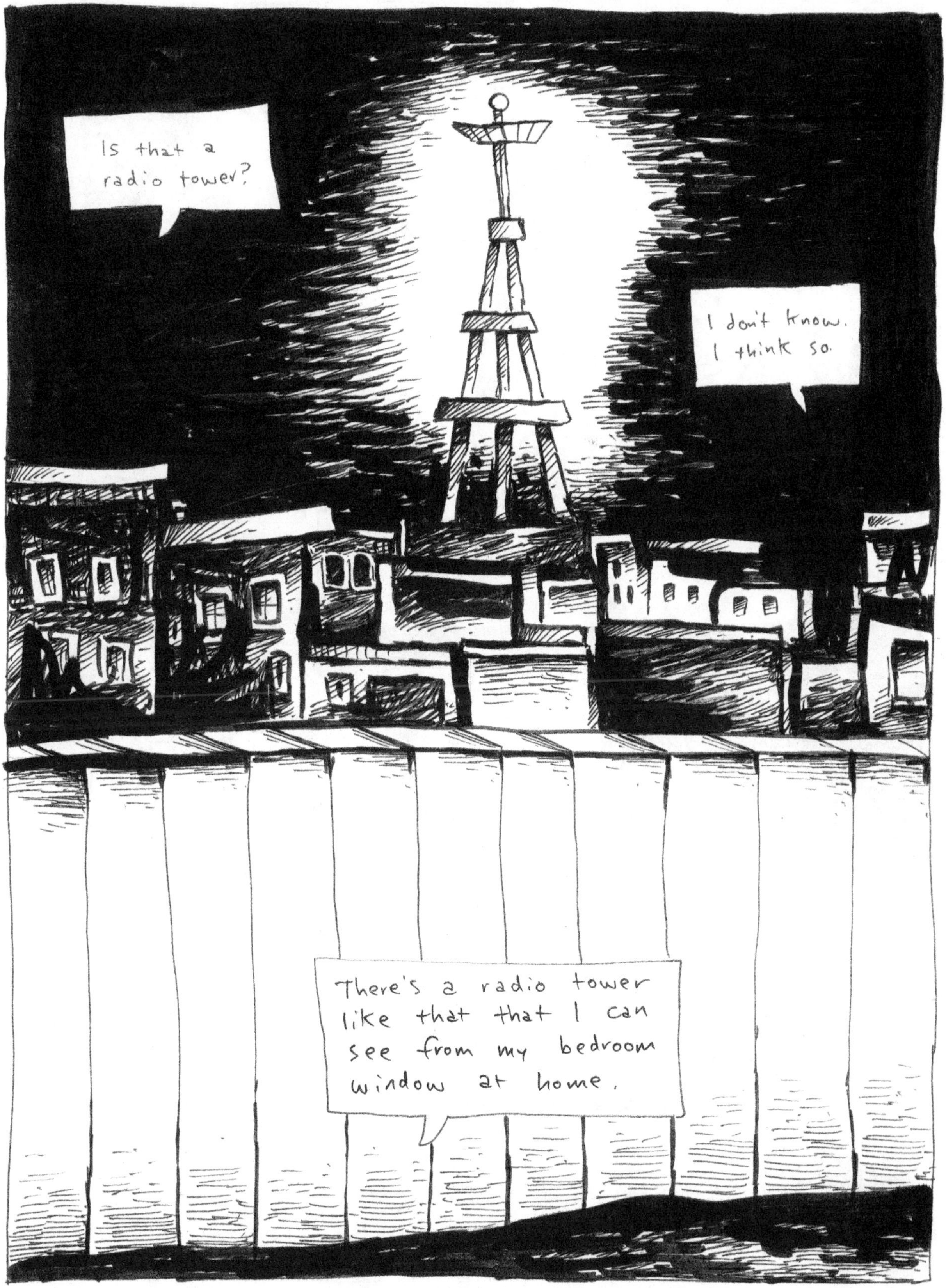
Is that a radio tower?
I don't know. I think so.
There's a radio tower like that that I can see from my bedroom window at home.

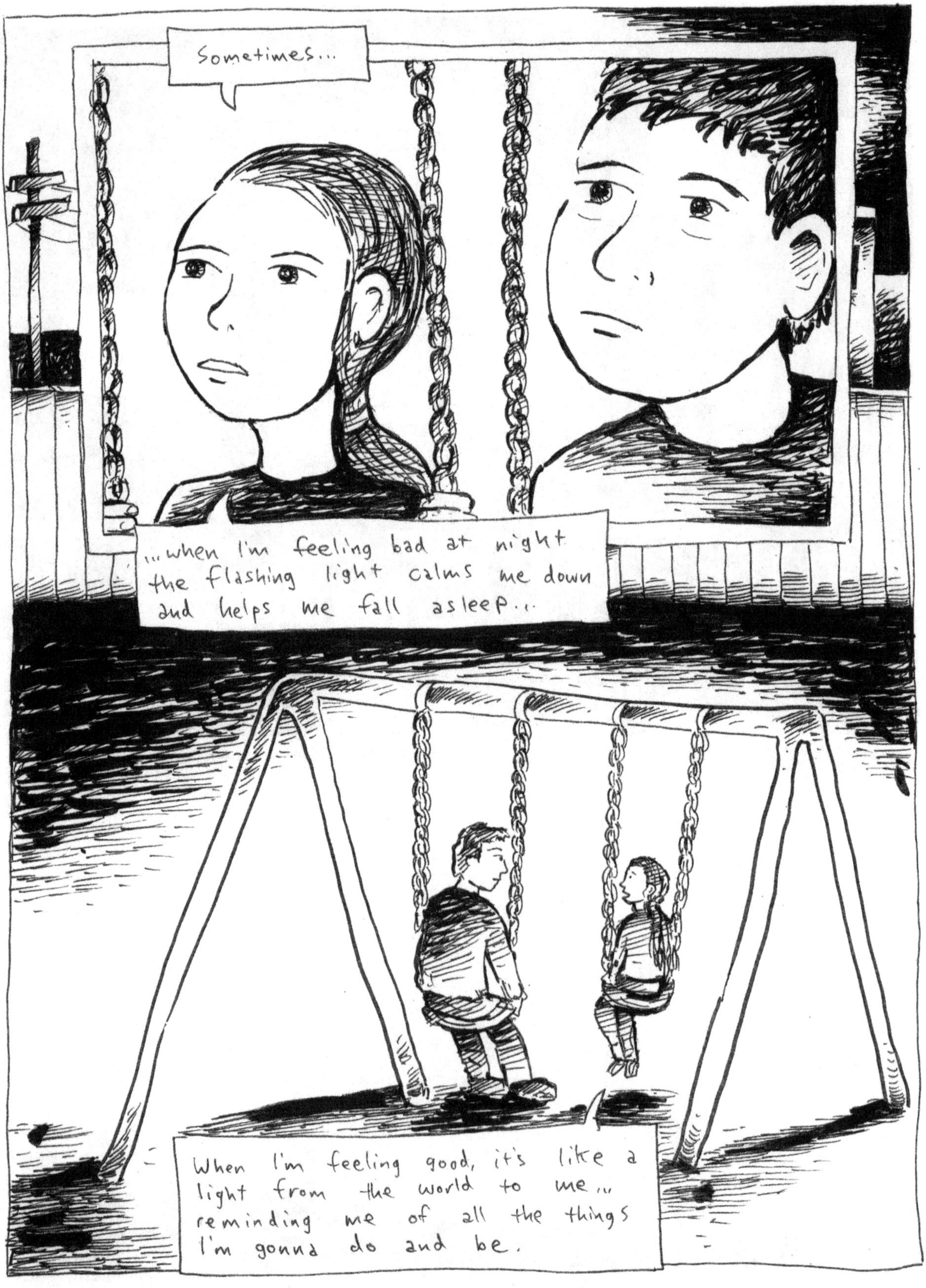
Sometimes...
...when I'm feeling bad at night the flashing light calms me down and helps me fall asleep...
When I'm feeling good, it's like a light from the world to me... reminding me of all the things I'm gonna do and be.

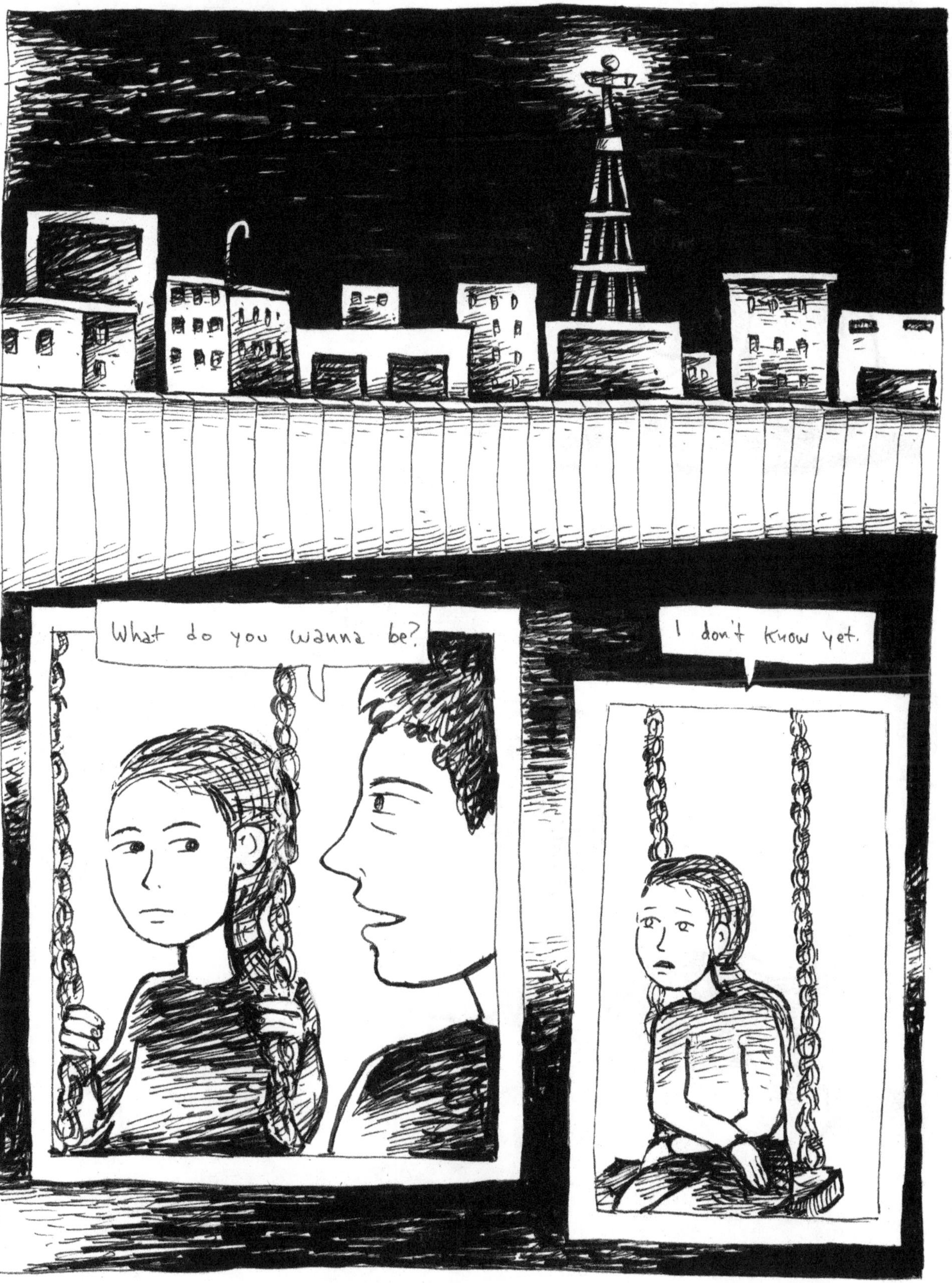
What do you wanna be?
I don't know yet.

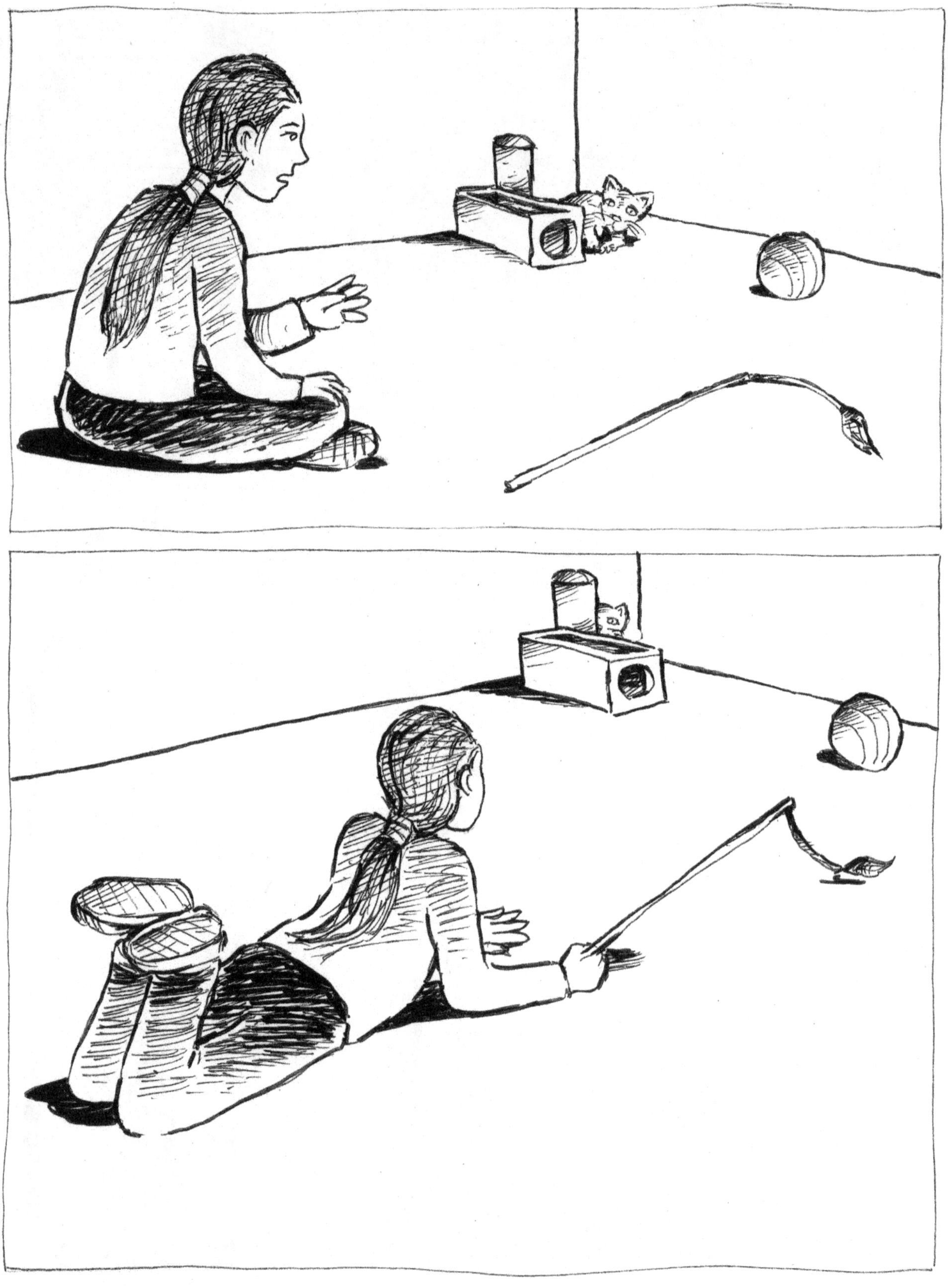

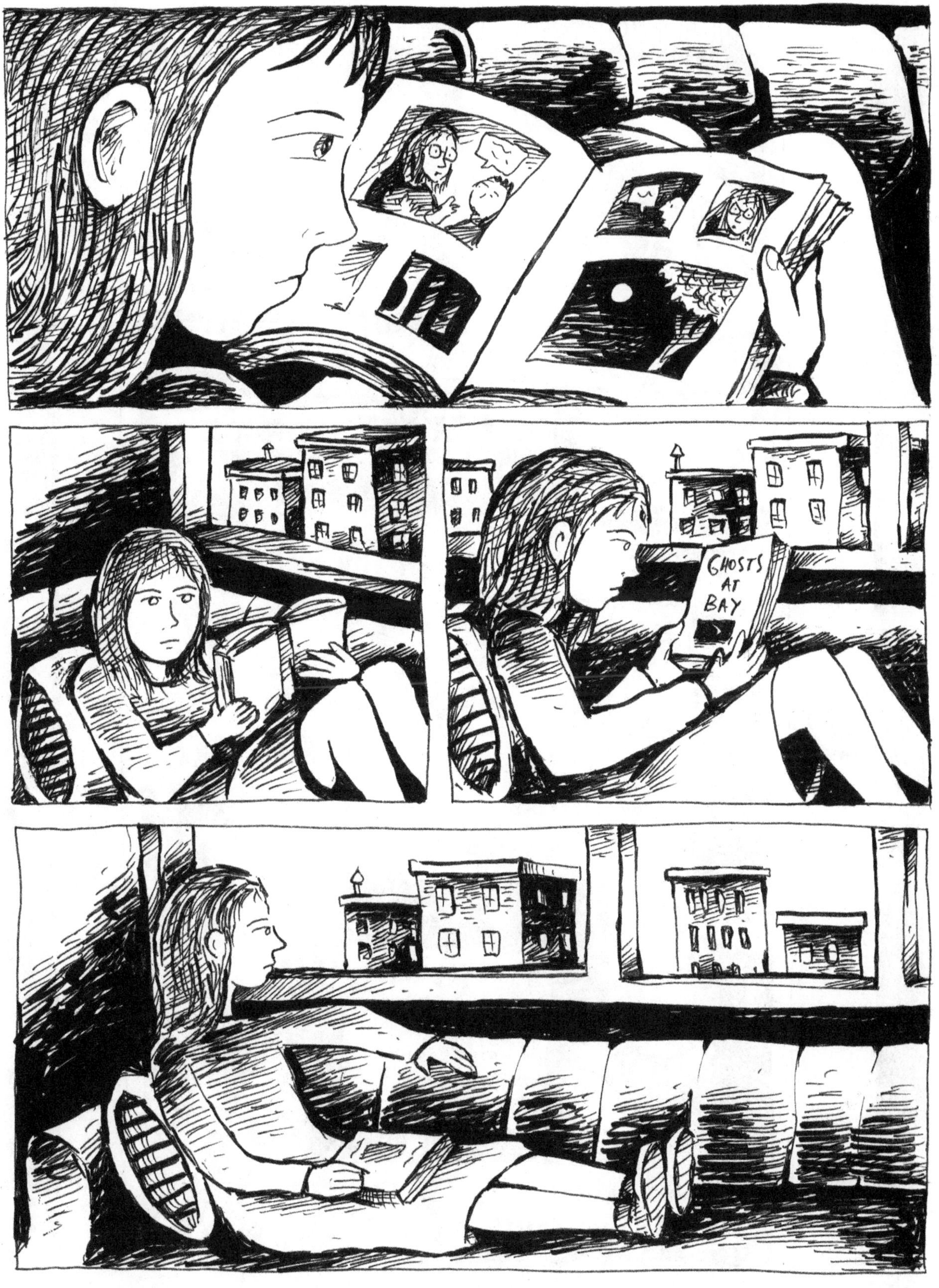
GHOSTS AT BAY

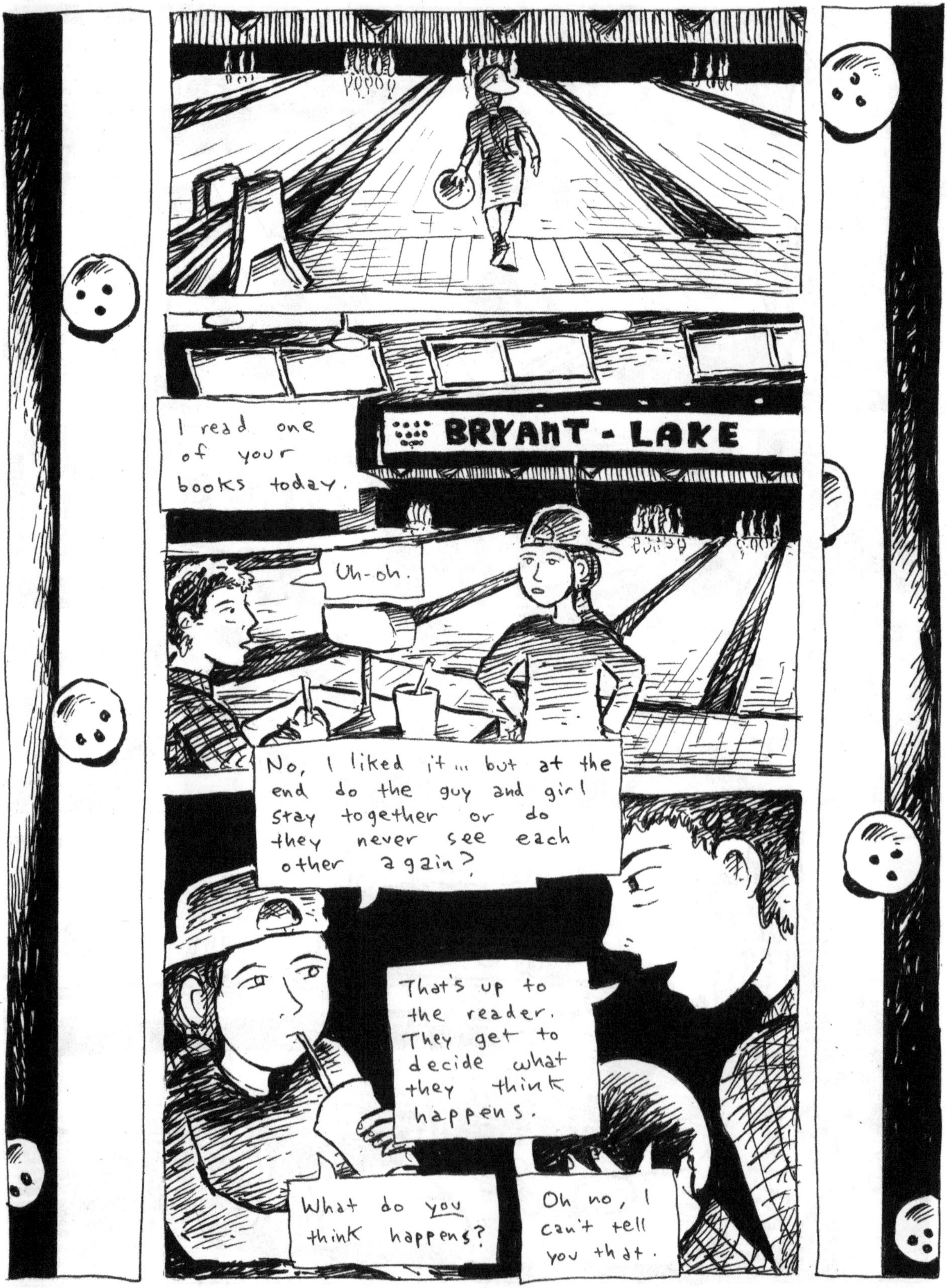
BRYANT - LAKE
I read one of your books today.
Uh-oh.
No, I liked it ... but at the end do the guy and girl stay together or do they never see each other again?
That's up to the reader. They get to decide what they think happens.
What do you think happens?
Oh no, I can't tell you that.

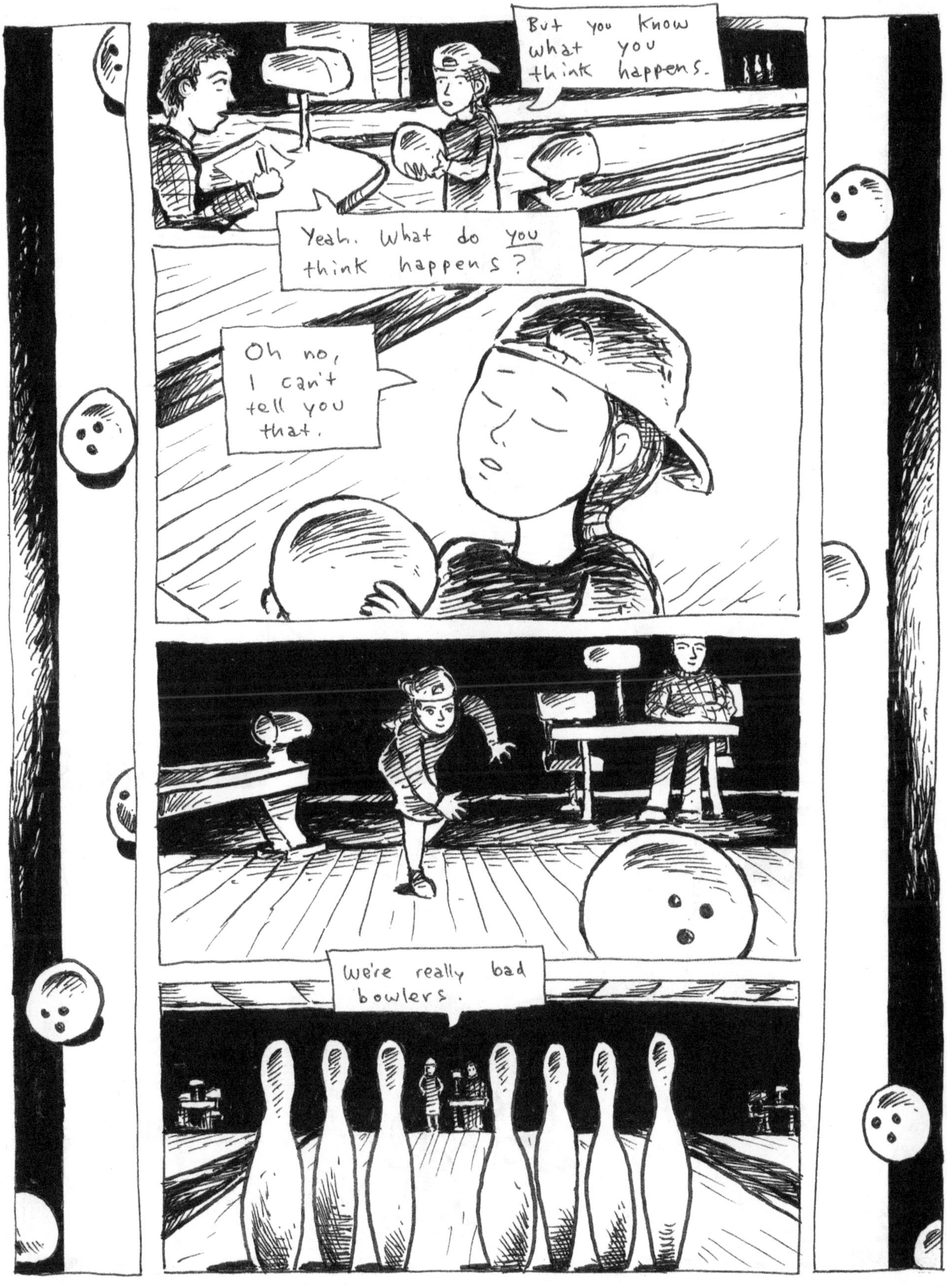
But you know what you think happens.
Yeah. What do you think happens?
Oh no, I can't tell you that.
We're really bad bowlers.

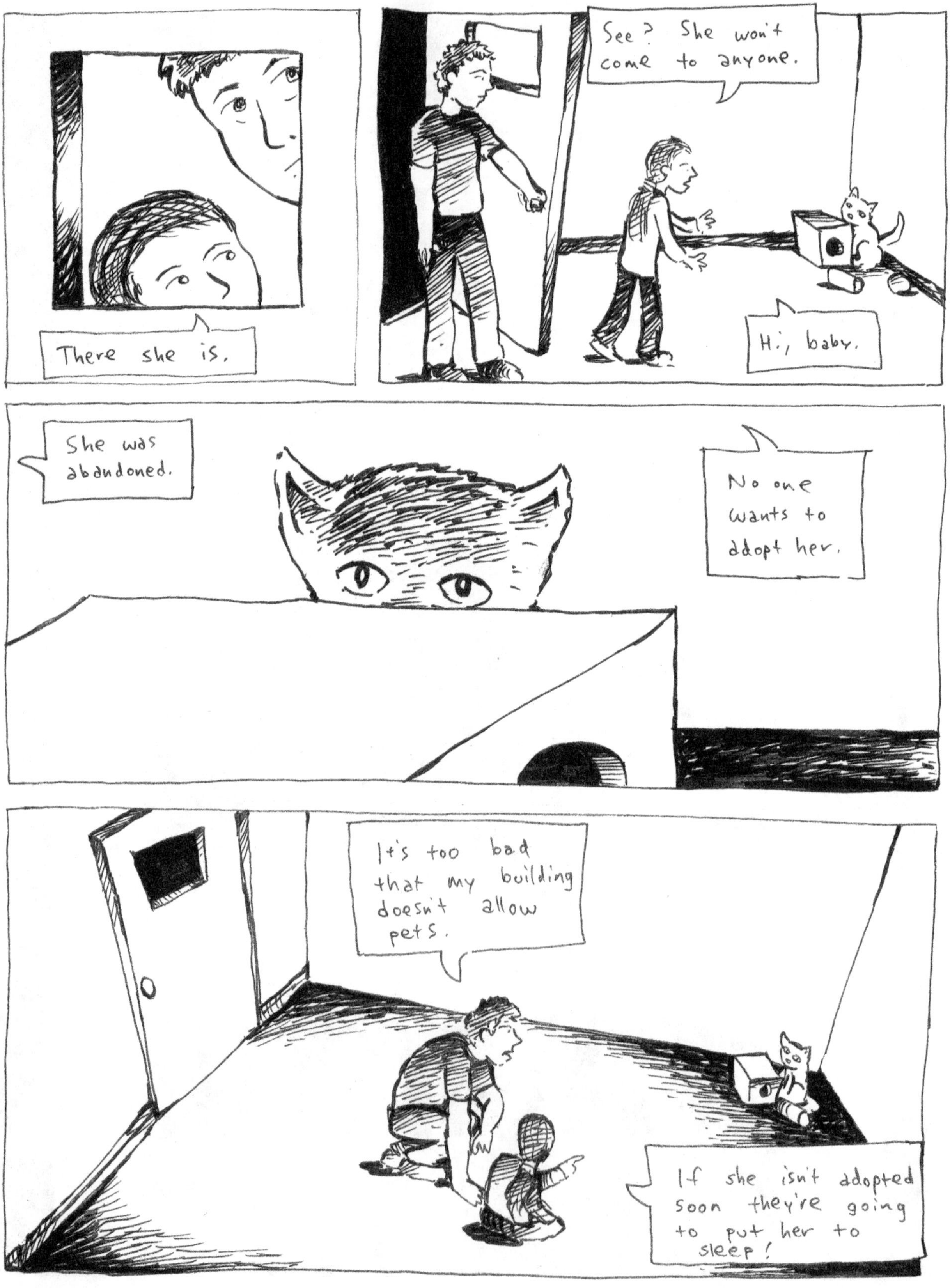
There she is.
See? She won't come to anyone.
Hi, baby.
She was abandoned.
No one wants to adopt her.
It's too bad that my building doesn't allow pets.
If she isn't adopted soon they're going to put her to sleep!

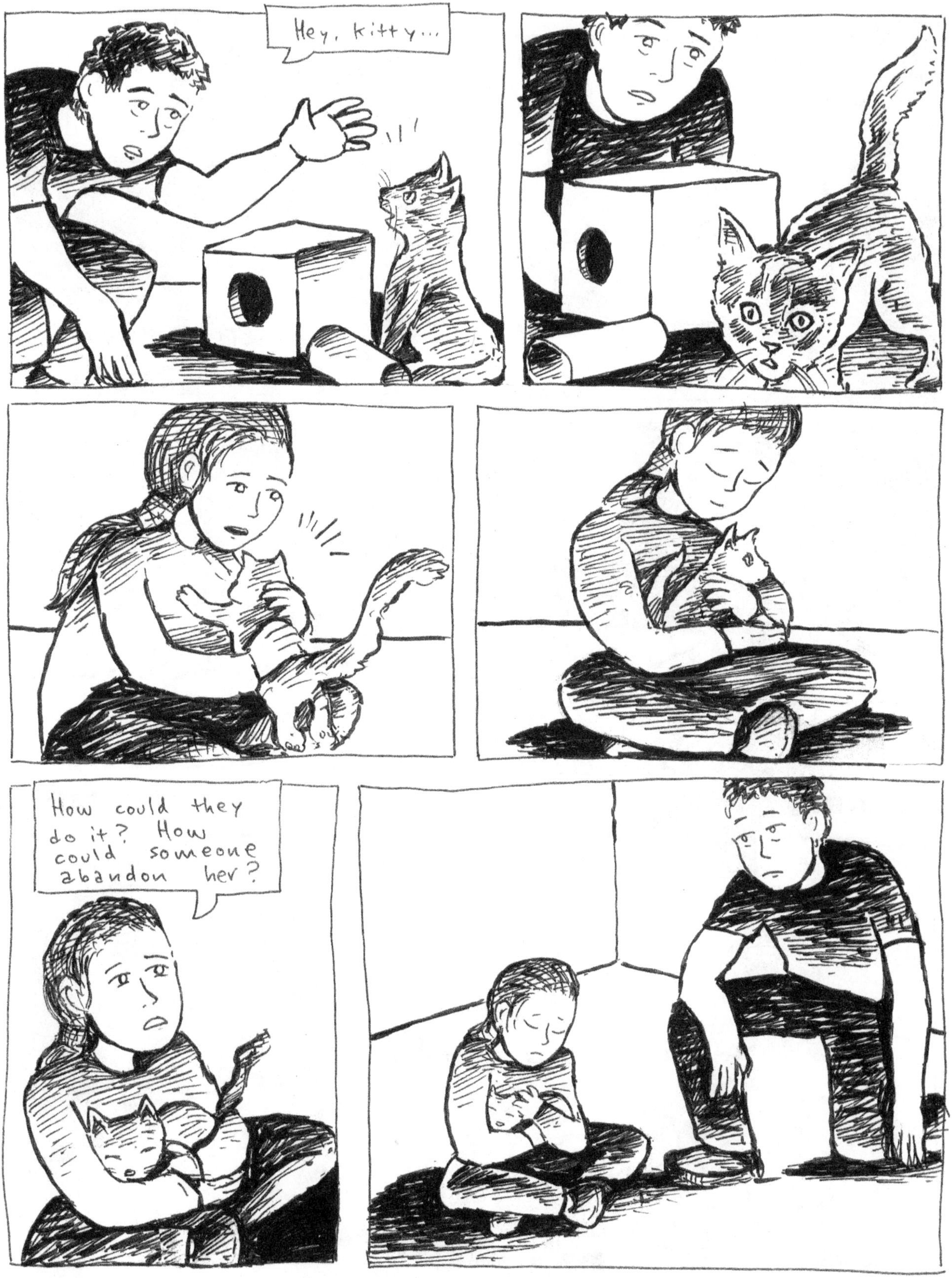
Hey, kitty...
How could they do it? How could someone abandon her?

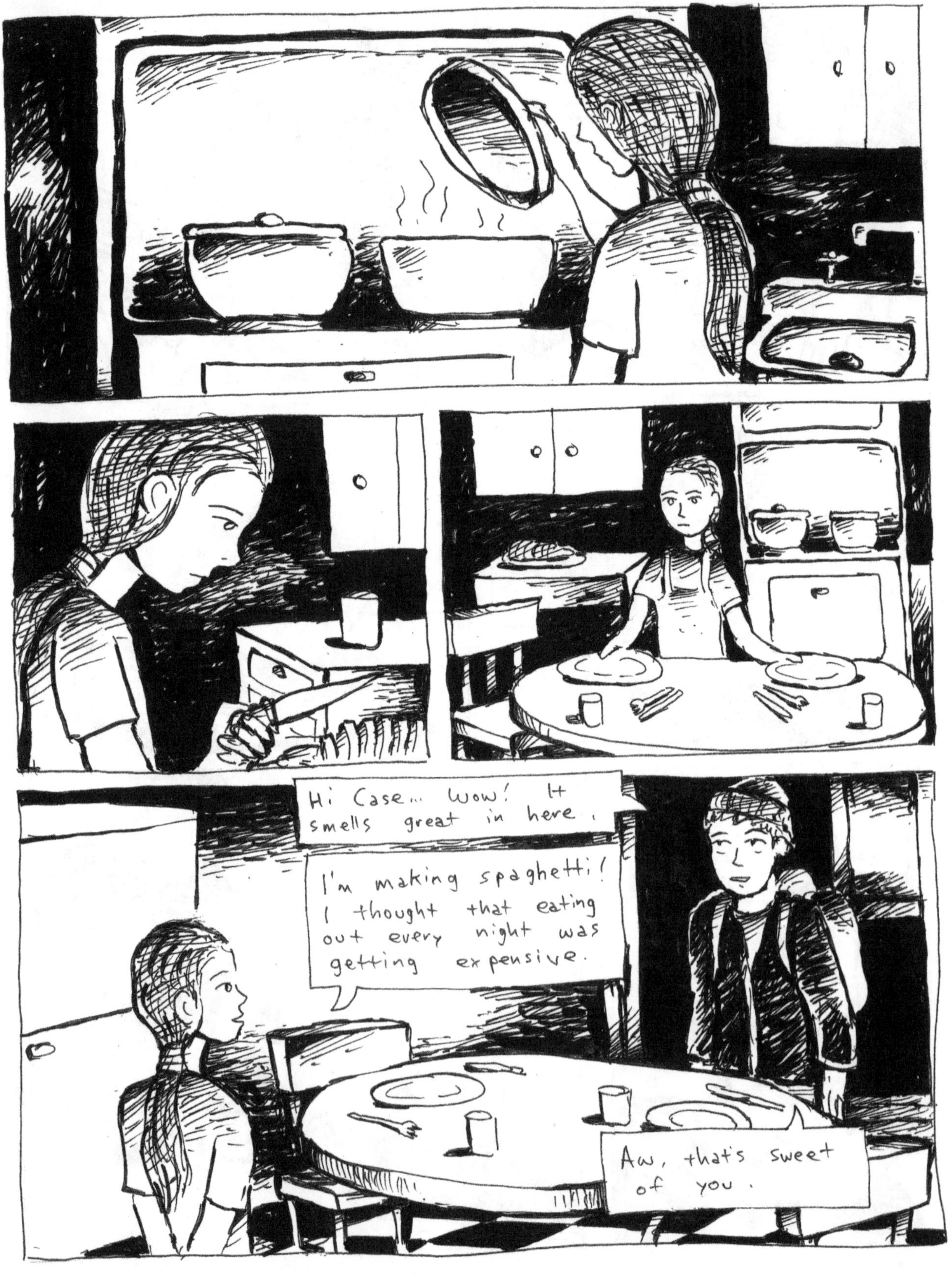
Hi Case... Wow! It smells great in here.
I'm making spaghetti! I thought that eating out every night was getting expensive.
Aw, that's sweet of you.

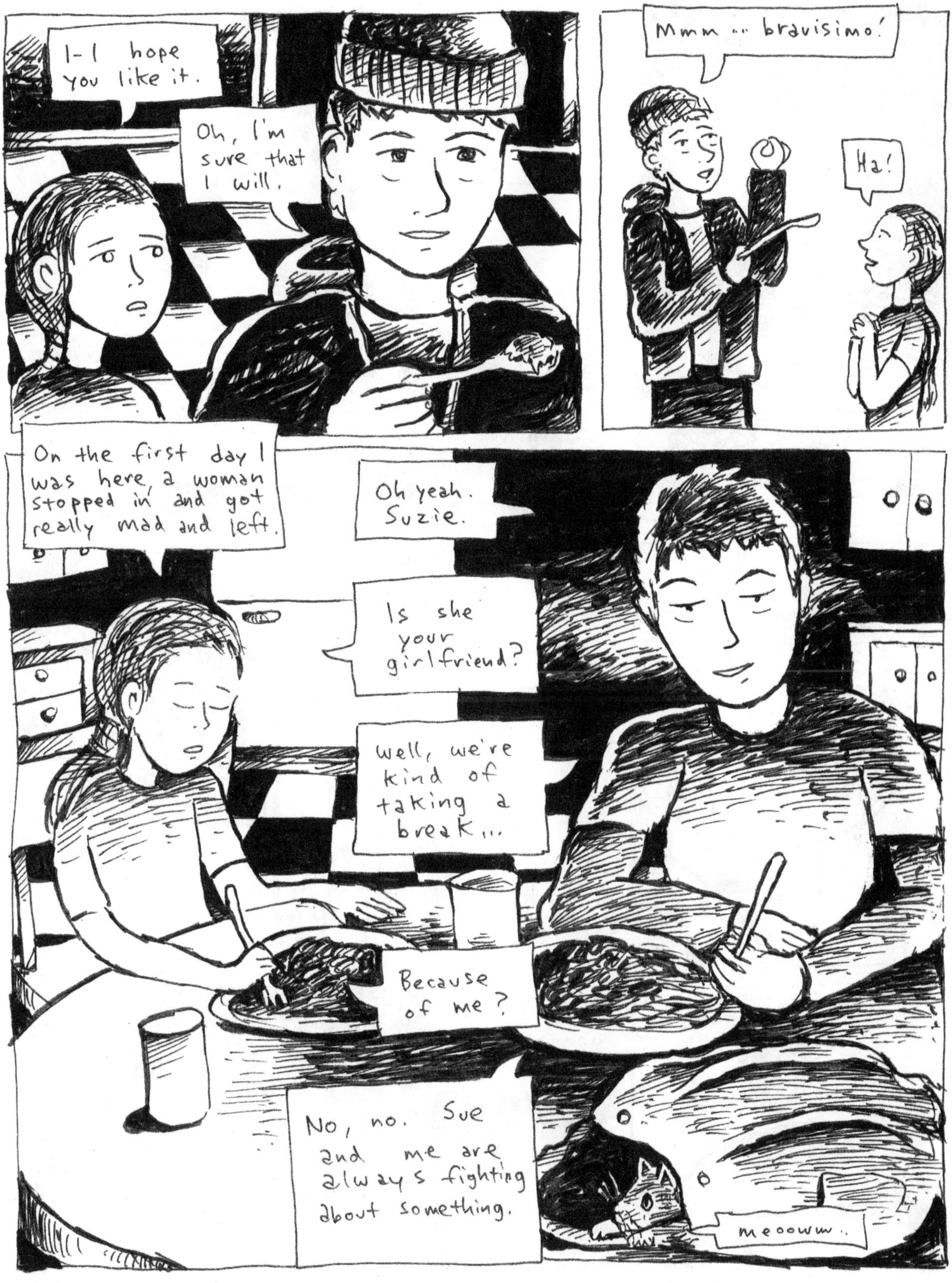
I-I hope you like it.
Oh, I'm sure that I will.
Mmm... bravisimo!
Ha!
On the first day I was here, a woman stopped in and got really mad and left.
Oh yeah. Suzie.
Is she your girlfriend?
Well, we're kind of taking a break...
Because of me?
No, no. Sue and me are always fighting about something.
meooww..

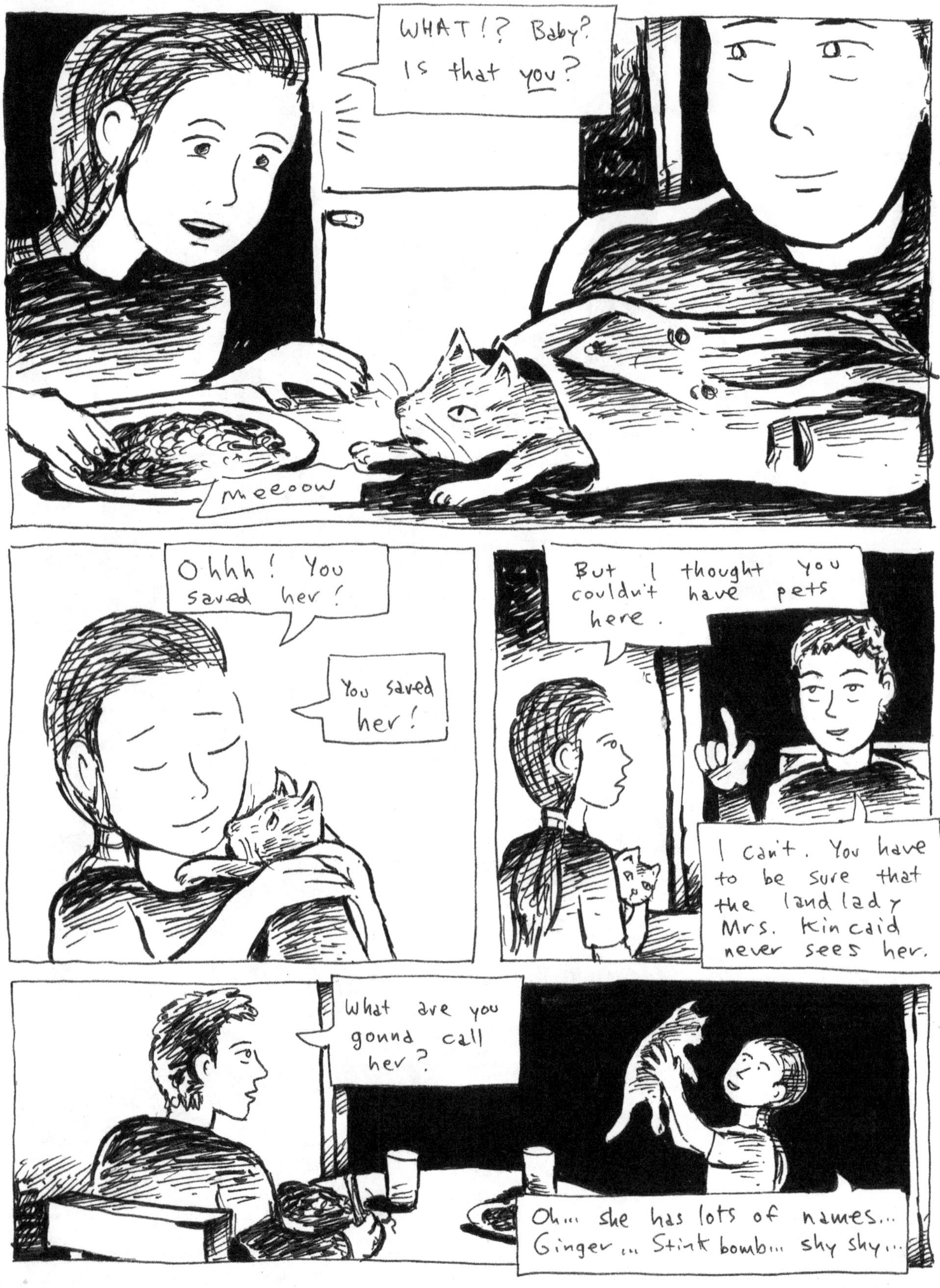
WHAT!? Baby? Is that you?
Meeoow
Ohhh! You saved her!
You saved her!
But I thought you couldn't have pets here.
I can't. You have to be sure that the landlady Mrs. Kincaid never sees her.
What are you gonna call her?
Oh... she has lots of names... Ginger... Stink bomb... shy shy...

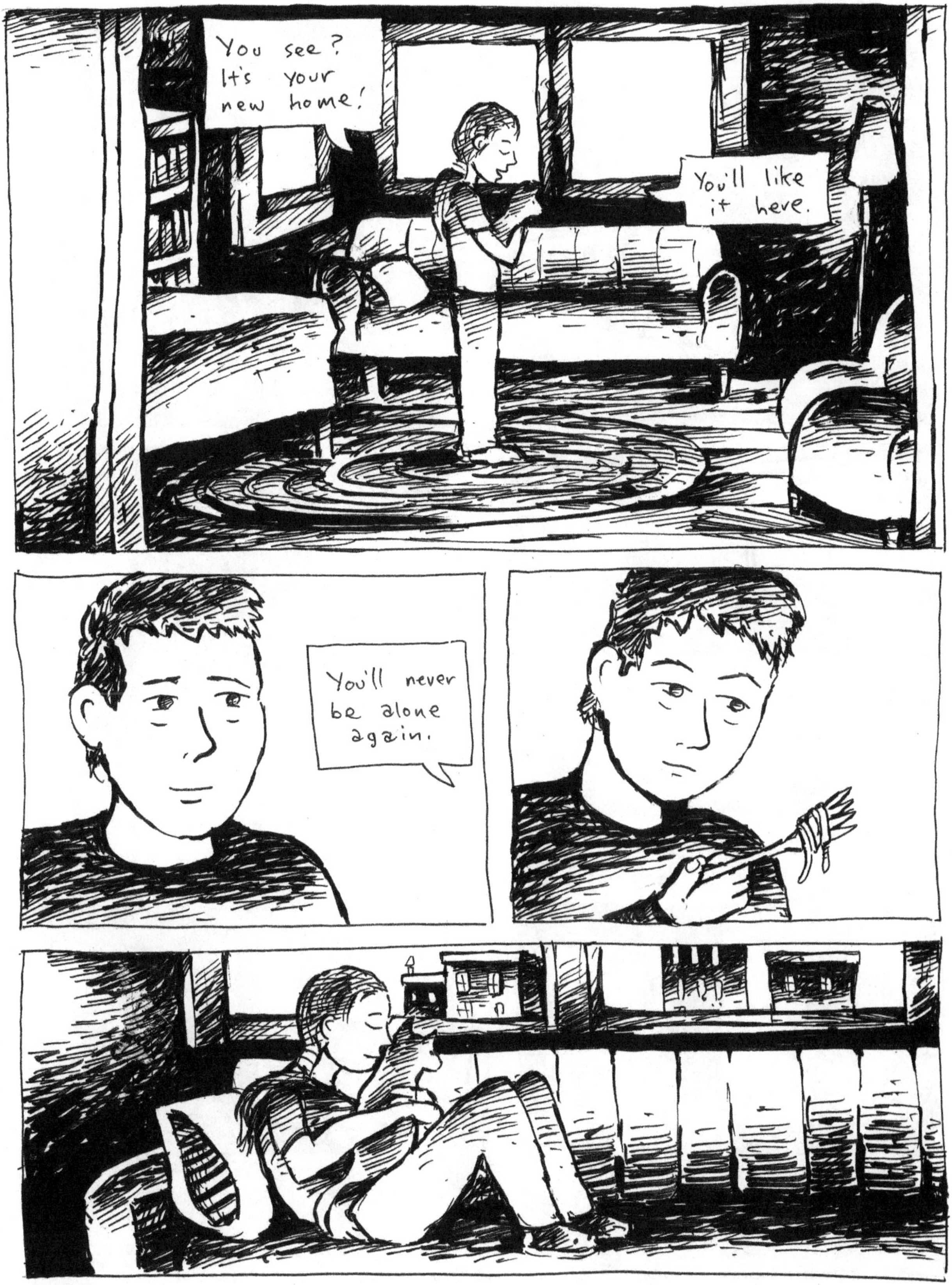
You see? It's your new home!
You'll like it here.
You'll never be alone again.

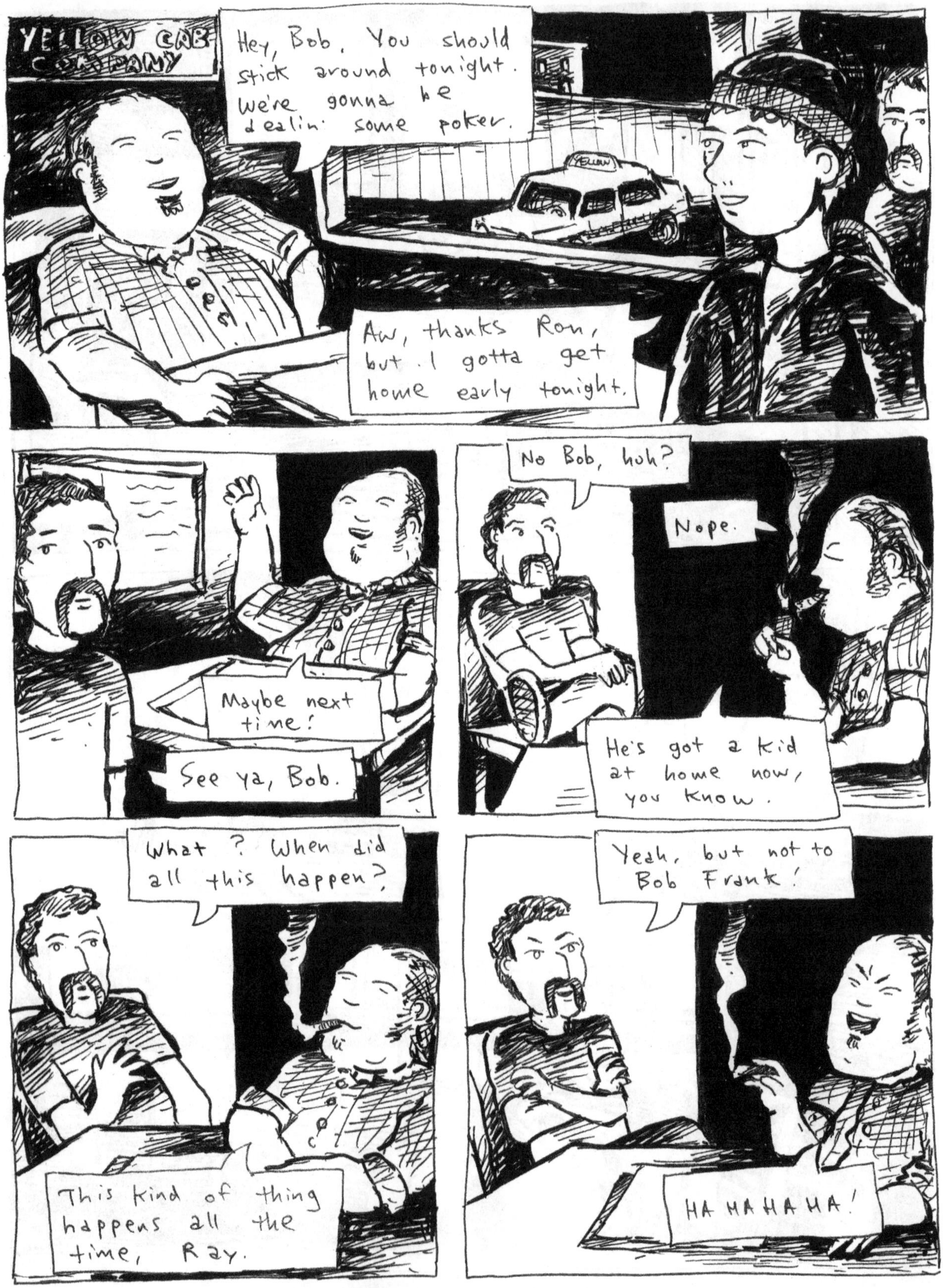
YELLOW CAB COMPANY
Hey, Bob. You should stick around tonight. We're gonna be dealin' some poker.
YELLOW
Aw, thanks Ron, but I gotta get home early tonight.
Maybe next time!
See ya, Bob.
No Bob, huh?
Nope.
He's got a kid at home now, you know.
What? When did all this happen?
This kind of thing happens all the time, Ray.
Yeah, but not to Bob Frank!
HA HA HA HA HA!

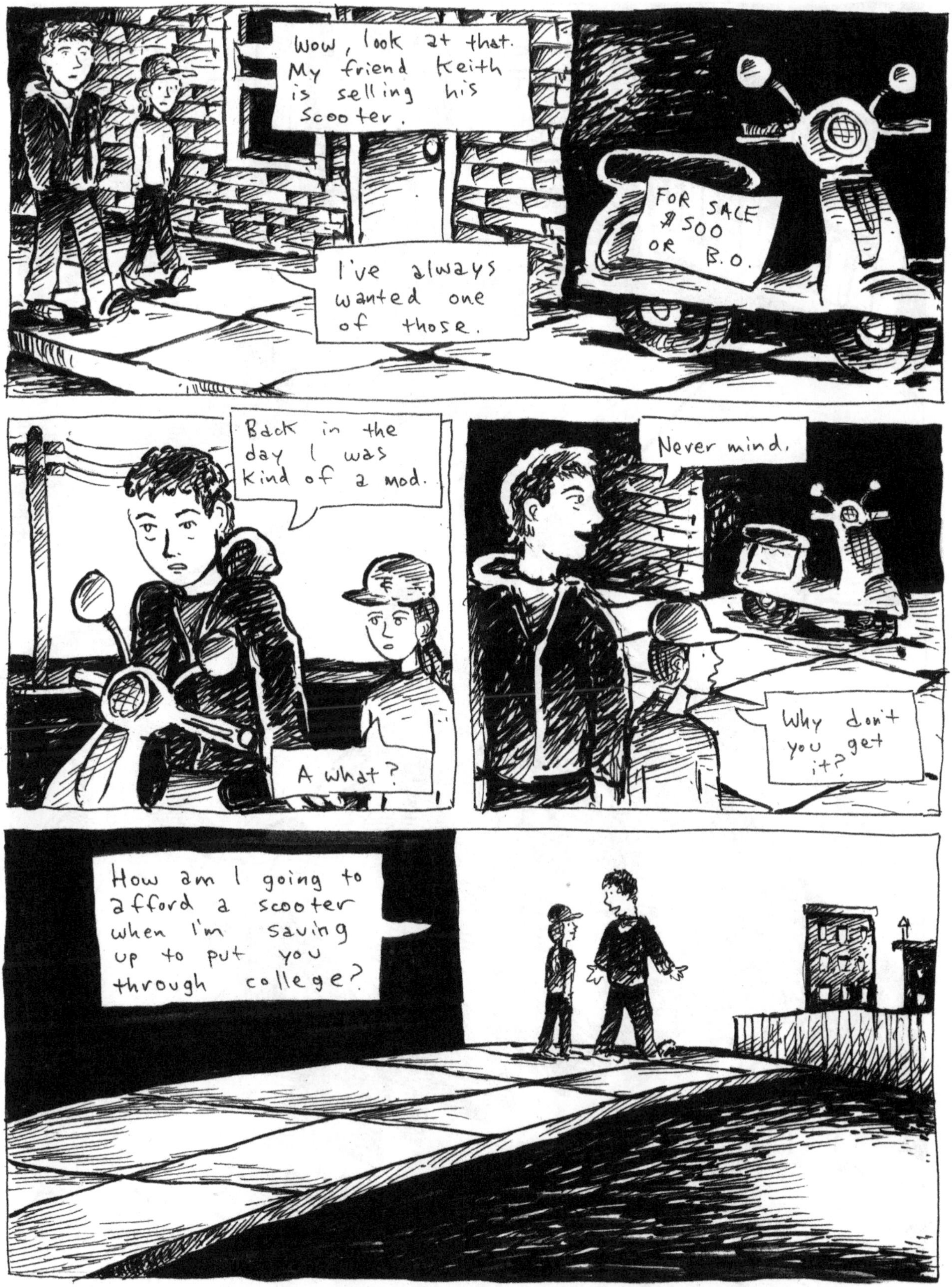
Wow, look at that. My friend Keith is selling his Scooter.
I've always wanted one of those.
FOR SALE $500 OR B.O.
Back in the day I was kind of a mod.
A what?
Never mind.
Why don't you get it?
How am I going to afford a scooter when I'm saving up to put you through college?

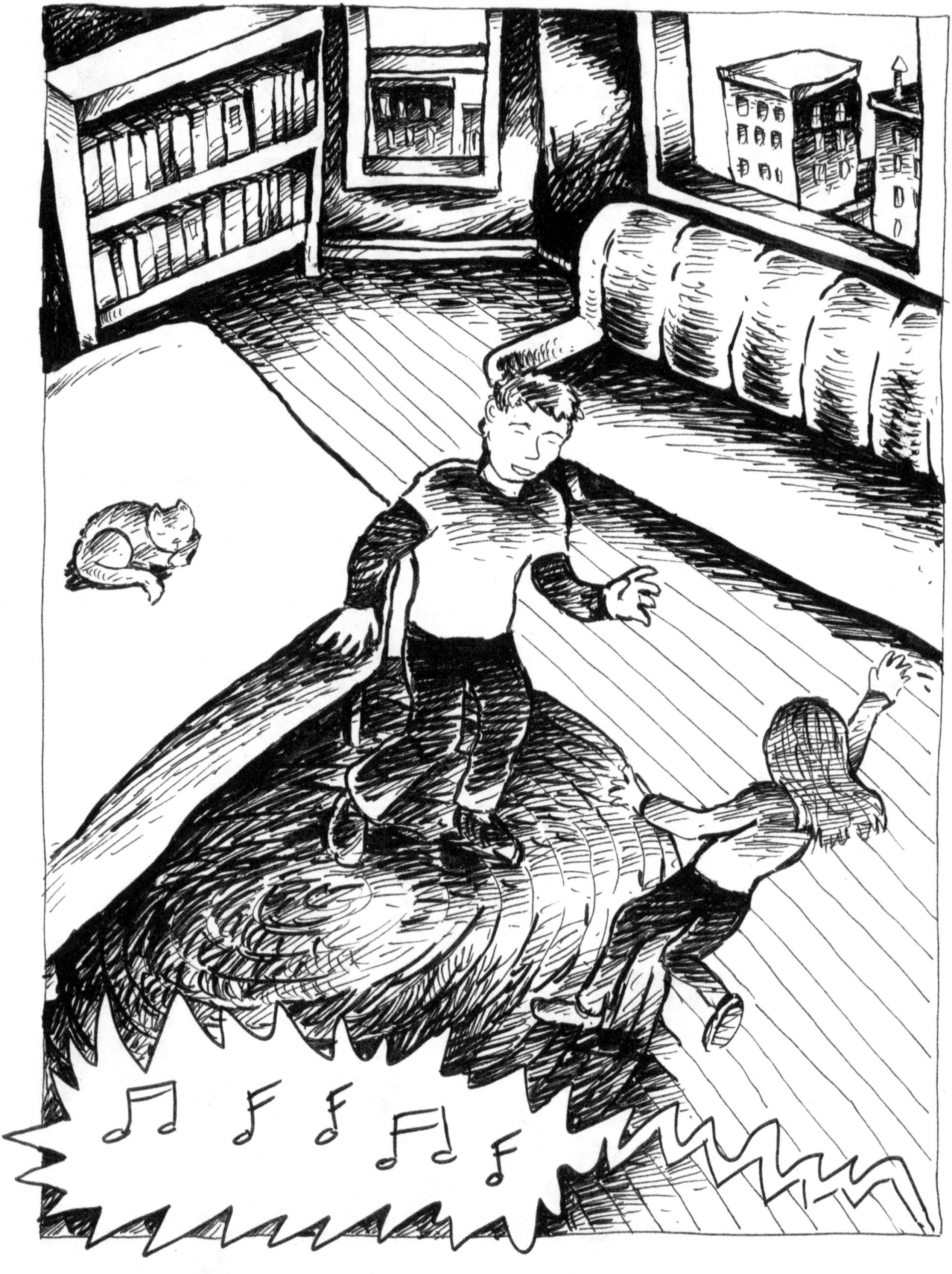

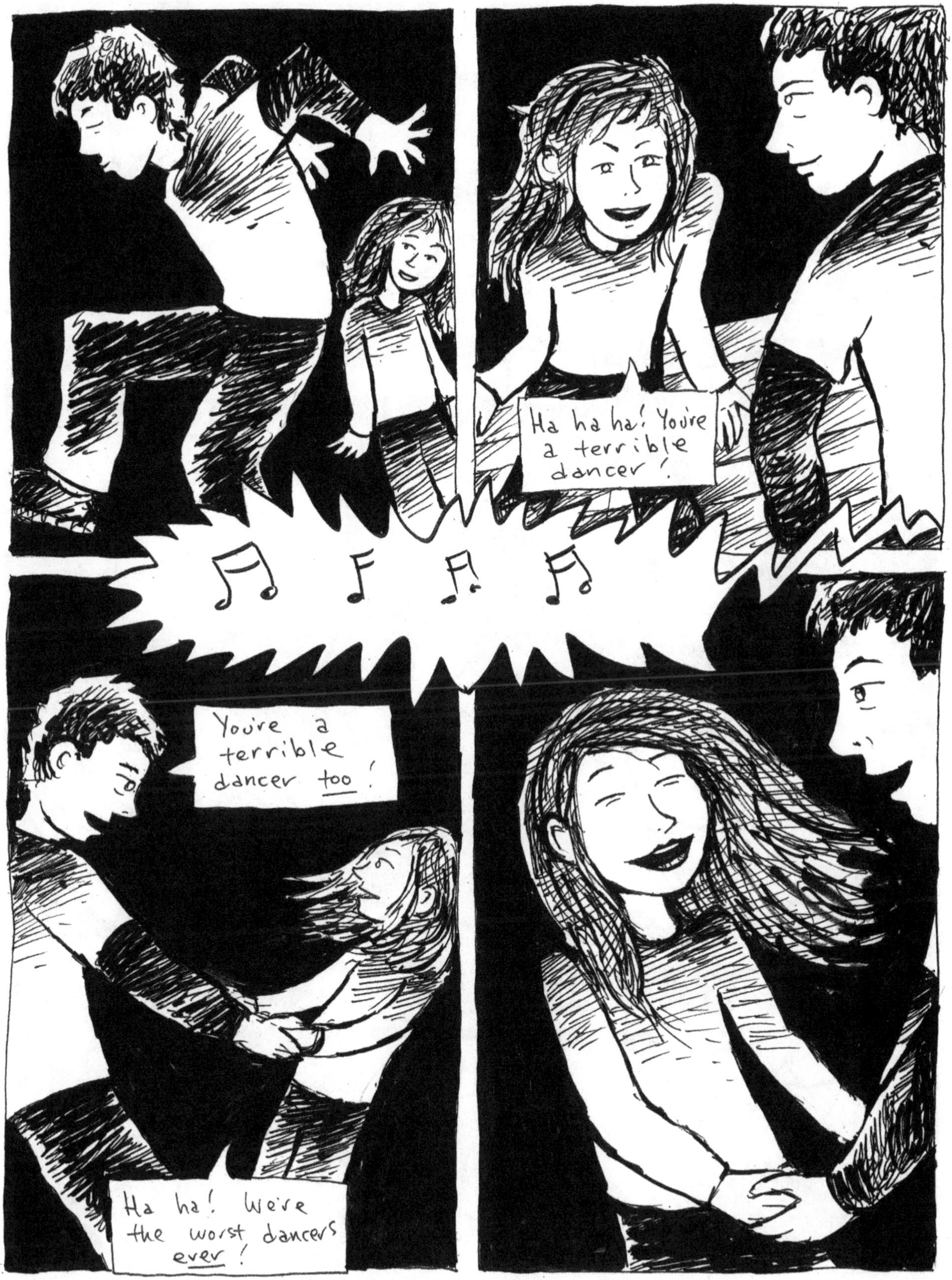
Ha ha ha! You're a terrible dancer!
You're a terrible dancer too!
Ha ha! We're the worst dancers ever!

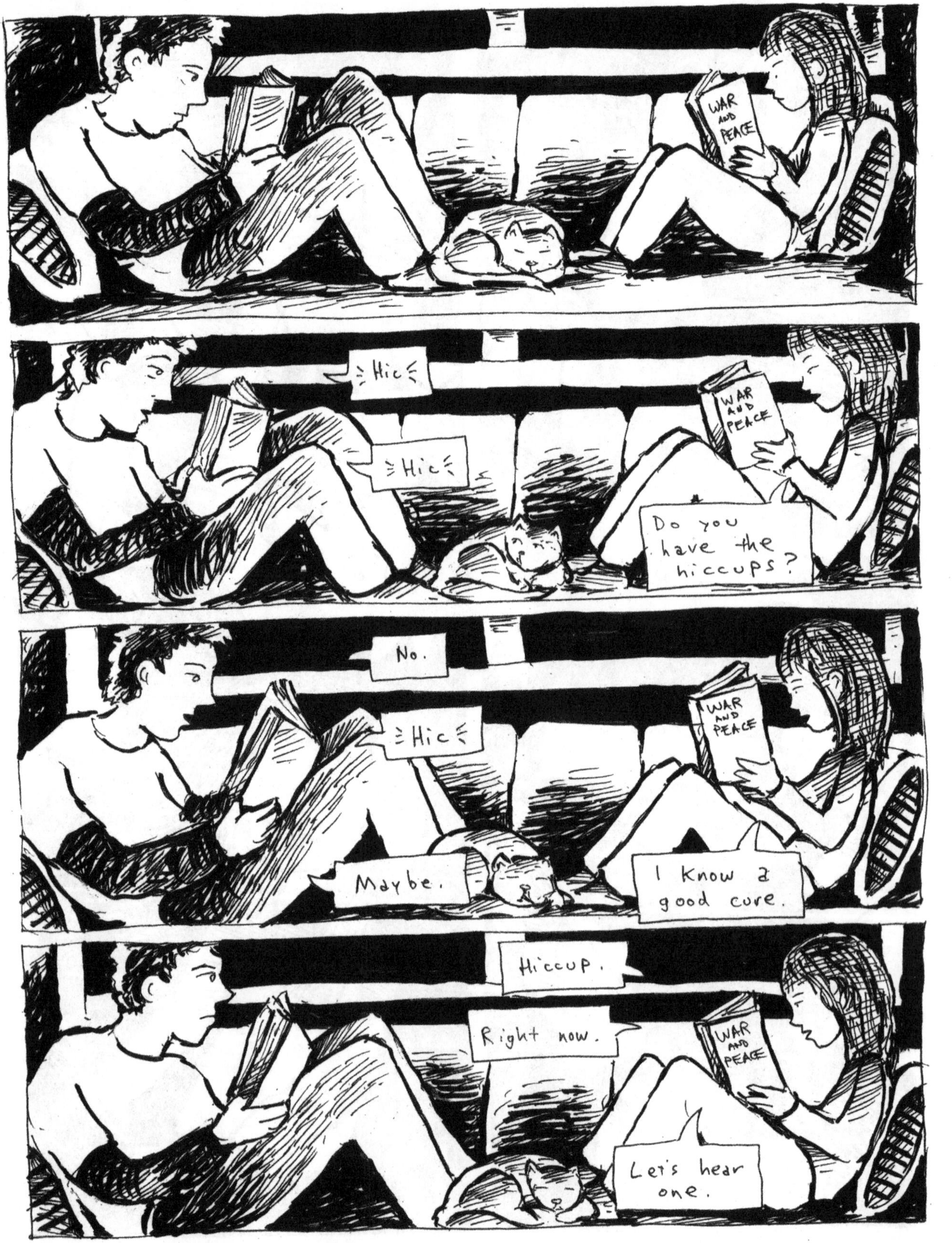
WAR AND PEACE
Hic
Hic
Do you have the hiccups?
No.
Hic
Maybe.
I know a good cure.
Hiccup.
Right now.
Let's hear one.

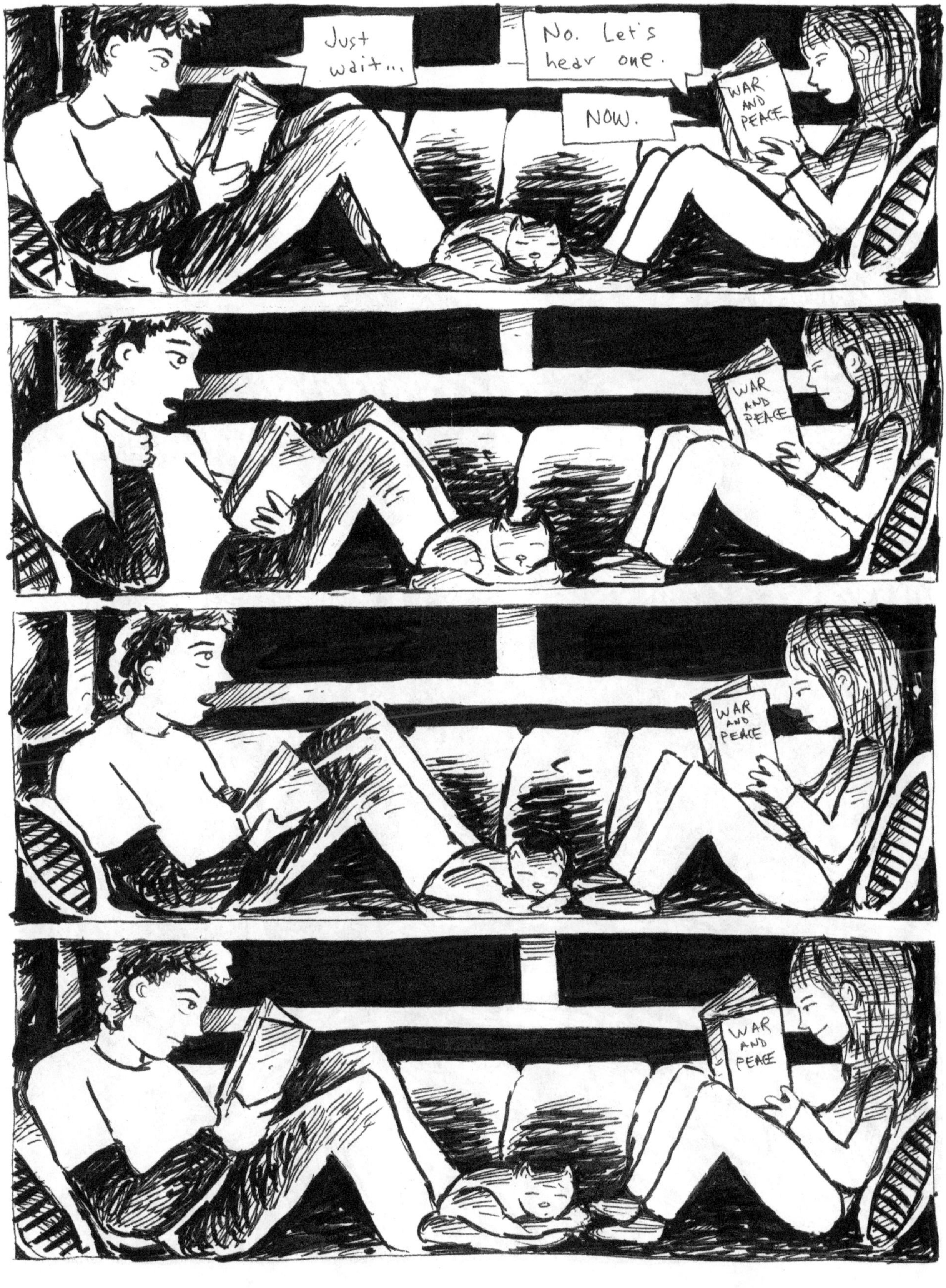
Just wait...
No. Let's hear one.
NOW.
WAR AND PEACE
WAR AND PEACE
WAR AND PEACE
WAR AND PEACE

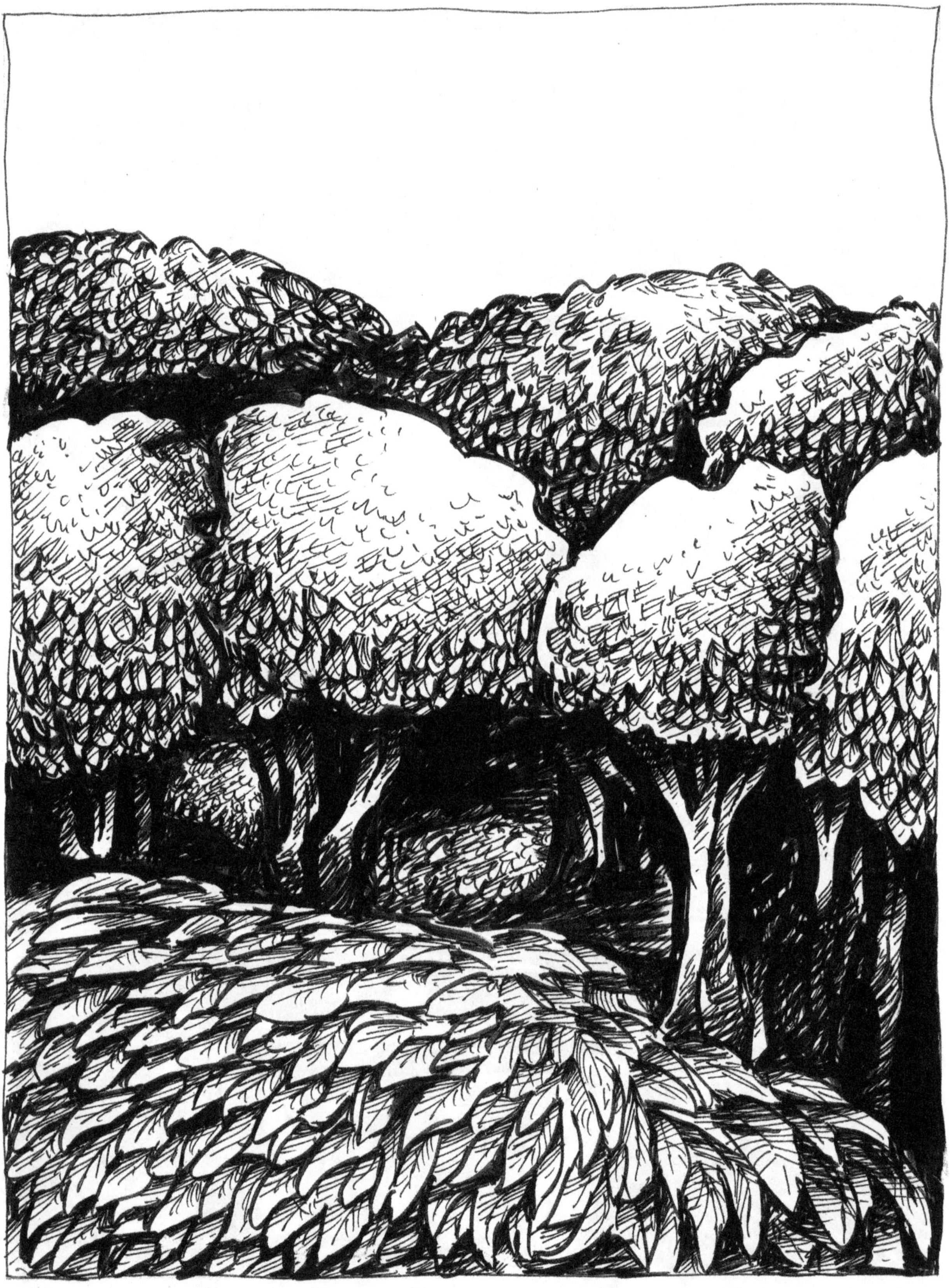

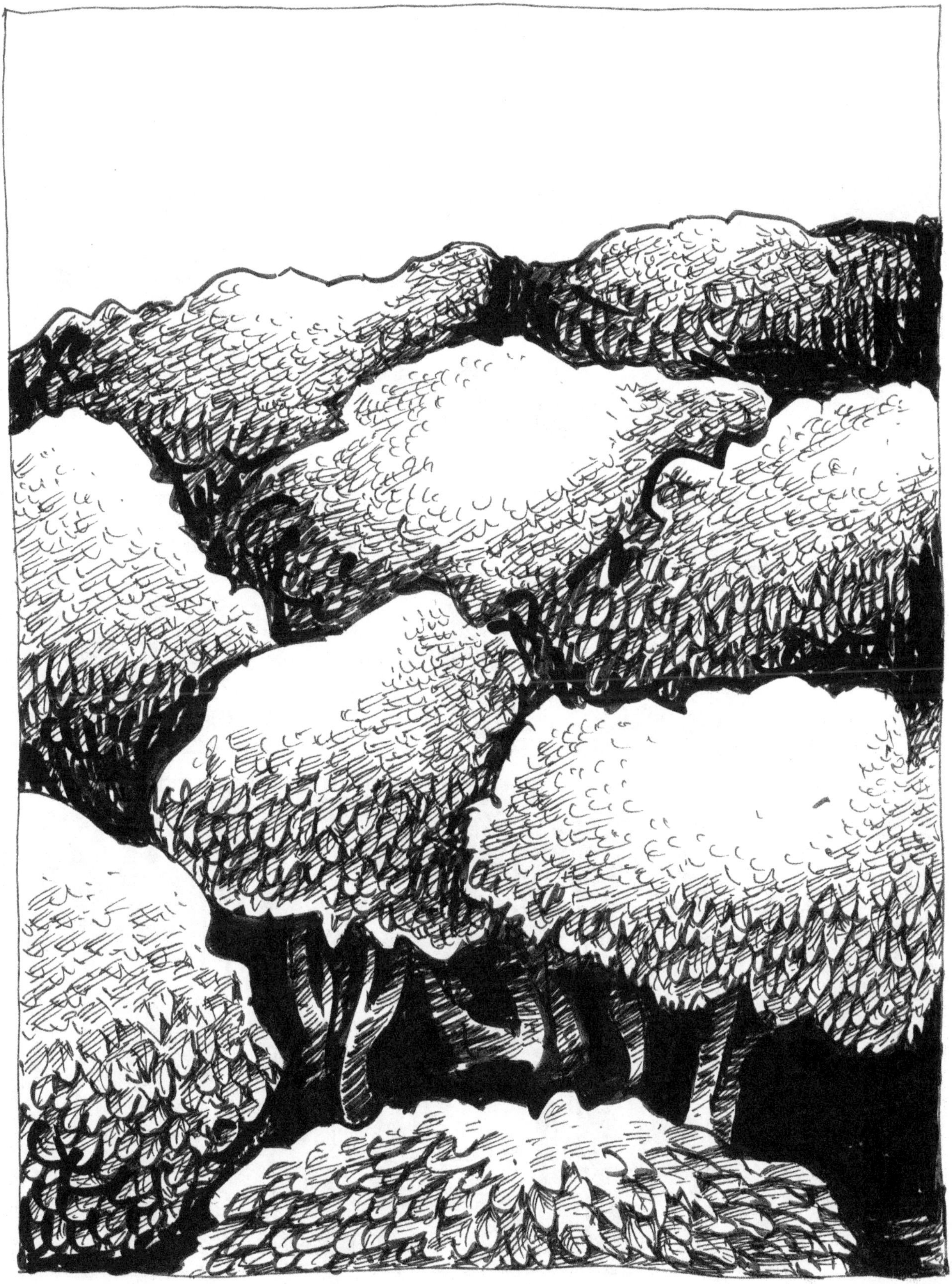

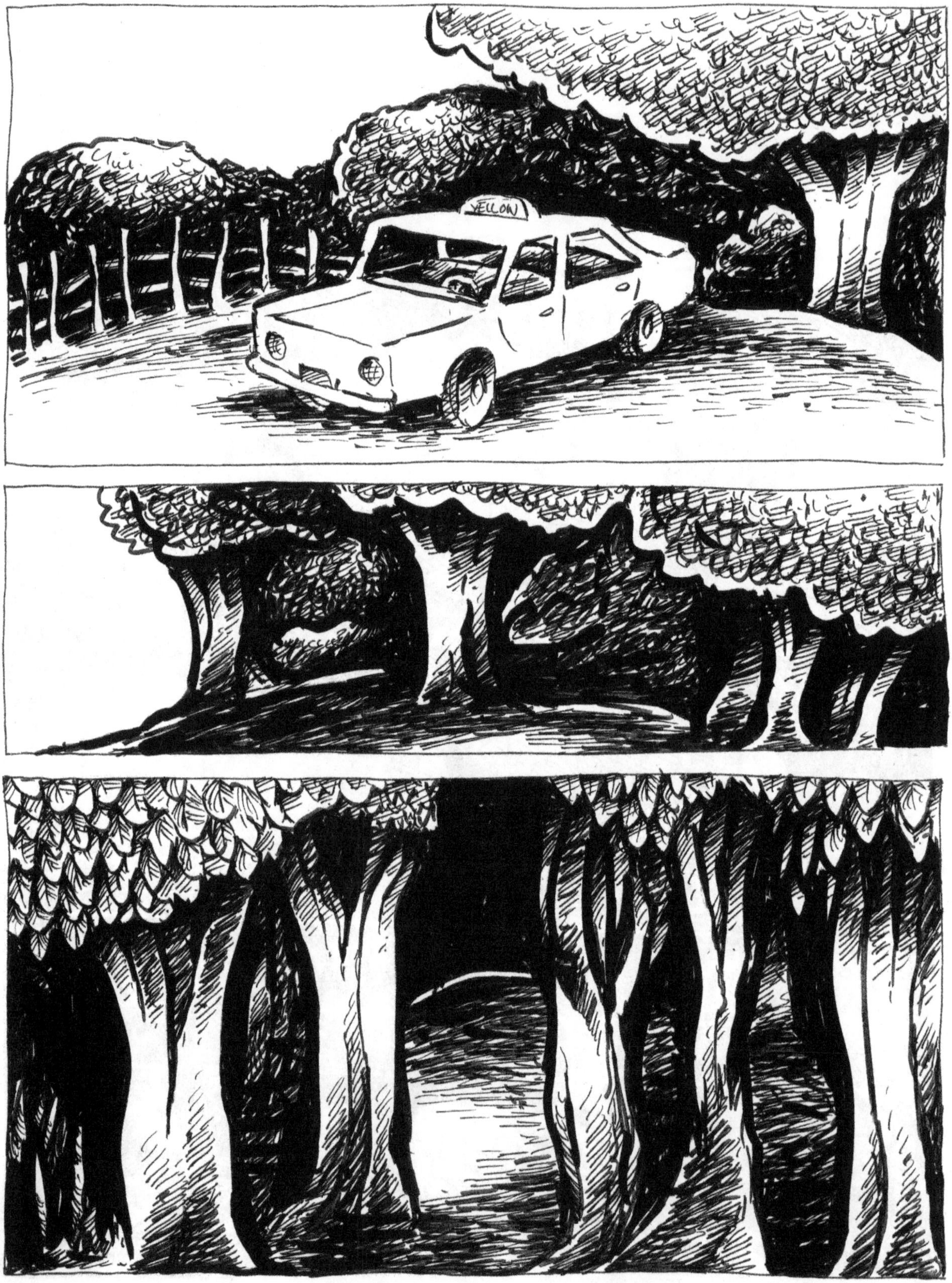
YELLOW

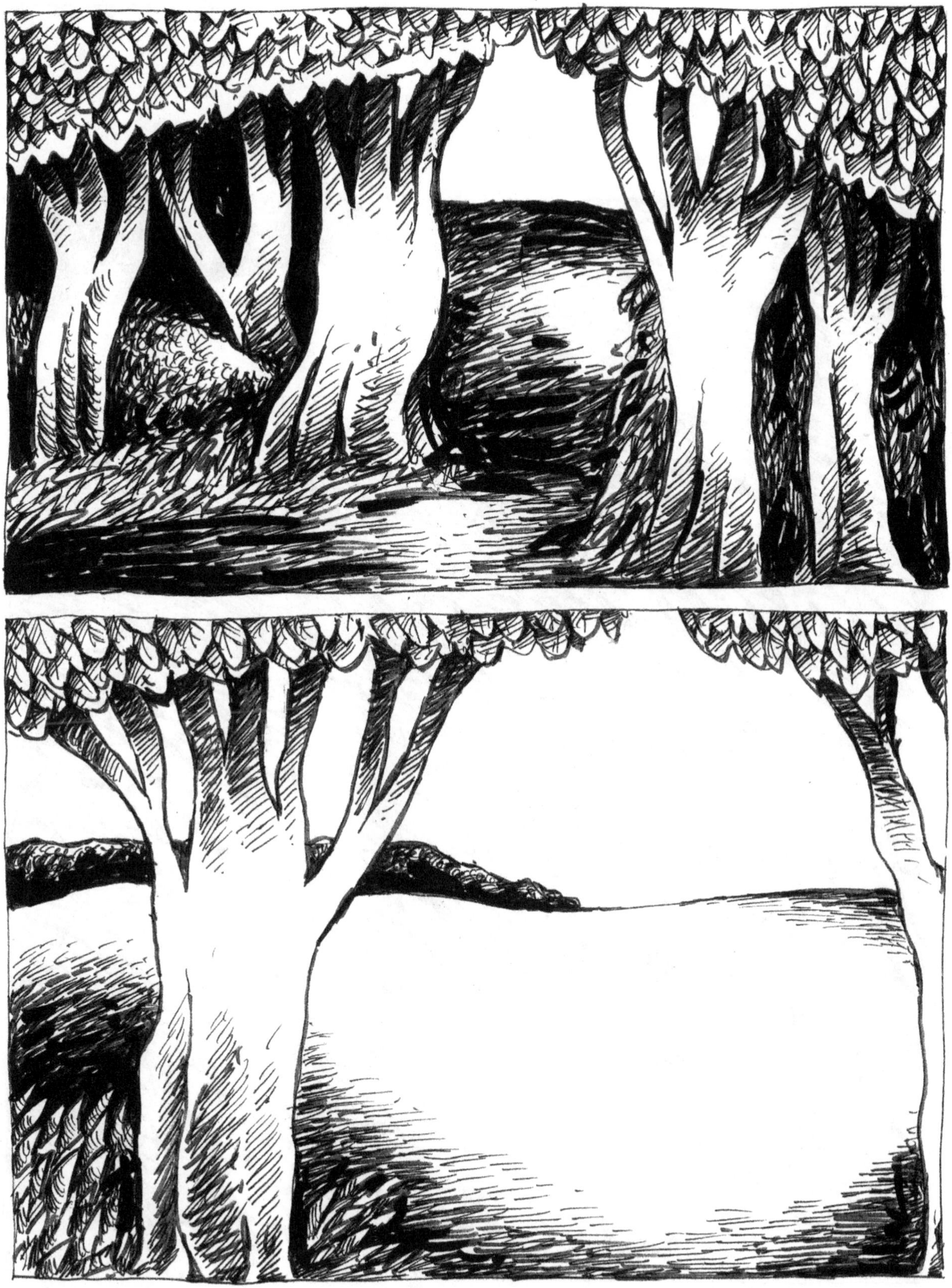

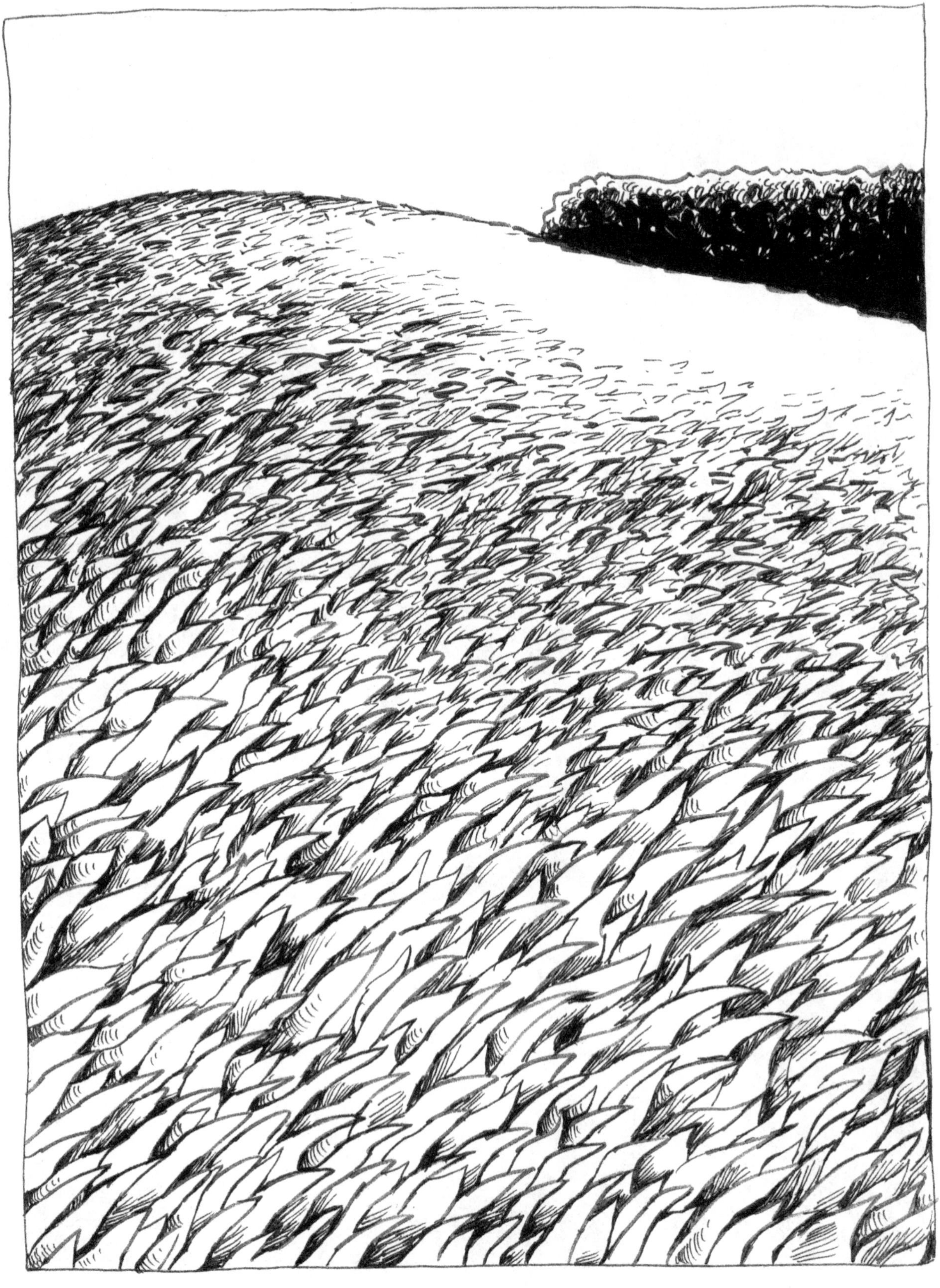

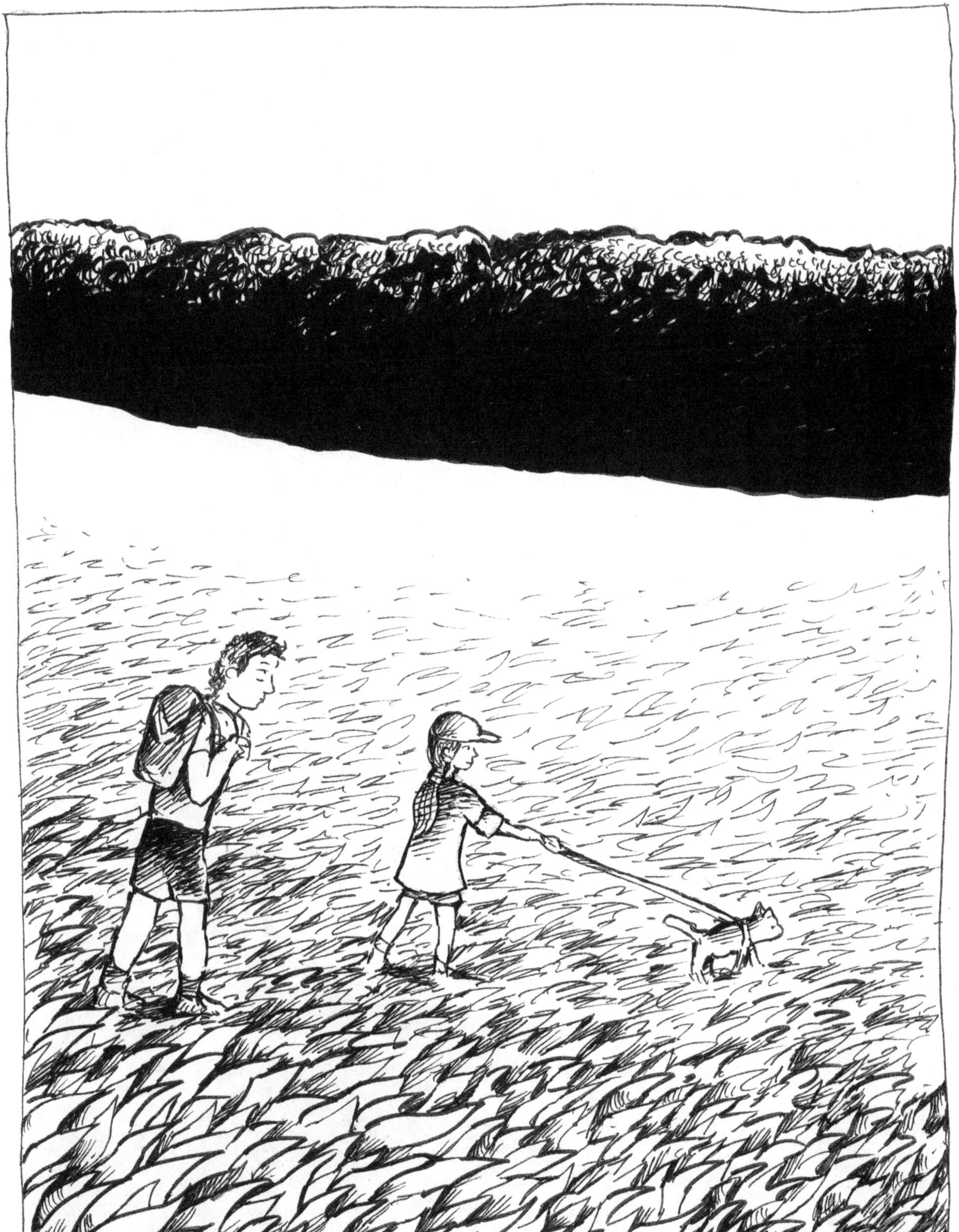

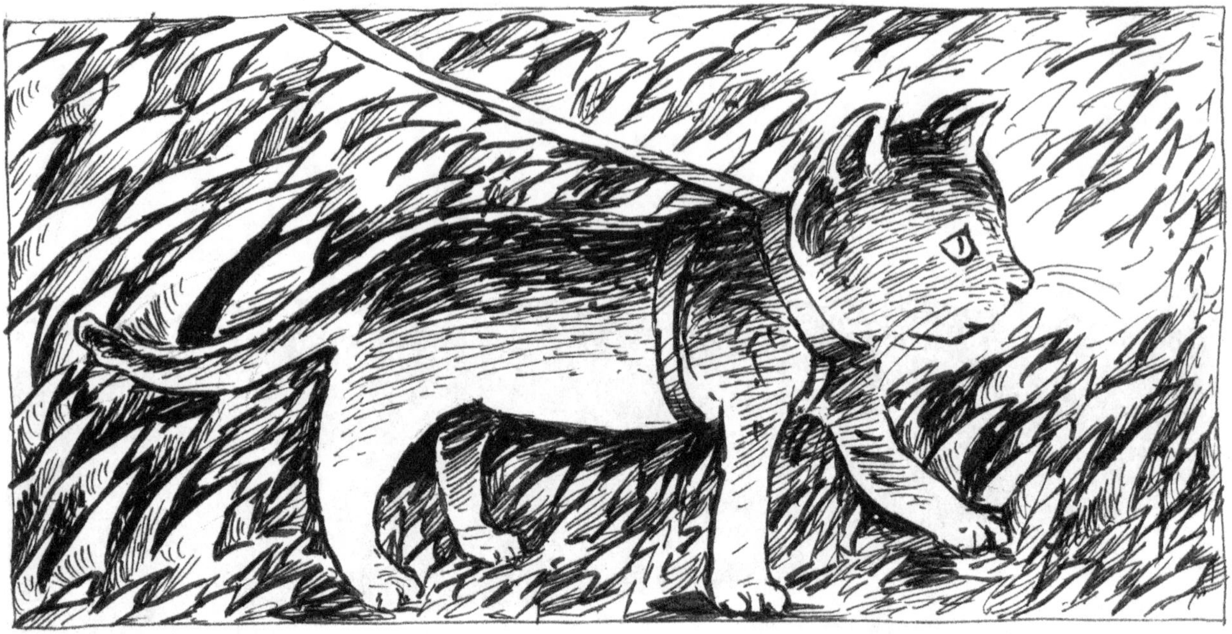

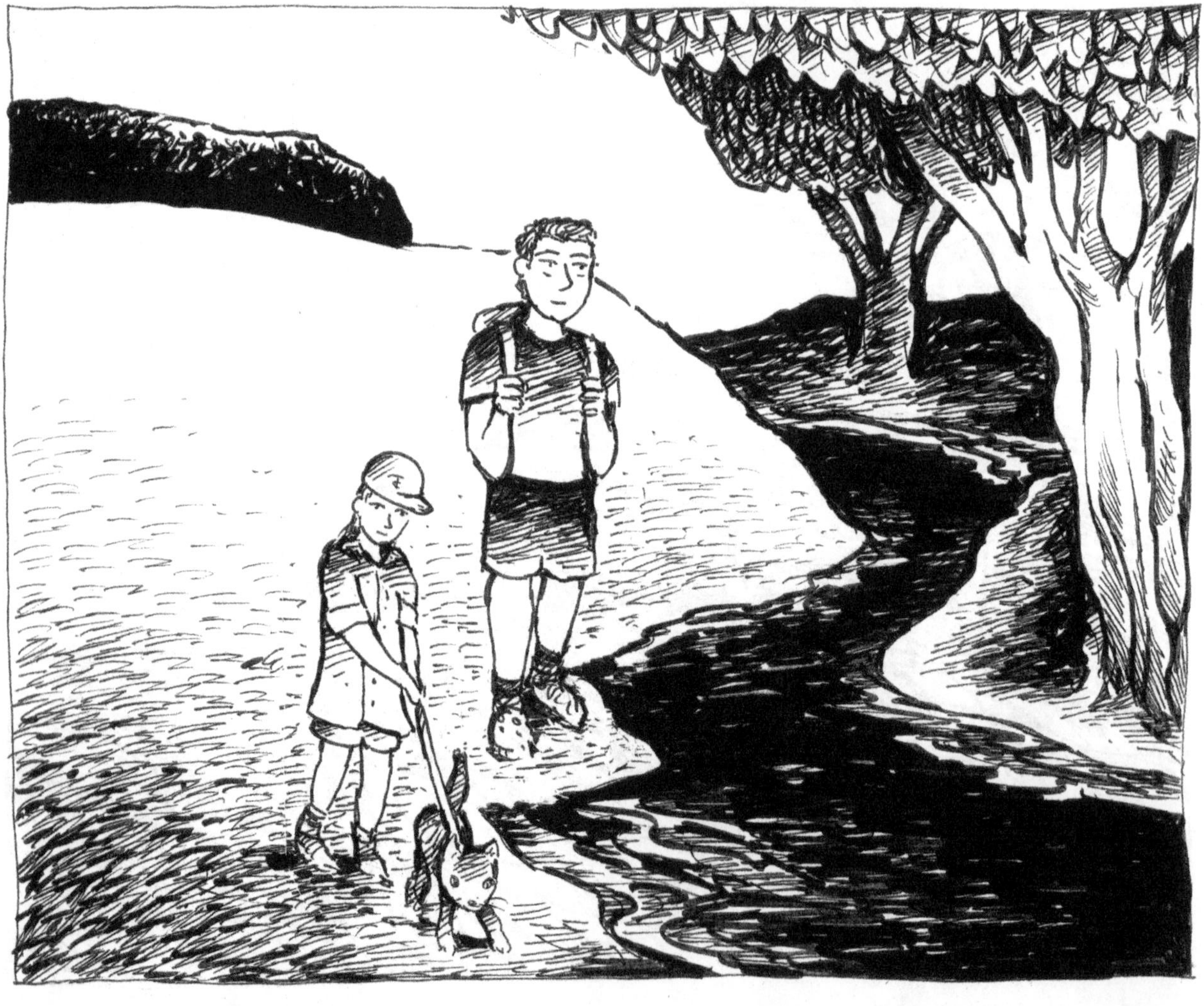

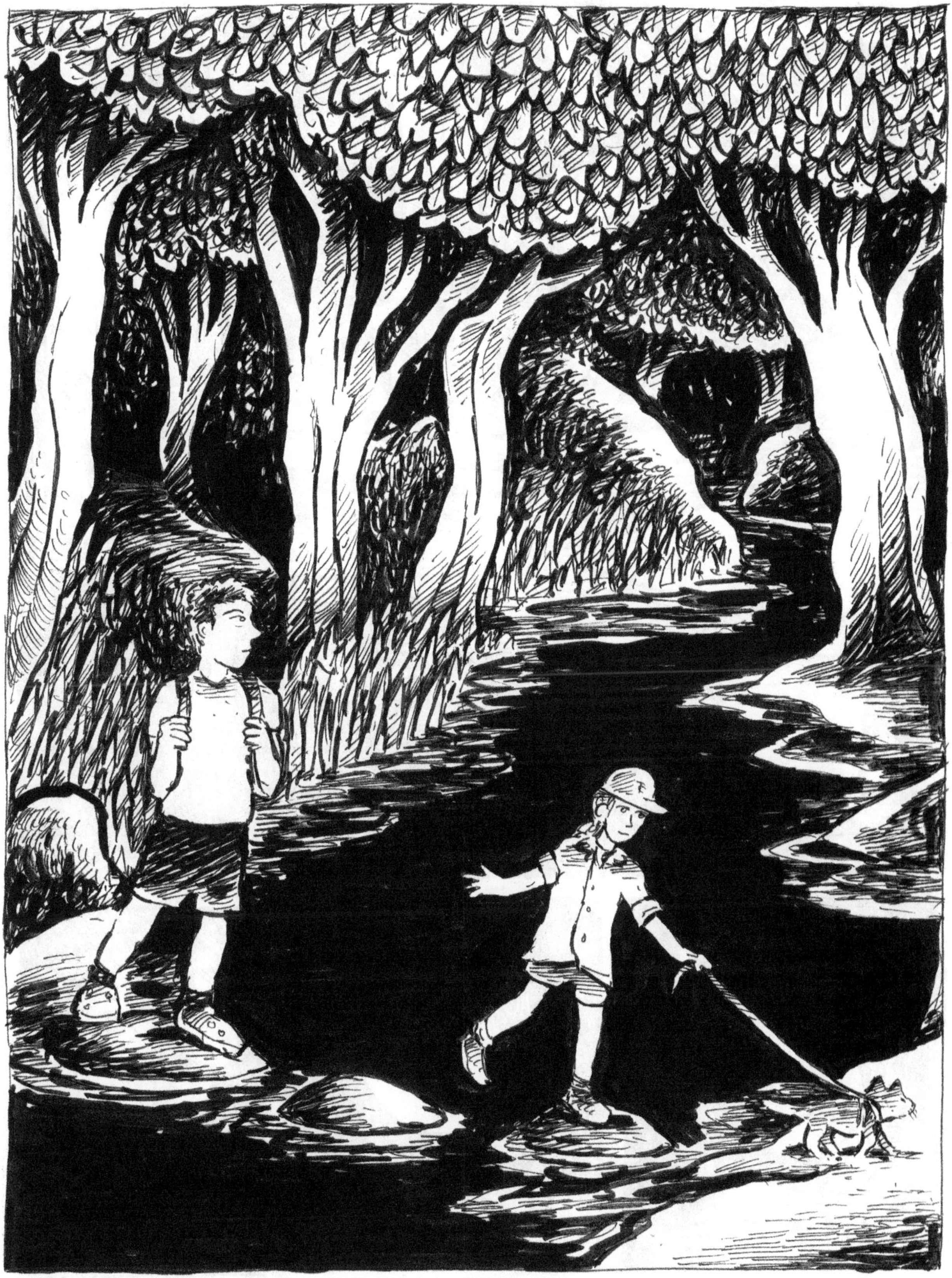

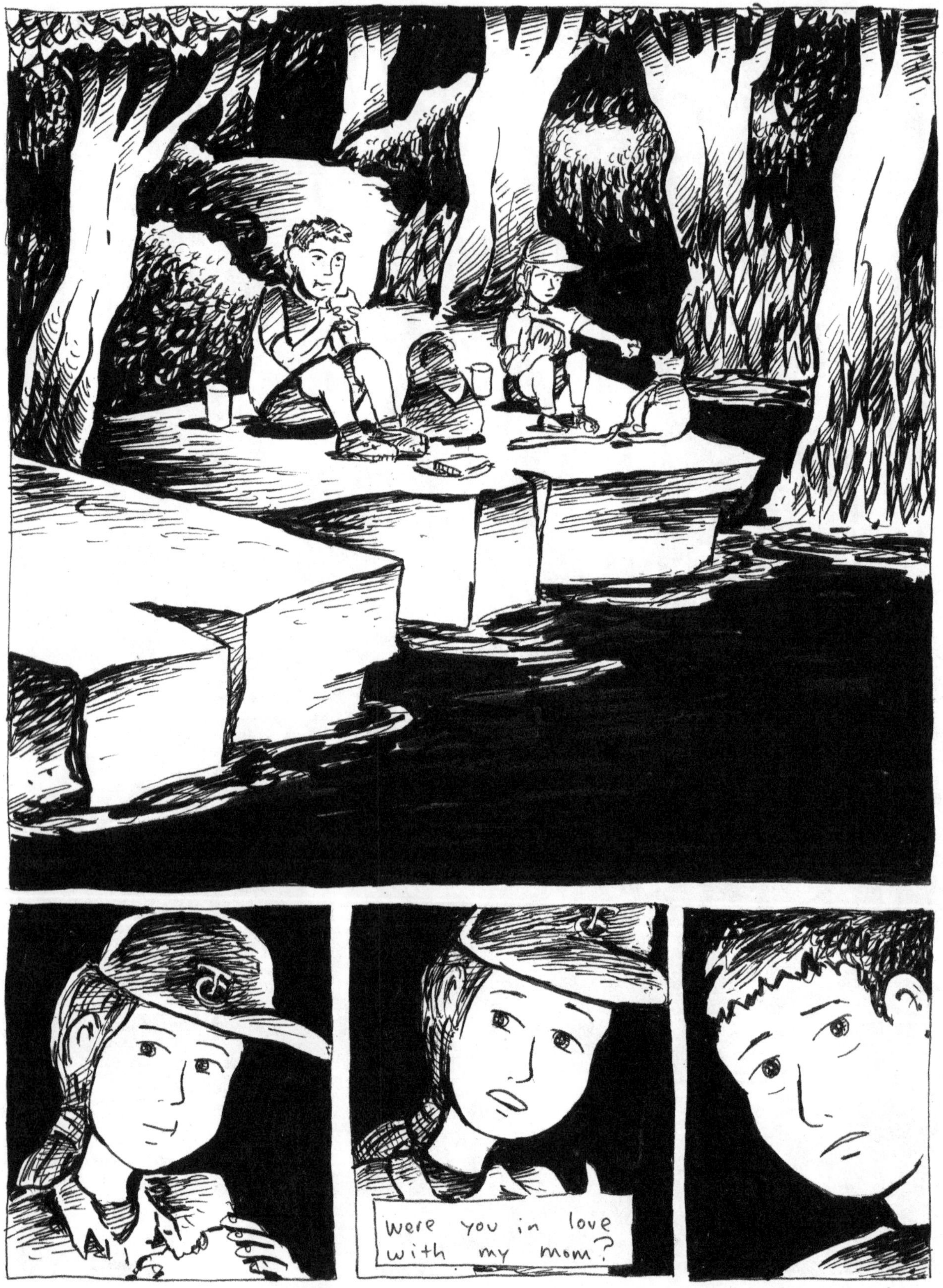
were you in love with my mom?

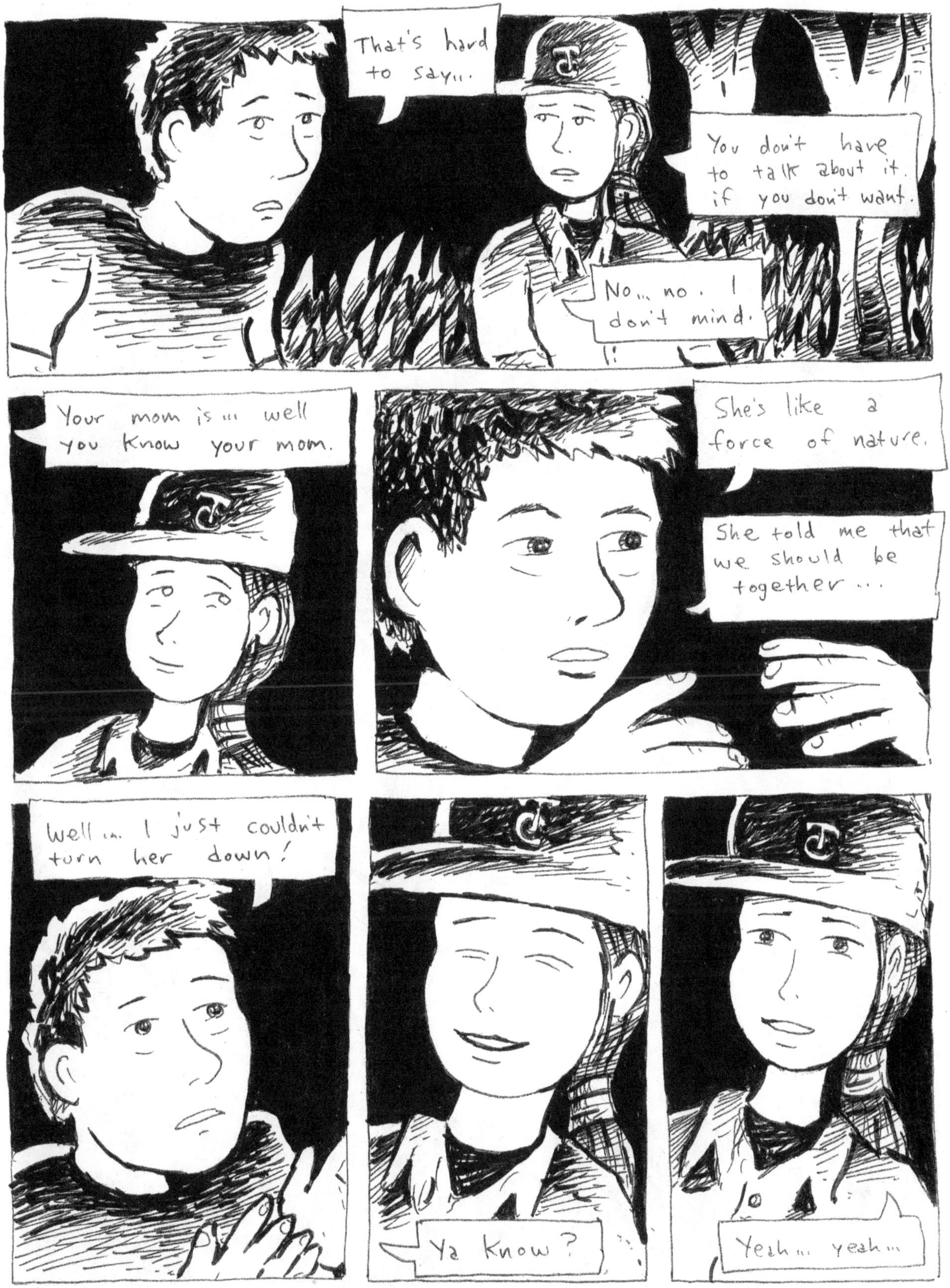
That's hard to say...
You don't have to talk about it if you don't want.
No... no. I don't mind.
Your mom is... well you know your mom.
She's like a force of nature.
She told me that we should be together...
Well... I just couldn't turn her down!
Ya know?
Yeah... yeah...

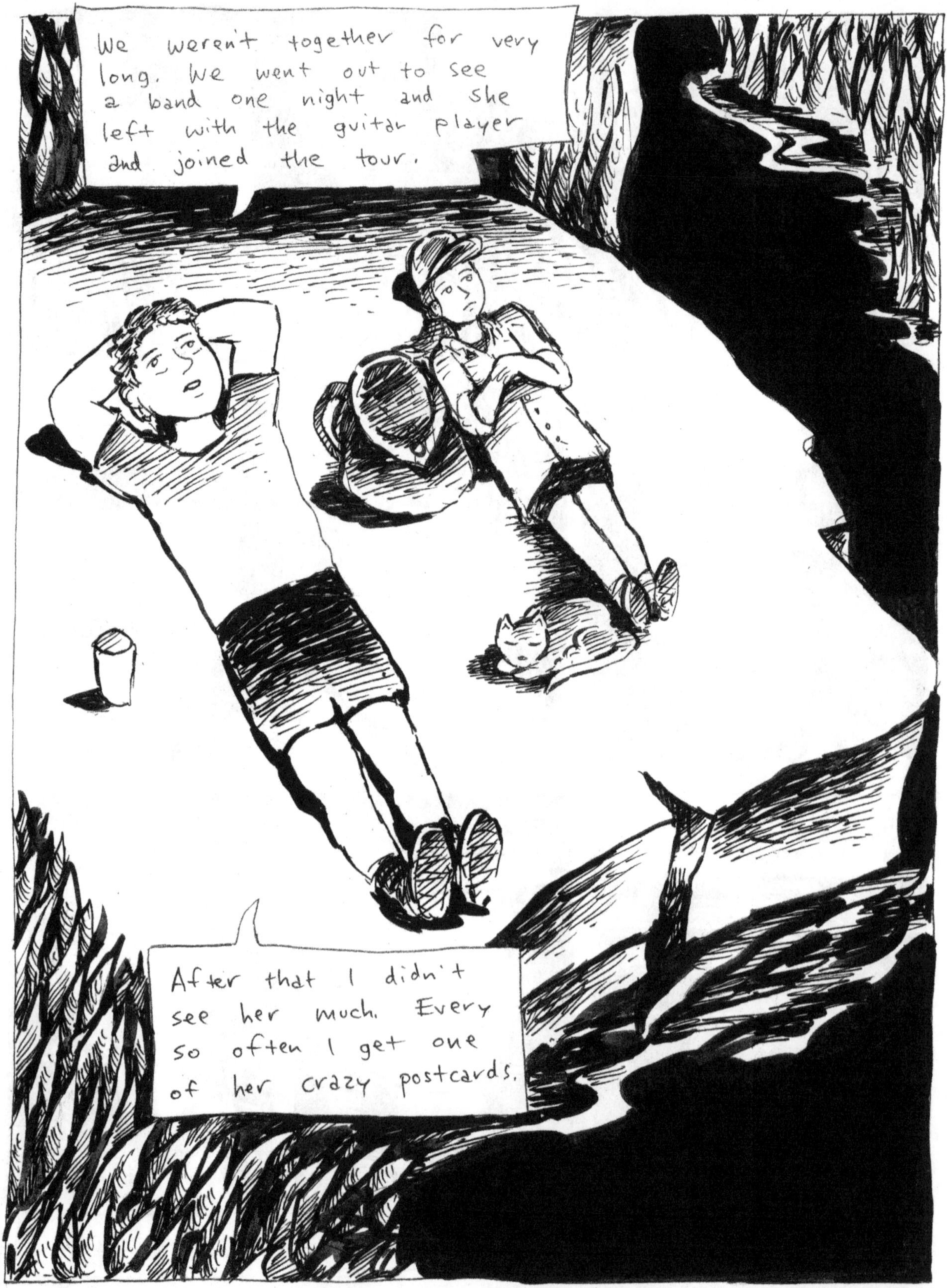

We weren't together for very long. We went out to see a band one night and she left with the guitar player and joined the tour.
After that I didn't see her much. Every so often I get one of her crazy postcards.

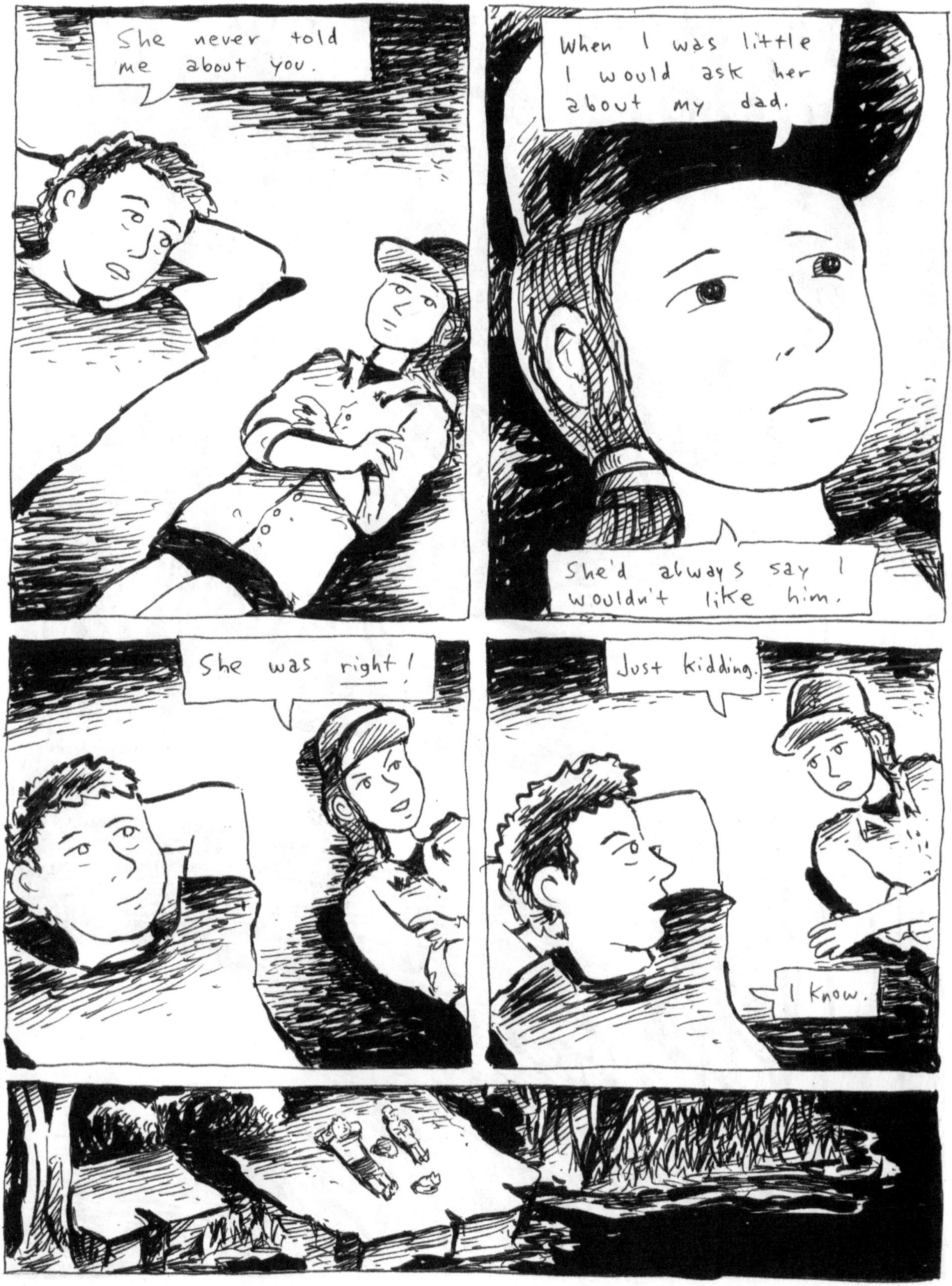
She never told me about you.
When I was little I would ask her about my dad.
She'd always say I wouldn't like him.
She was right!
Just kidding.
I know.

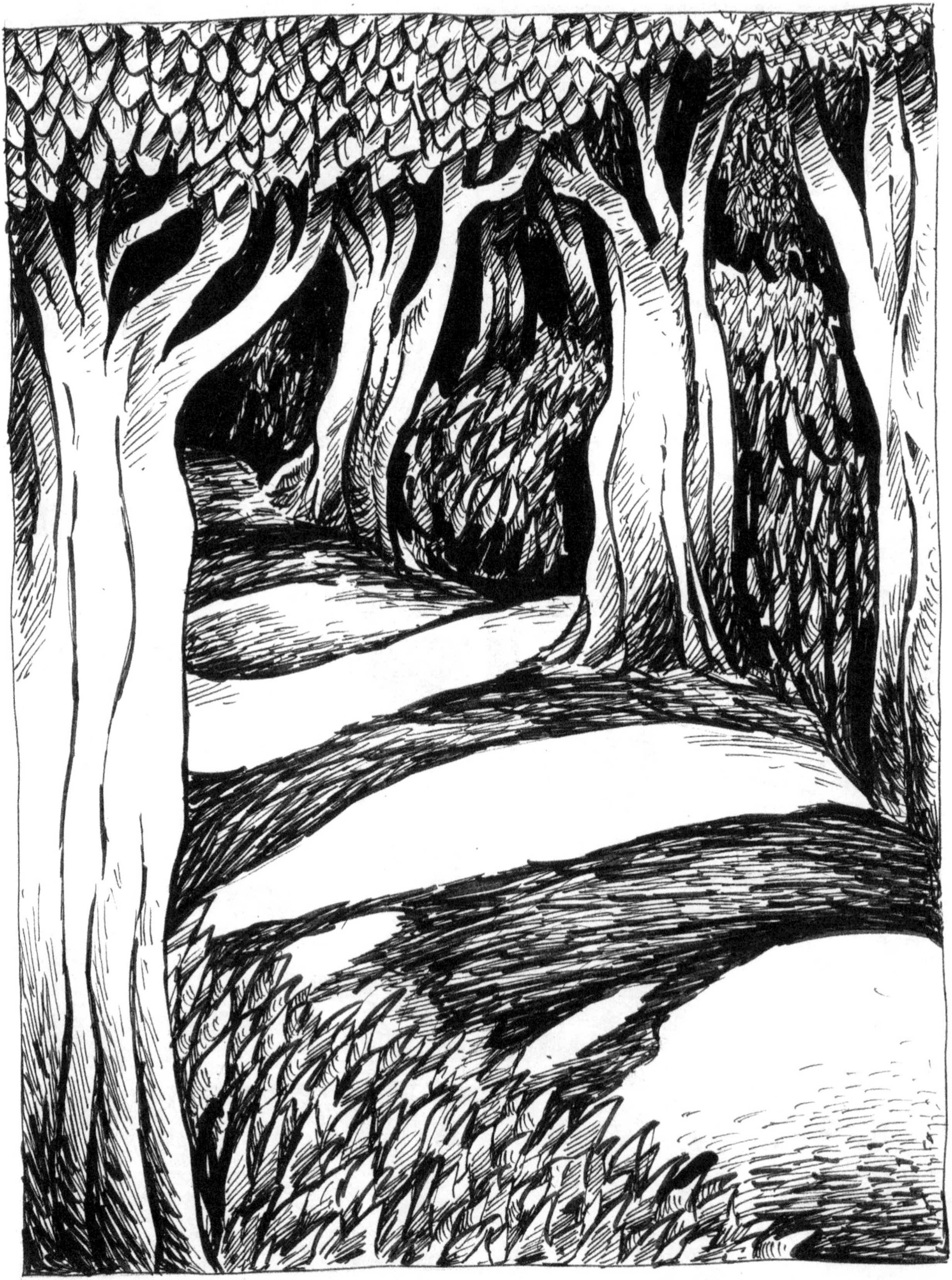

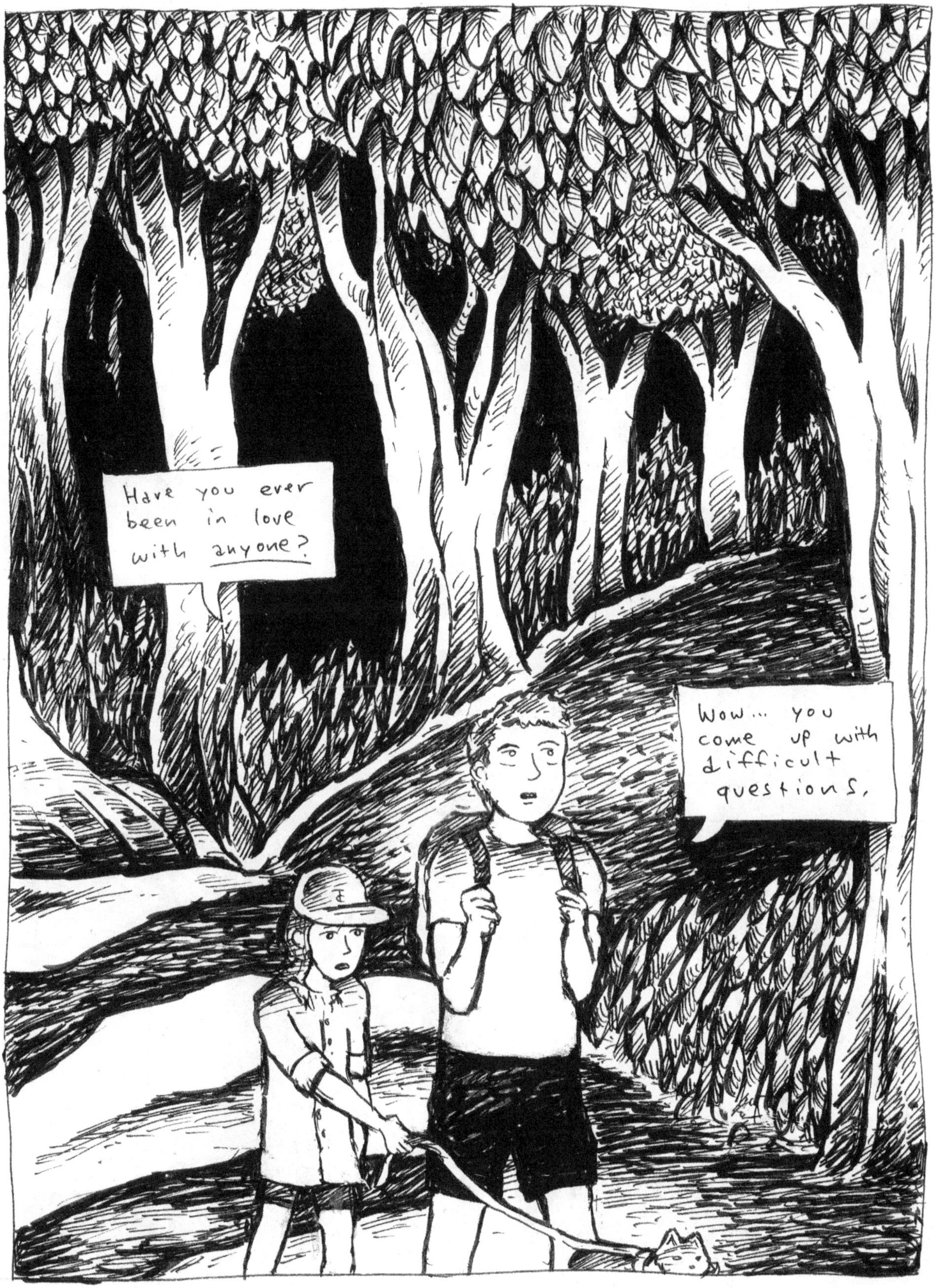
Have you ever been in love with anyone?
Wow... you come up with difficult questions.

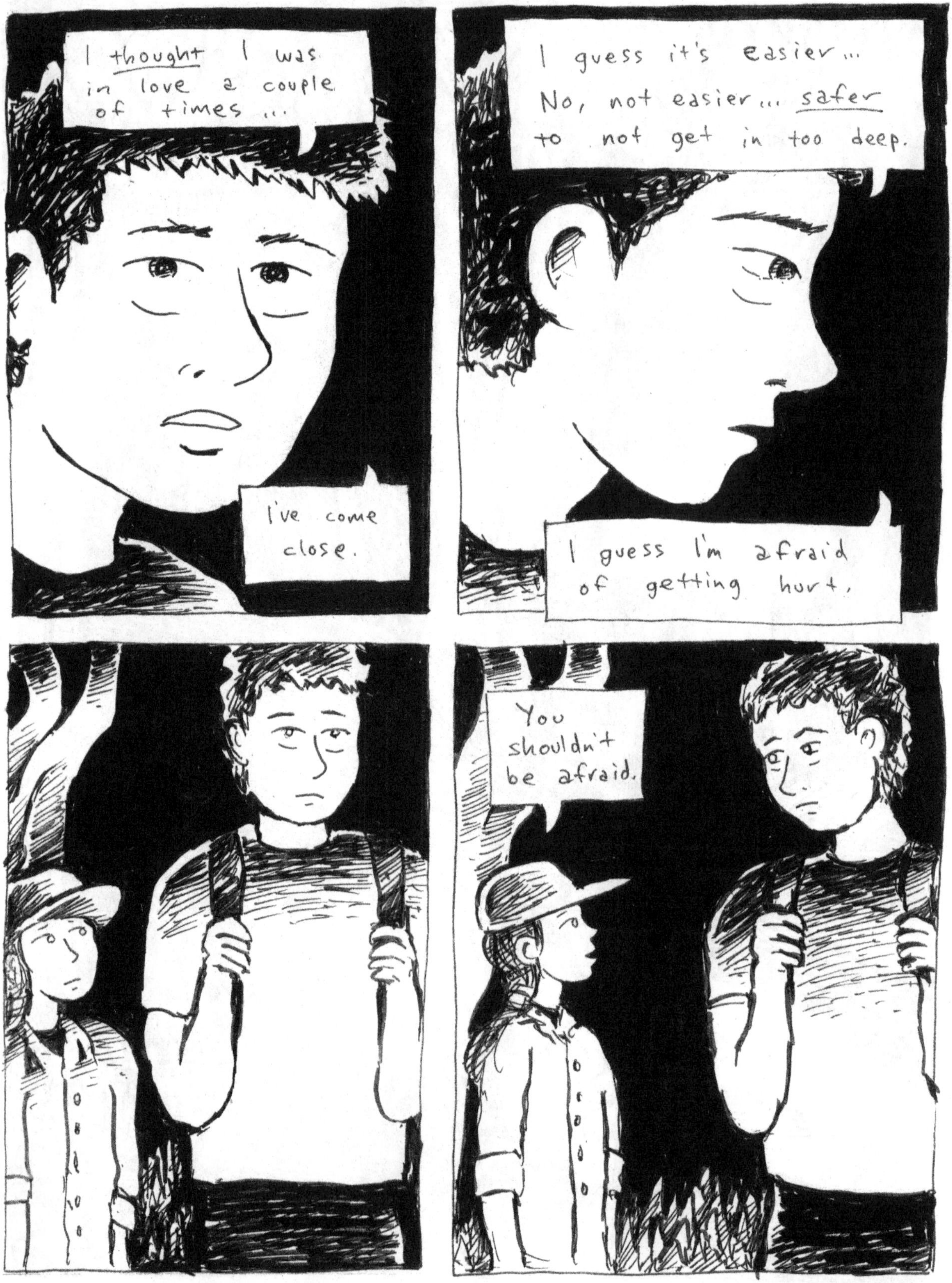
I thought I was in love a couple of times ...
I've come close.
I guess it's easier...
No, not easier... safer to not get in too deep.
I guess I'm afraid of getting hurt.
You shouldn't be afraid.

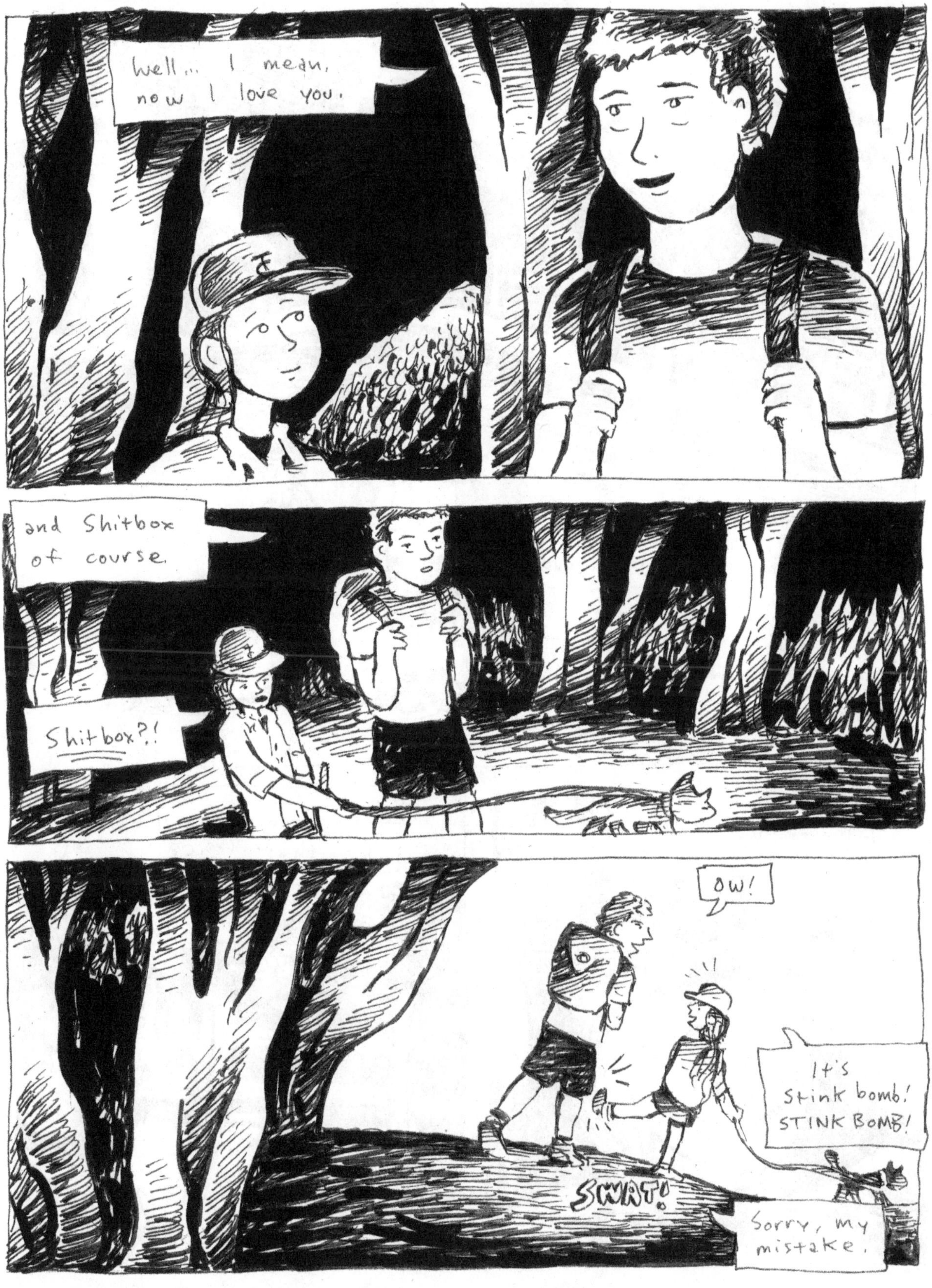
Well... I mean, now I love you.
and Shitbox of course.
Shitbox?!
OW!
It's Stink bomb! STINK BOMB!
SWAT!
Sorry, my mistake.

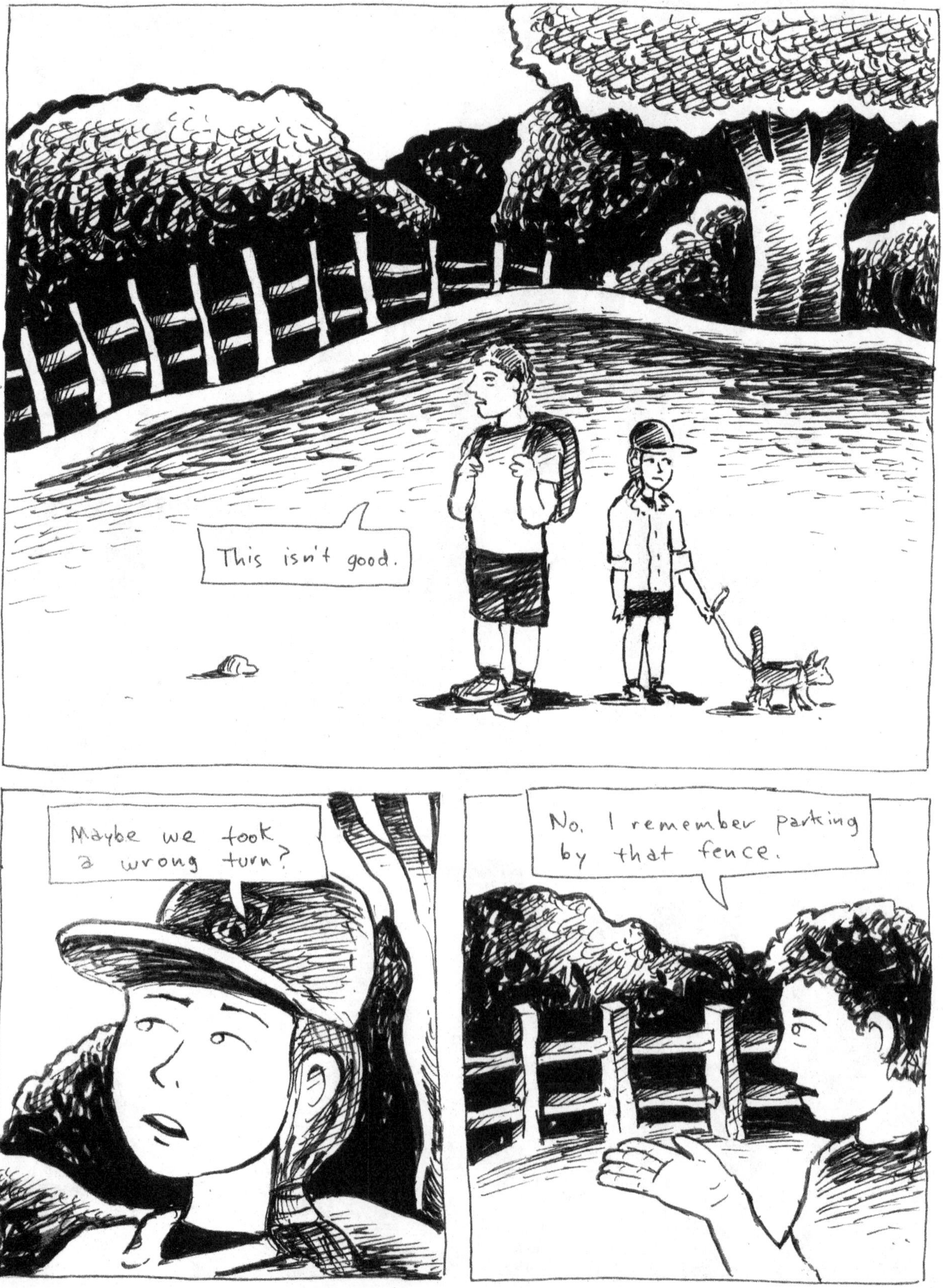
This isn't good.
Maybe we took a wrong turn?
No. I remember parking by that fence.

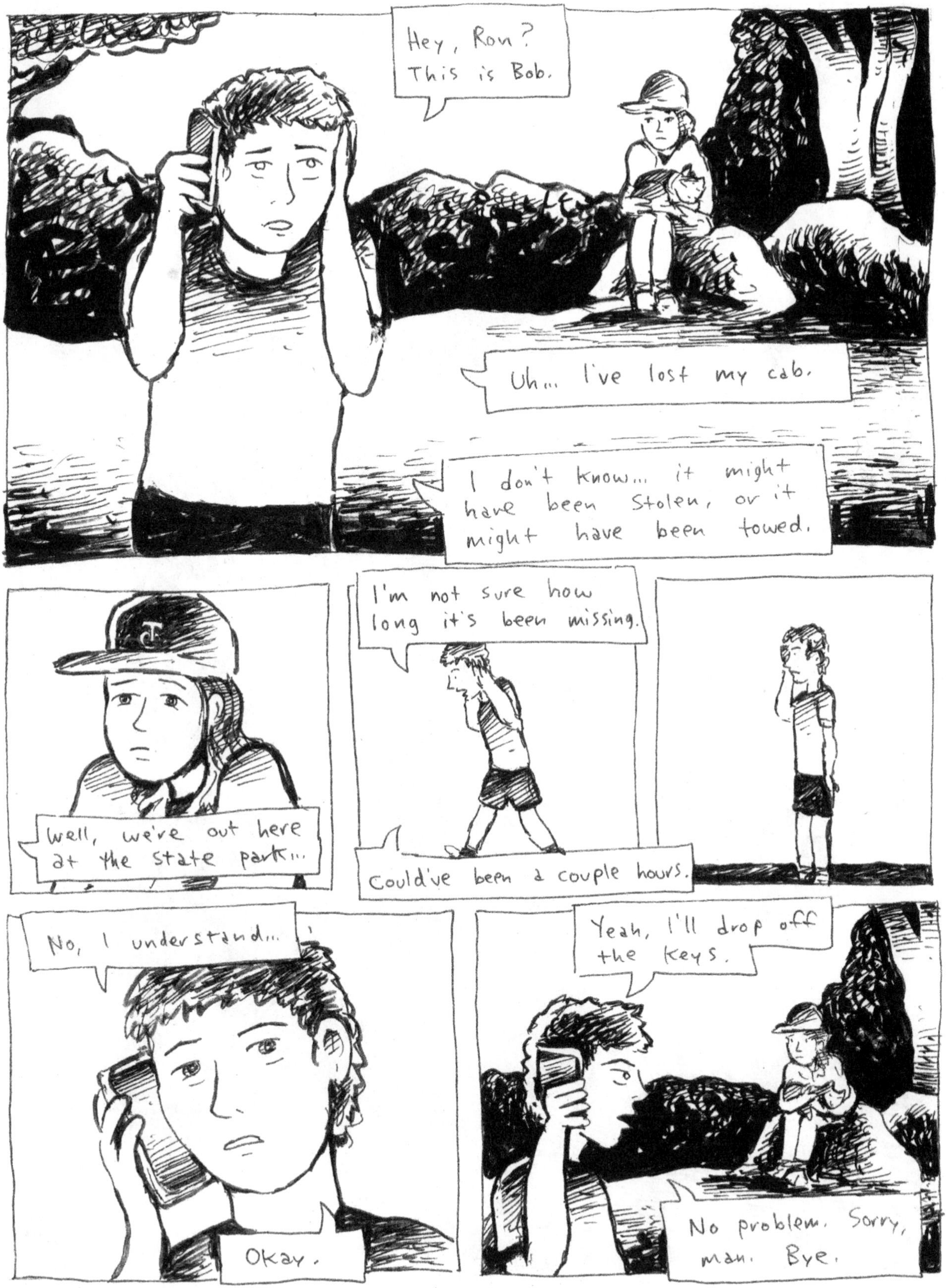
Hey, Ron? This is Bob.
Uh... I've lost my cab.
I don't know... it might have been stolen, or it might have been towed.
Well, we're out here at the state park...
I'm not sure how long it's been missing.
Could've been a couple hours.
No, I understand...
Okay.
Yeah, I'll drop off the keys.
No problem. Sorry, man. Bye.

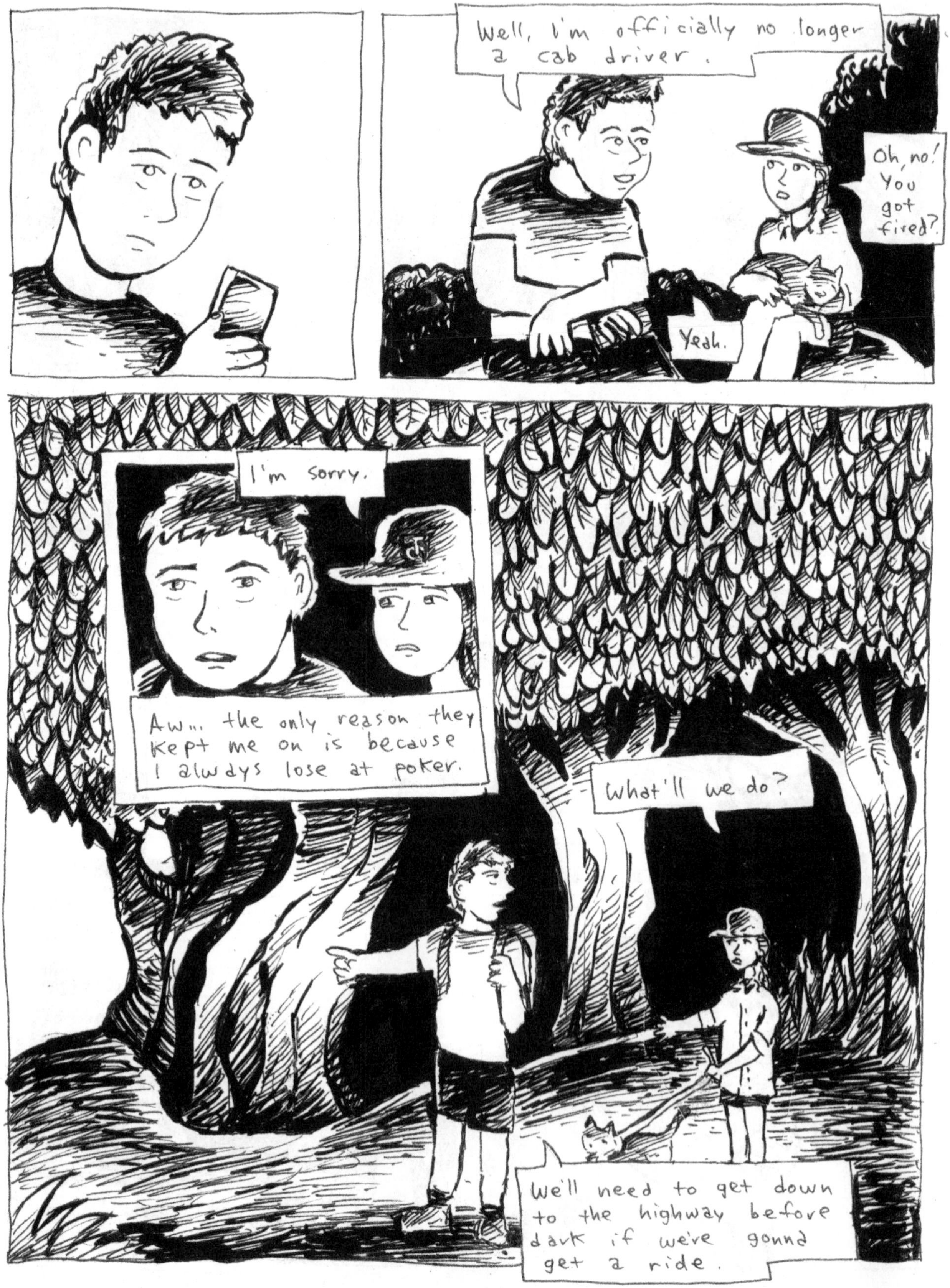
Well, I'm officially no longer a cab driver.
Oh, no! You got fired?
Yeah.
I'm sorry.
Aw... the only reason they kept me on is because I always lose at poker.
What'll we do?
We'll need to get down to the highway before dark if we're gonna get a ride.

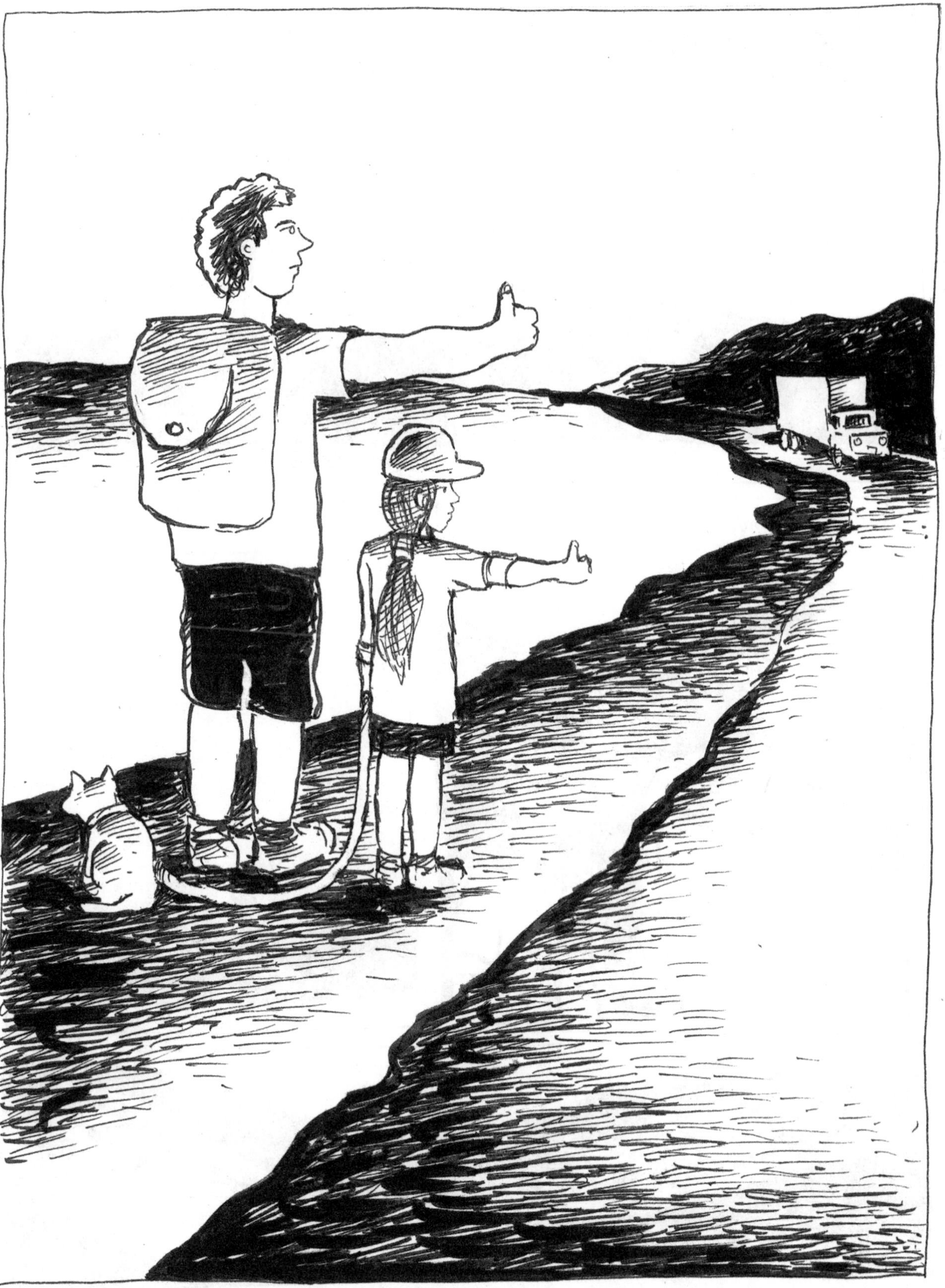

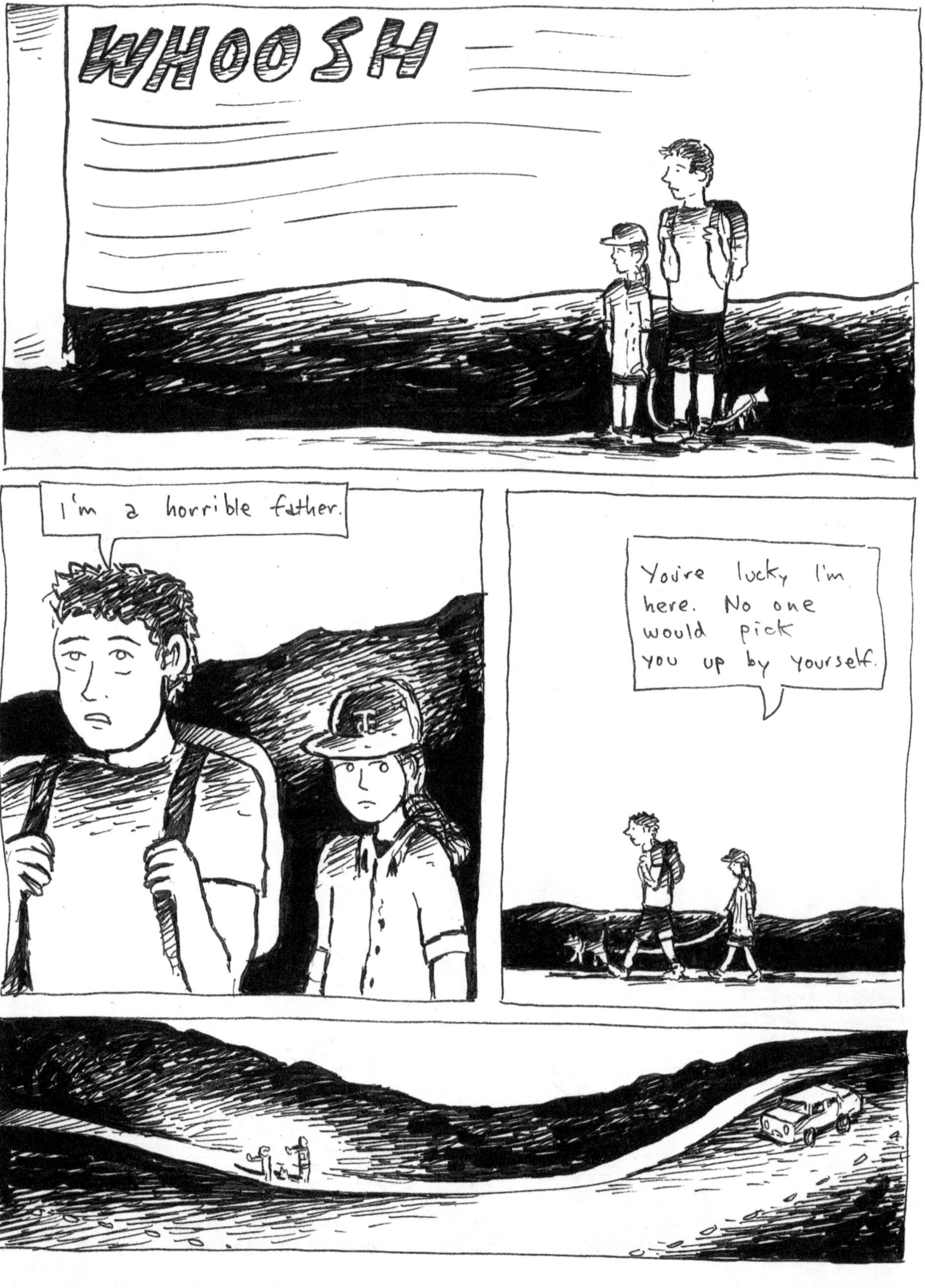
WHOOSH
I'm a horrible father.
You're lucky I'm here. No one would pick you up by yourself.

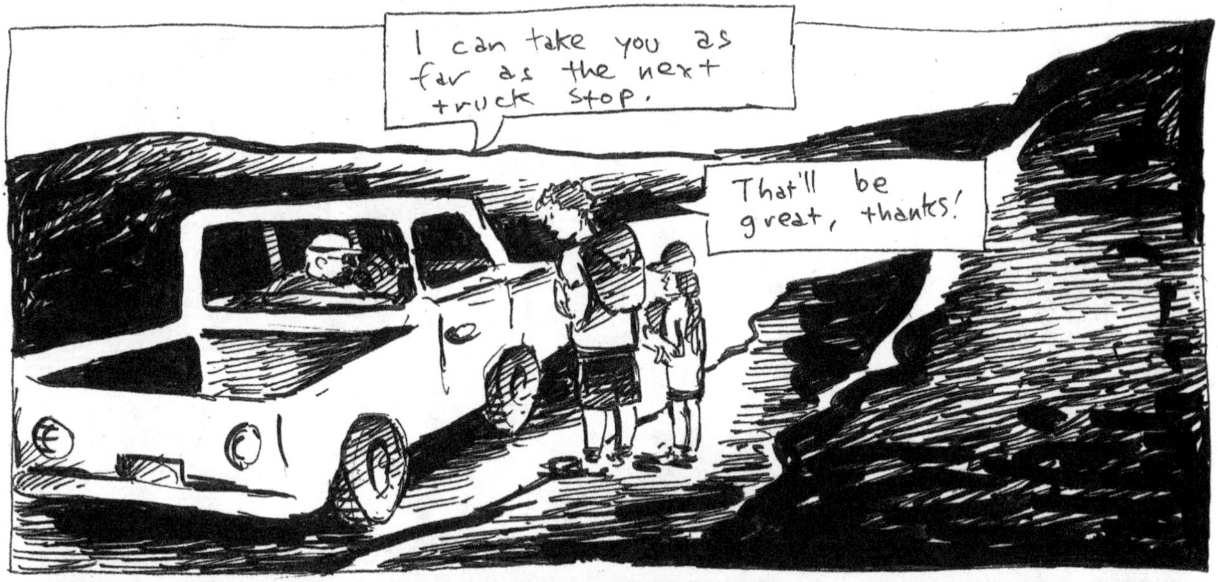
I can take you as far as the next truck stop.
That'll be great, thanks!

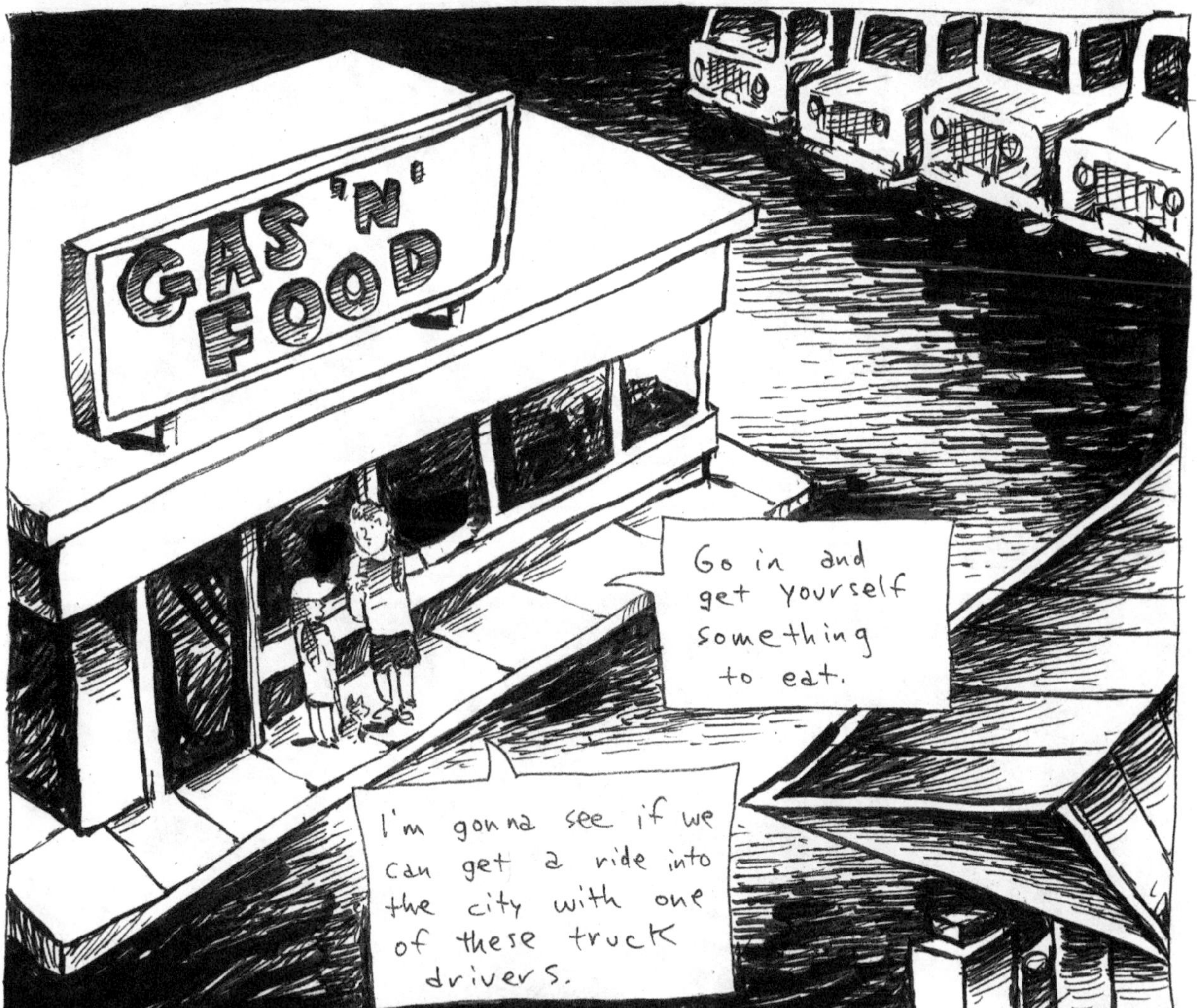
GAS 'N' FOOD
Go in and get yourself something to eat.
I'm gonna see if we can get a ride into the city with one of these truck drivers.

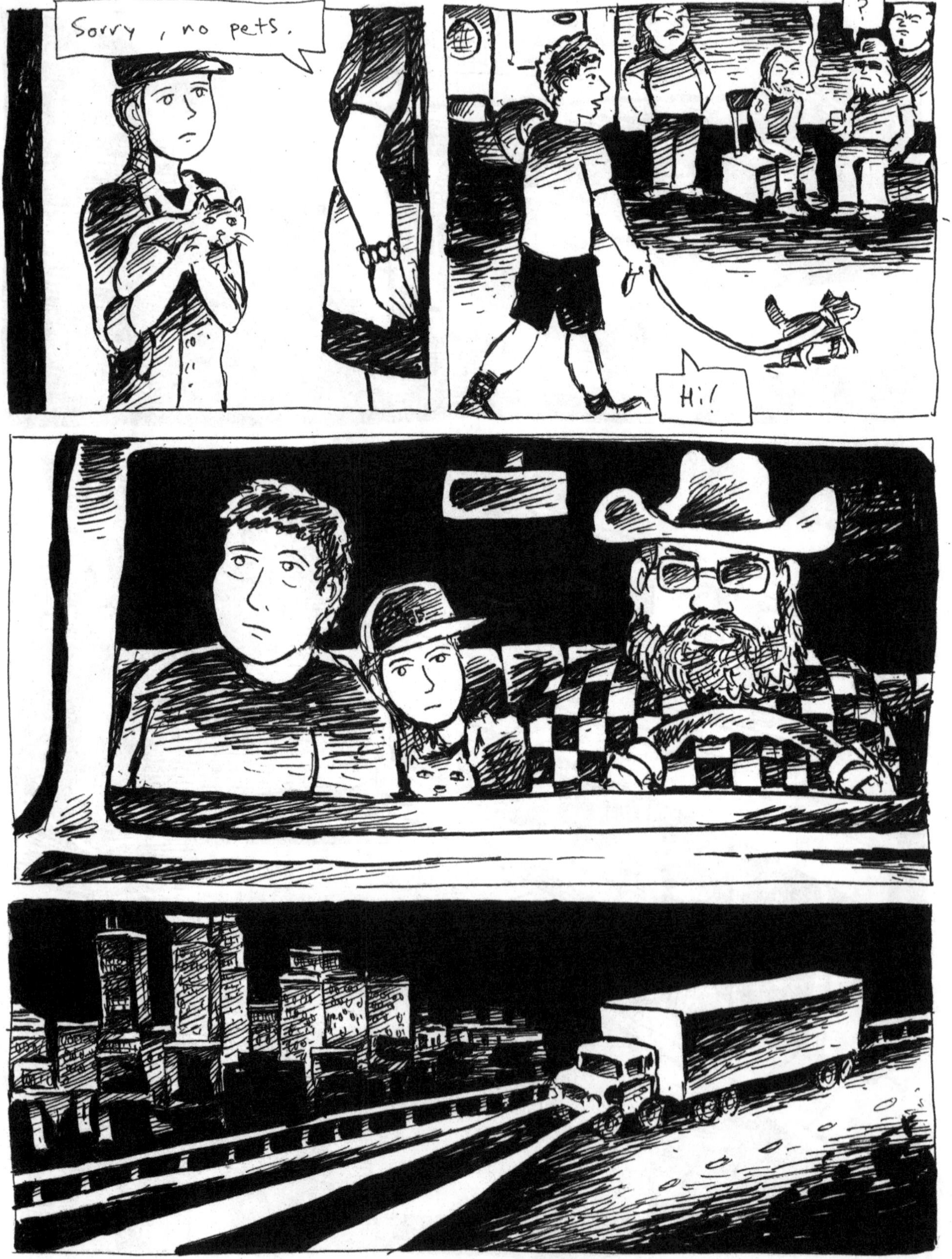
Sorry, no pets.
Hi!
?

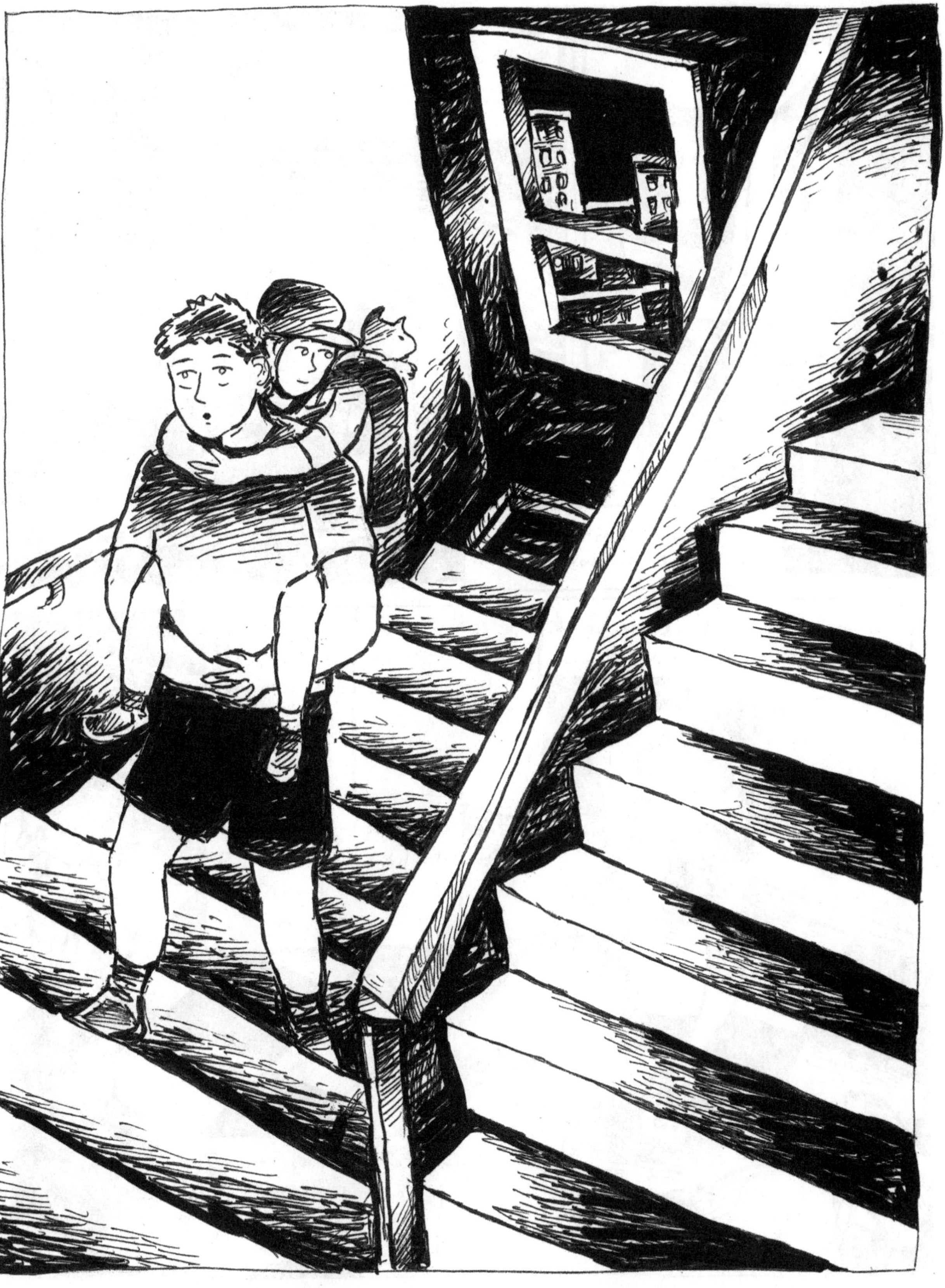

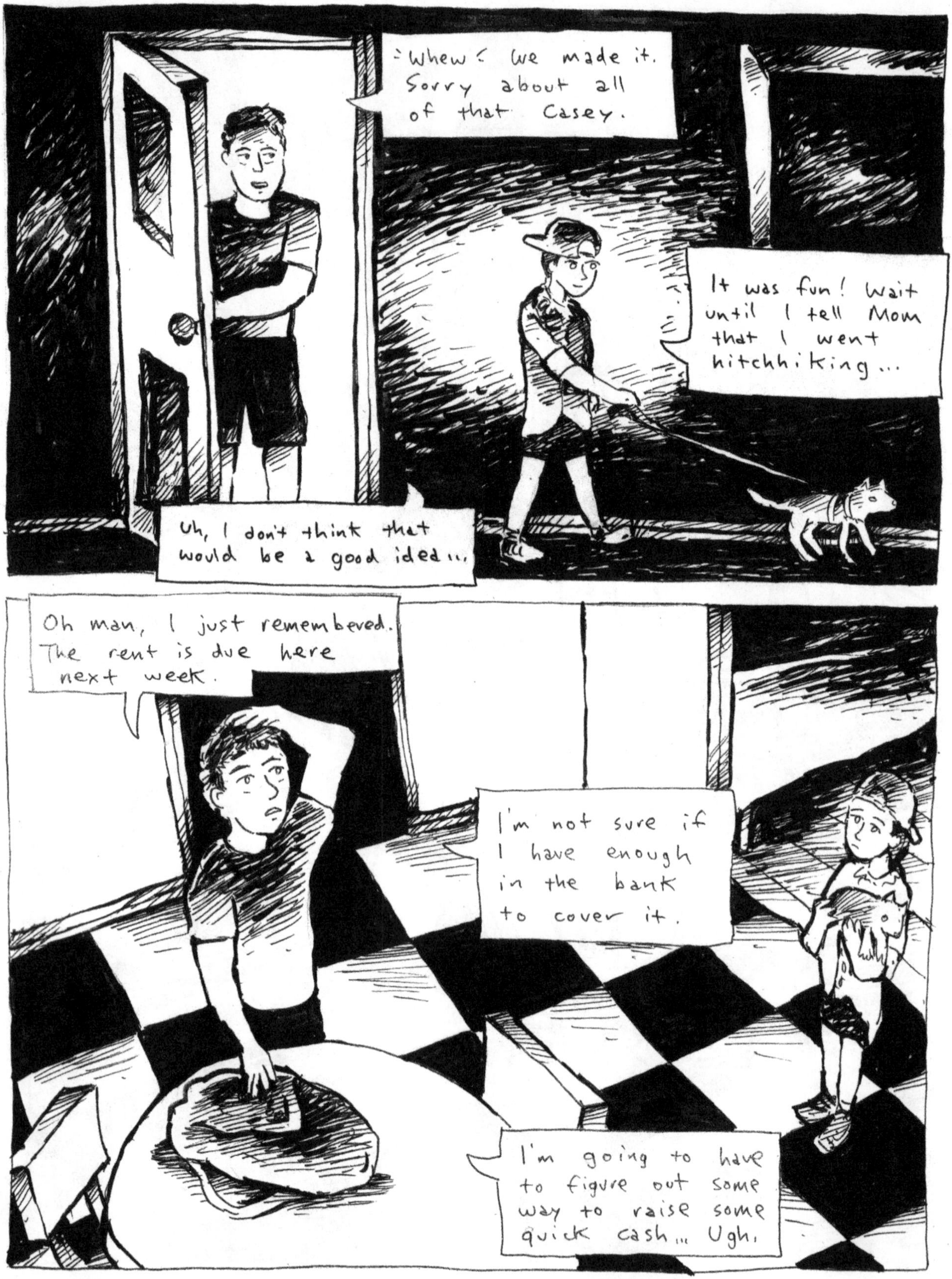
Whew! We made it. Sorry about all of that Casey.
It was fun! Wait until I tell Mom that I went hitchhiking...
Uh, I don't think that would be a good idea...
Oh man, I just remembered. The rent is due here next week.
I'm not sure if I have enough in the bank to cover it.
I'm going to have to figure out some way to raise some quick cash... Ugh.

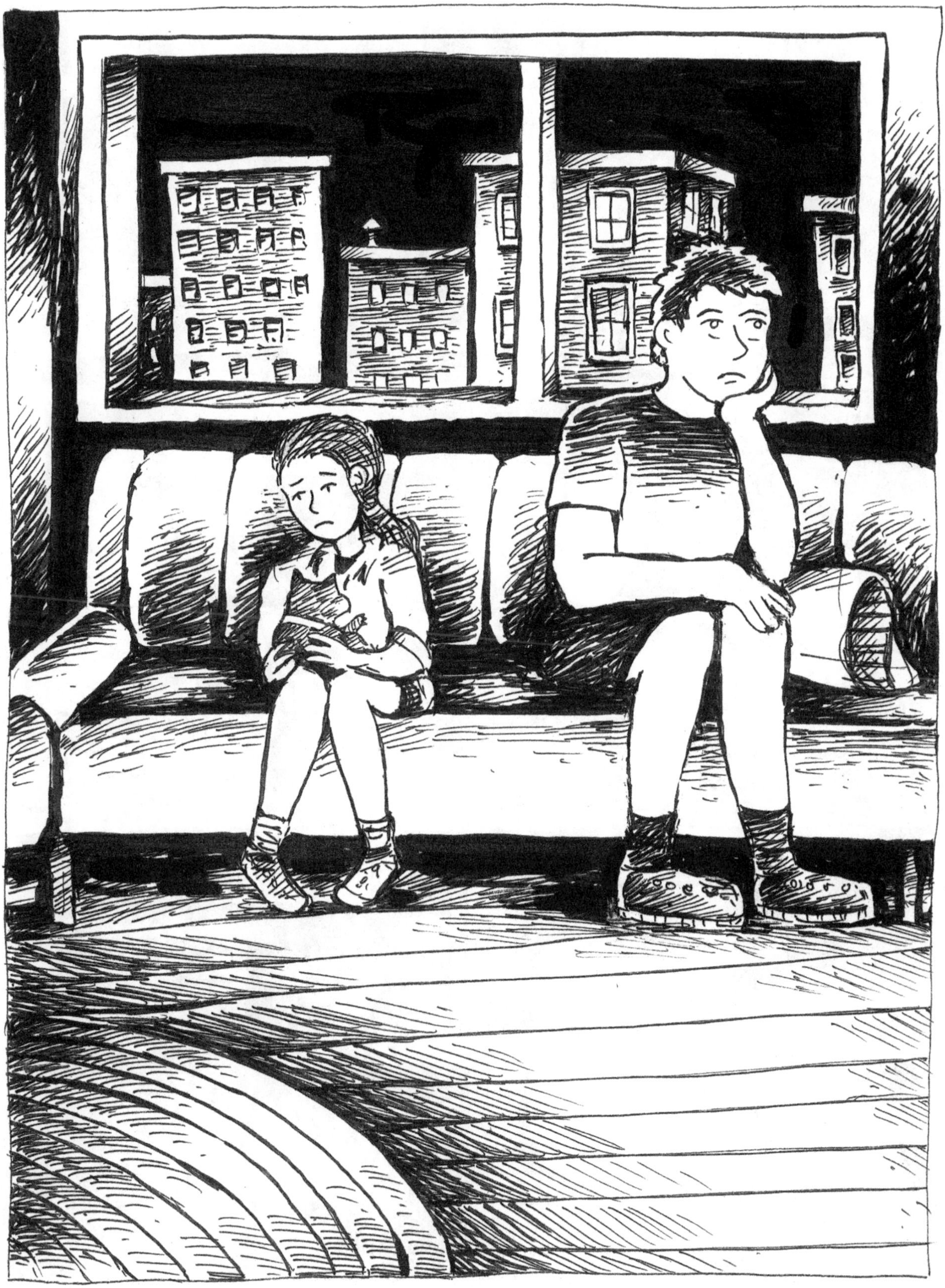

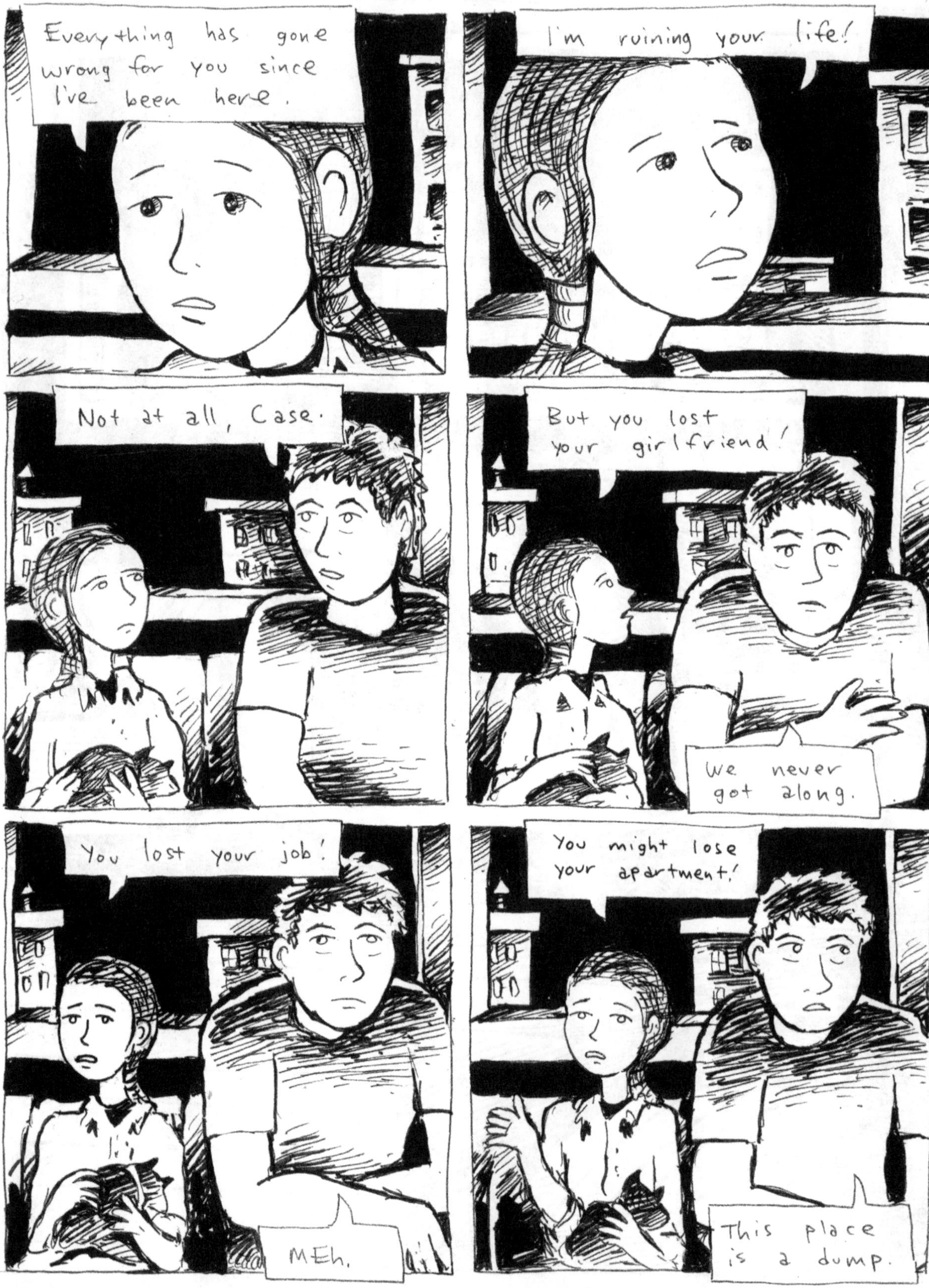
Everything has gone wrong for you since I've been here.
I'm ruining your life!
Not at all, Case.
But you lost your girlfriend!
We never got along.
You lost your job!
MEh.
You might lose your apartment!
This place is a dump.

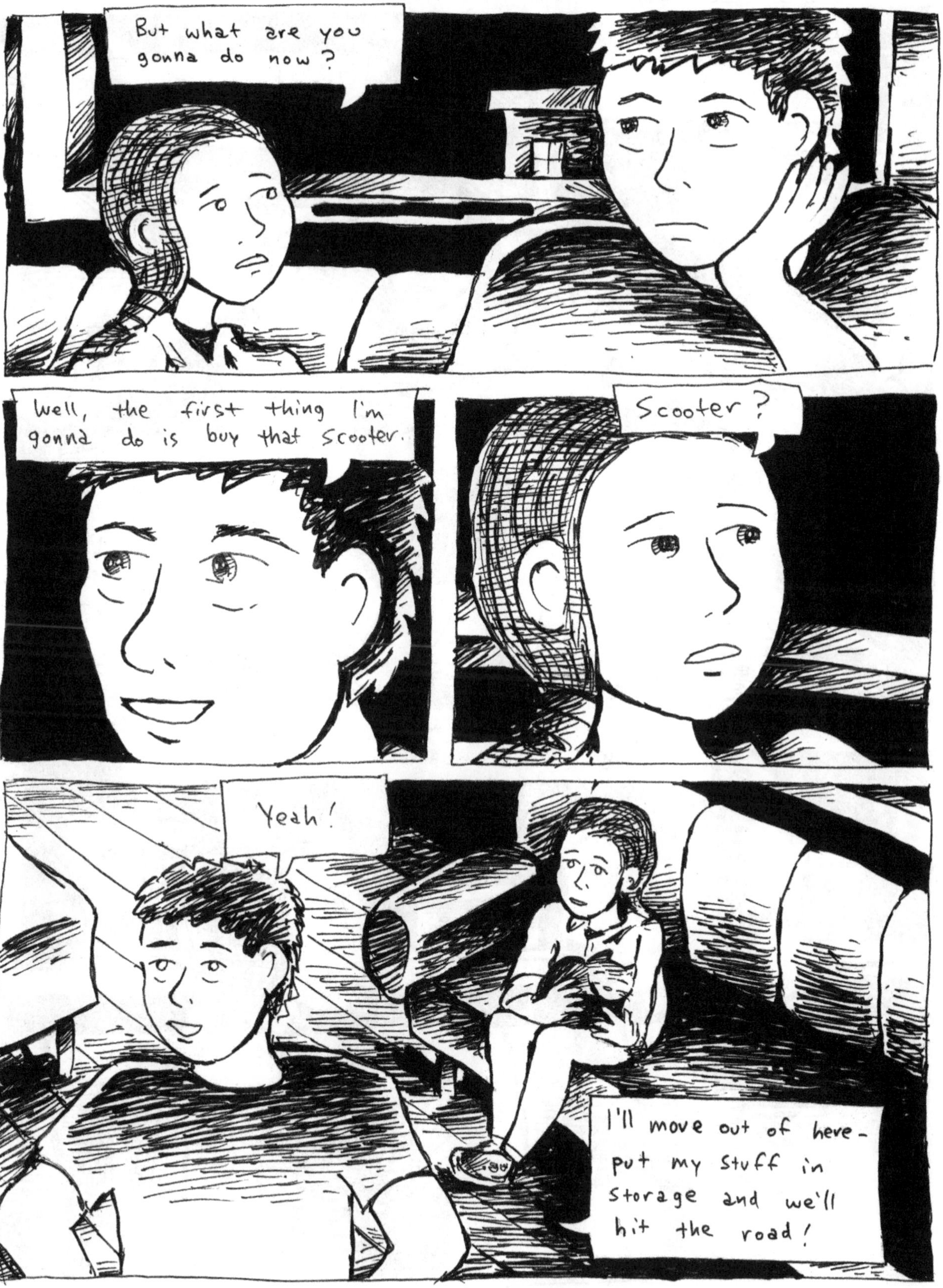
But what are you gonna do now?
Well, the first thing I'm gonna do is buy that scooter.
Scooter?
Yeah!
I'll move out of here-put my stuff in storage and we'll hit the road!

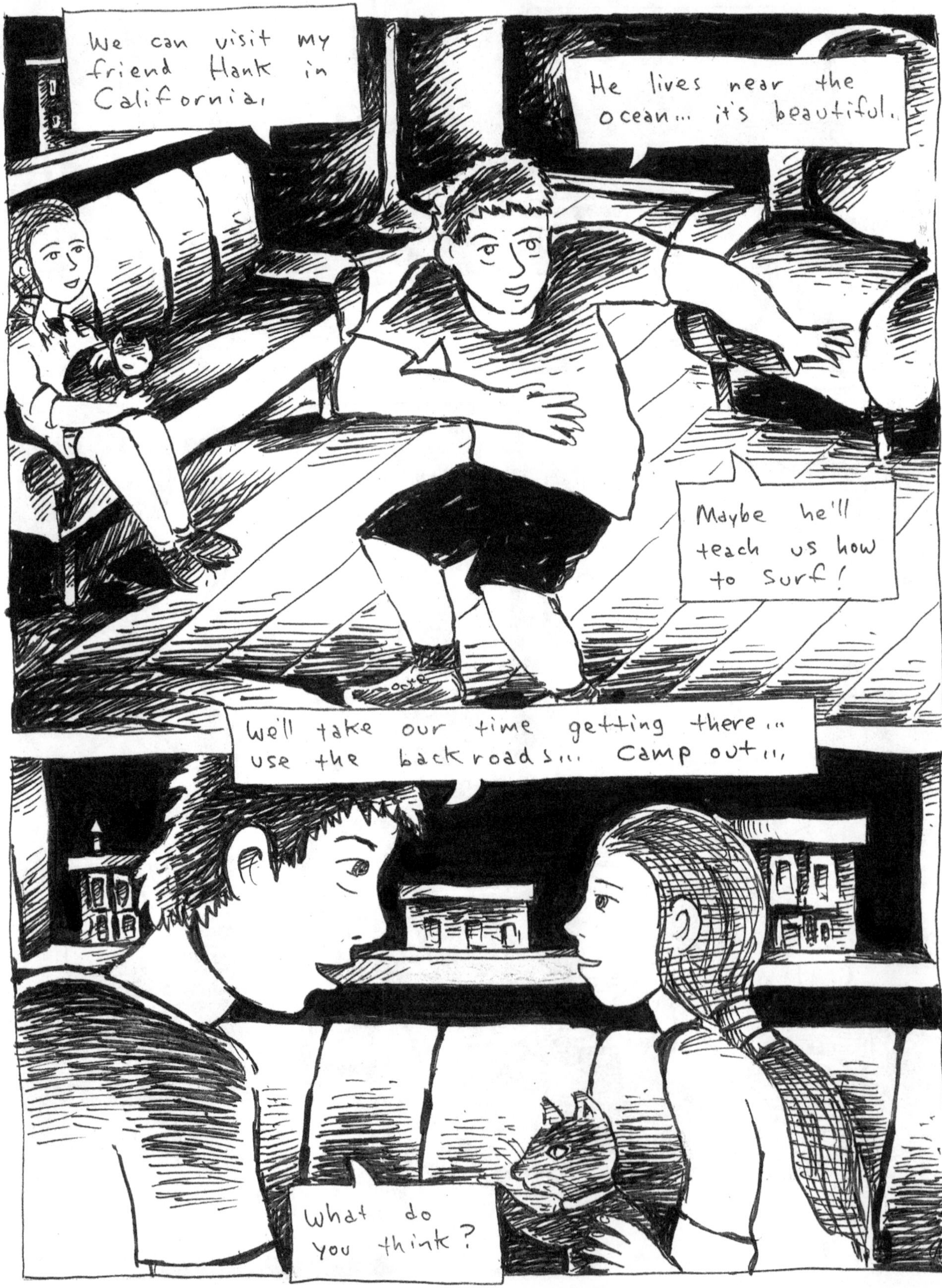
We can visit my friend Hank in California.
He lives near the ocean... it's beautiful.
Maybe he'll teach us how to surf!
We'll take our time getting there... use the backroads... Camp out...
What do you think?

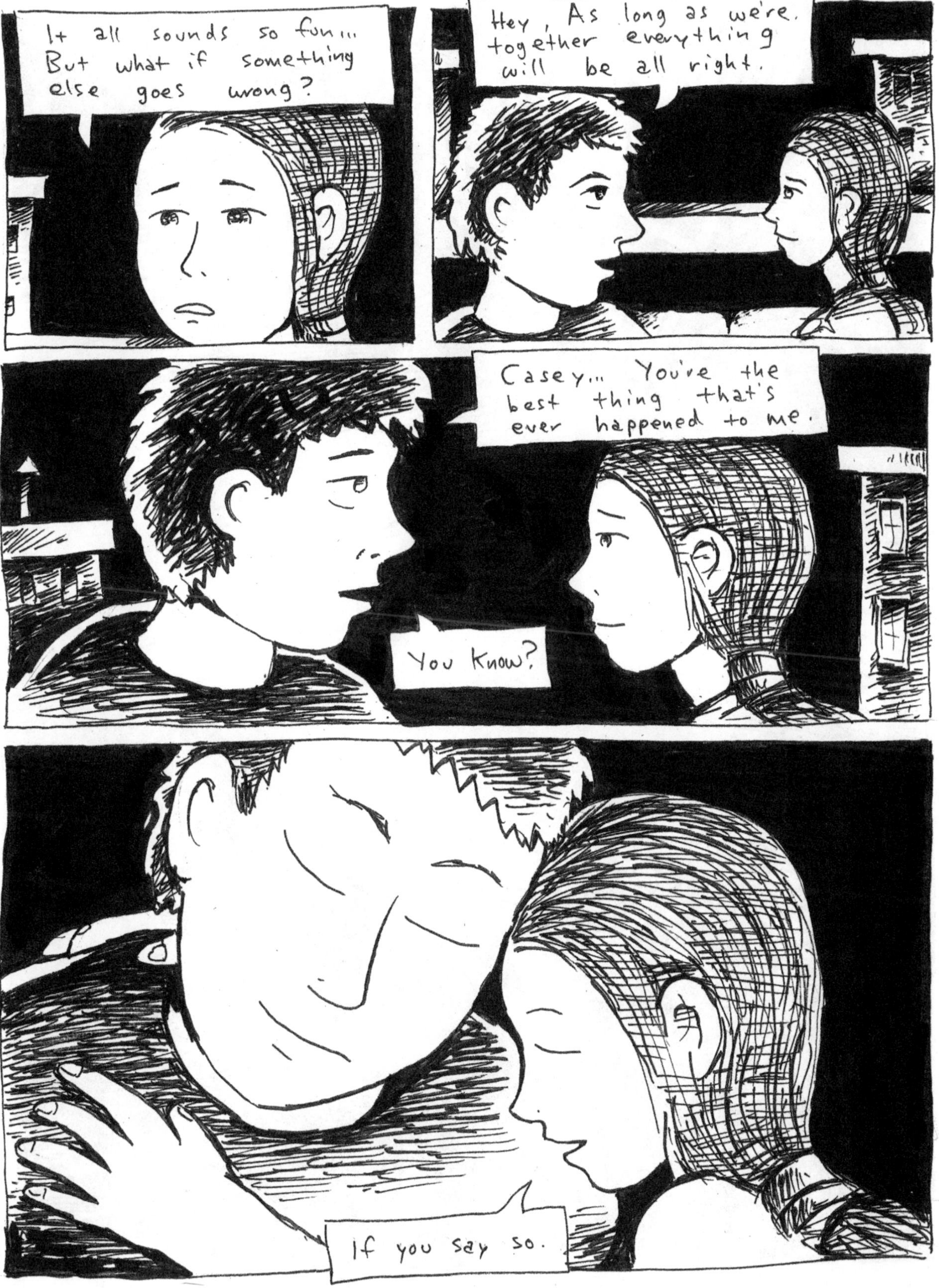
It all sounds so fun... But what if something else goes wrong?
Hey, As long as we're together everything will be all right.
Casey... You're the best thing that's ever happened to me.
You know?
If you say so.

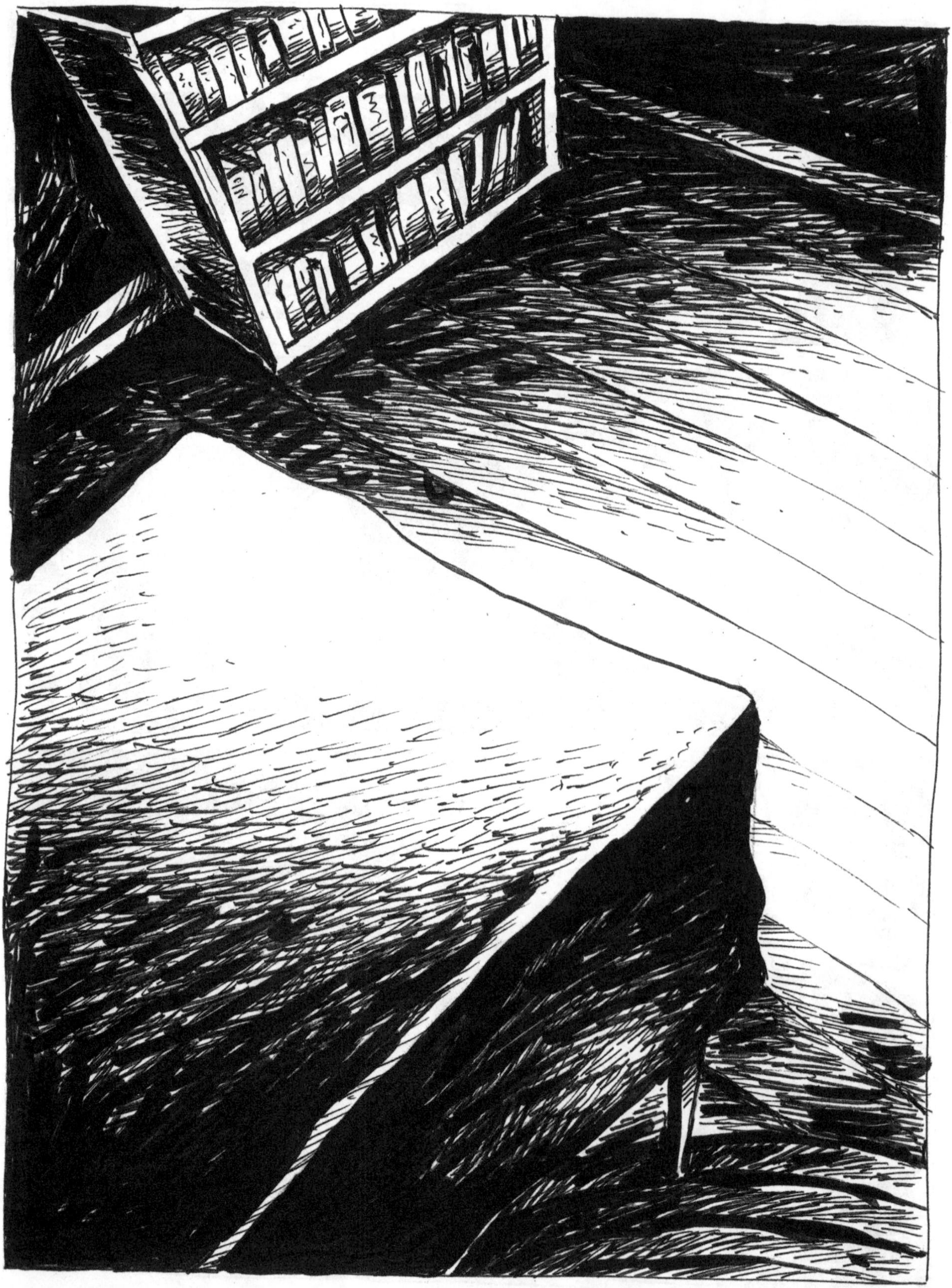

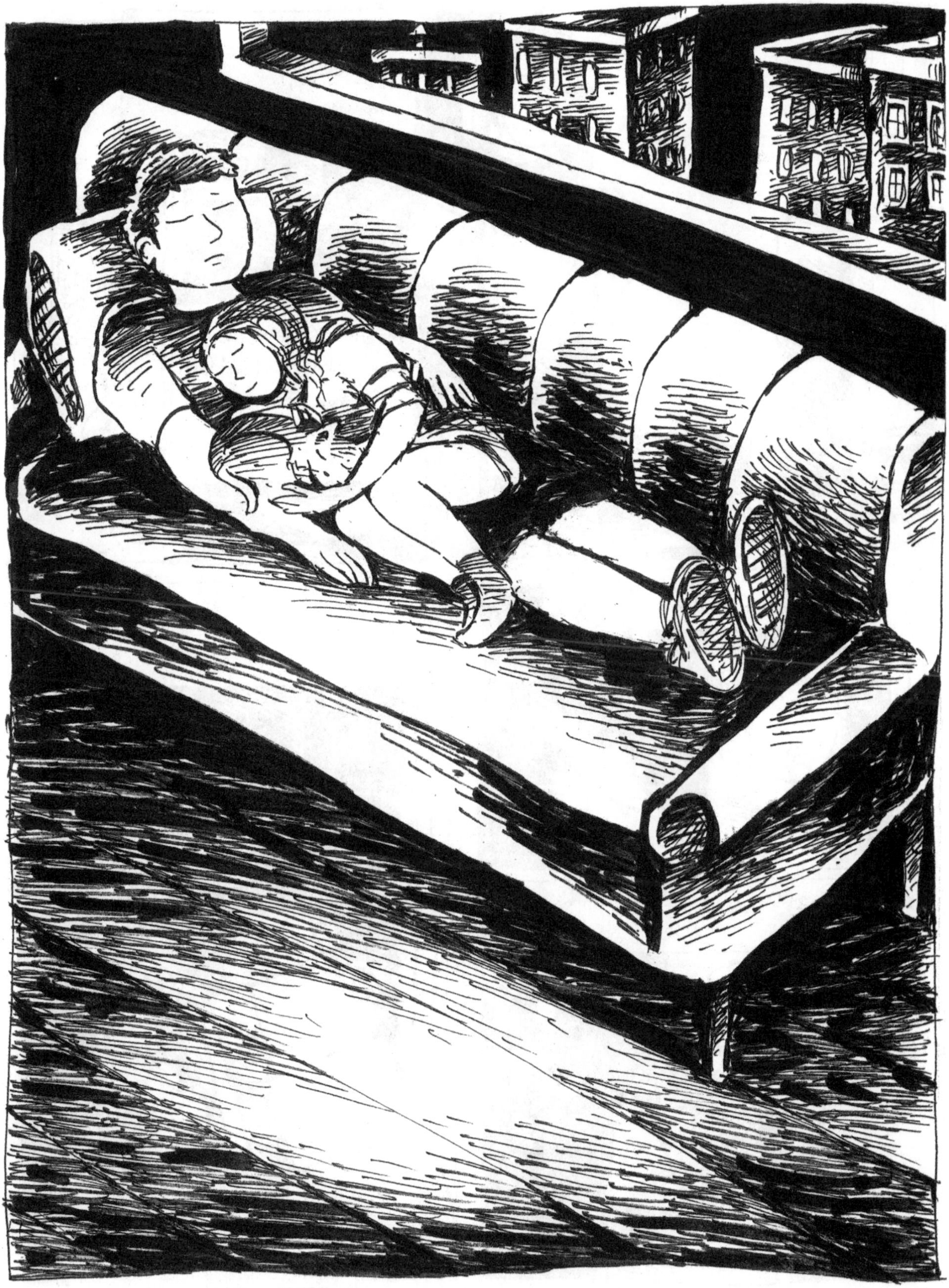

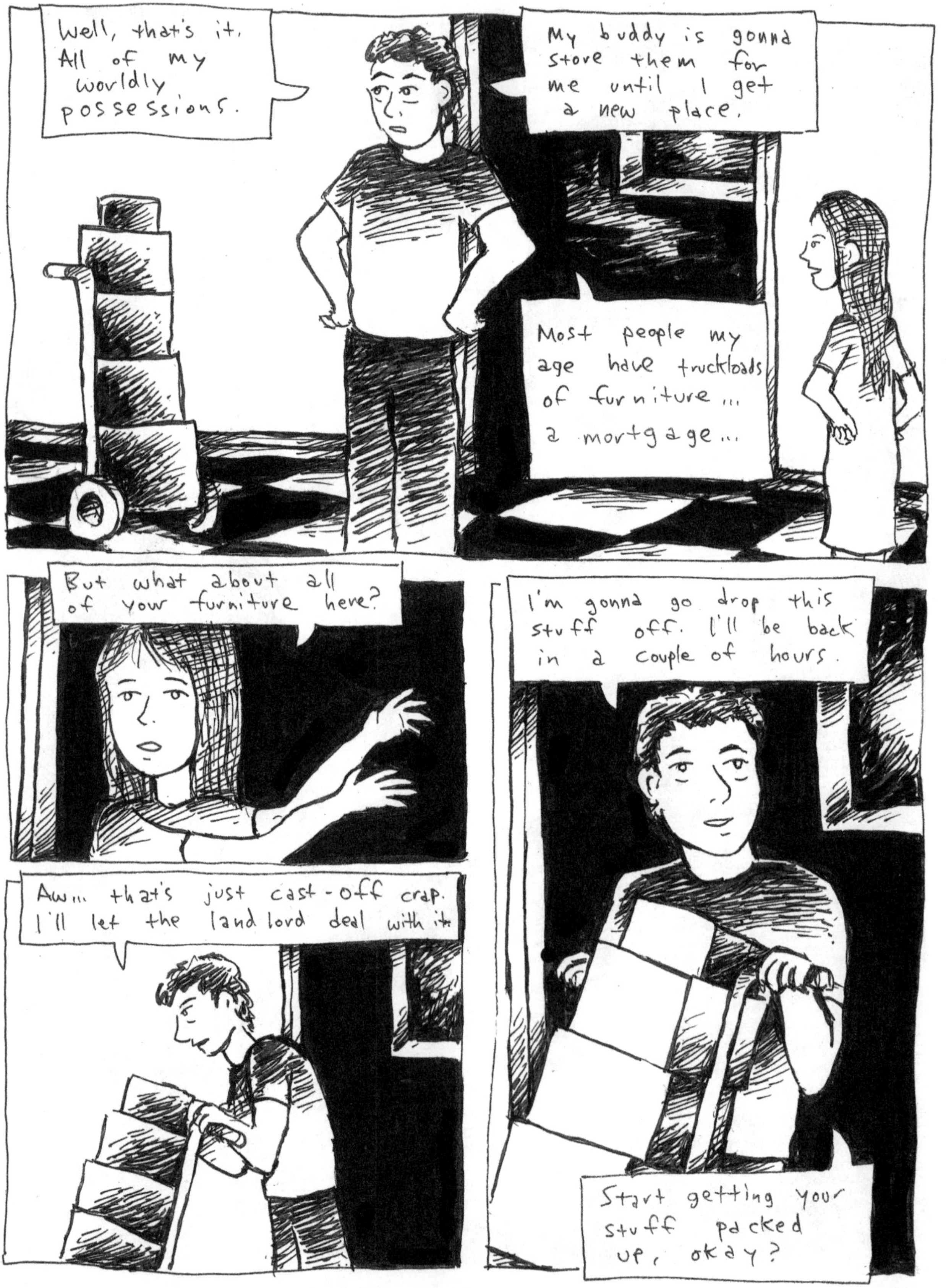
Well, that's it. All of my worldly possessions.
My buddy is gonna store them for me until I get a new place.
Most people my age have truckloads of furniture... a mortgage...
But what about all of your furniture here?
Aw... that's just cast-off crap. I'll let the landlord deal with it.
I'm gonna go drop this stuff off. I'll be back in a couple of hours.
Start getting your stuff packed up, okay?

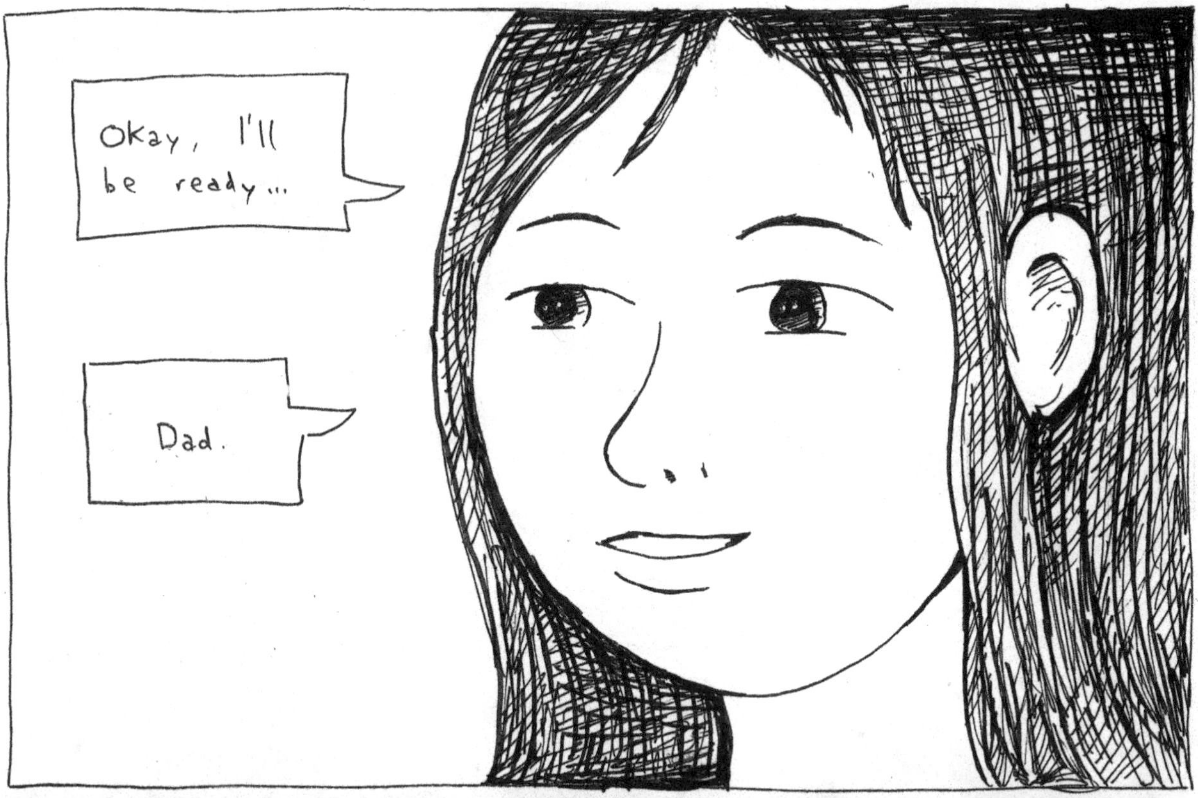
Okay, I'll be ready...
Dad.

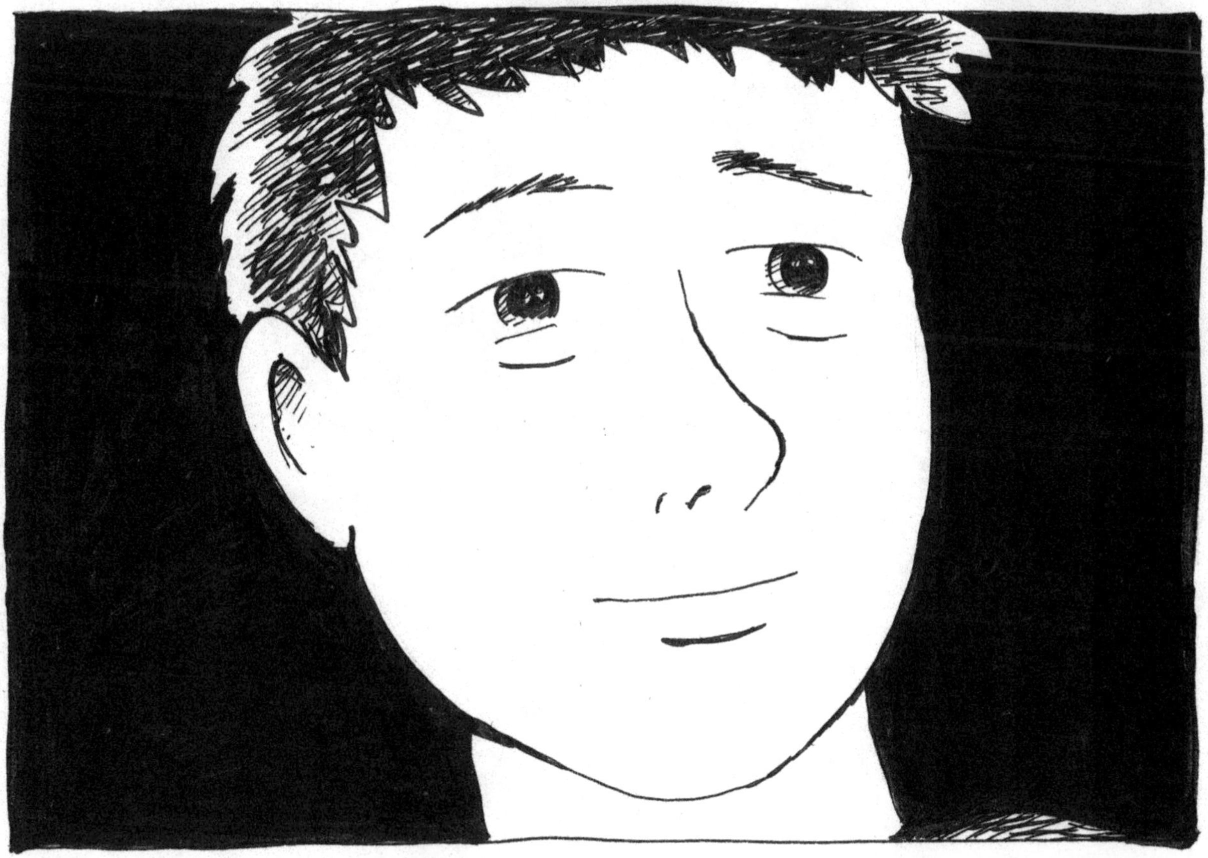

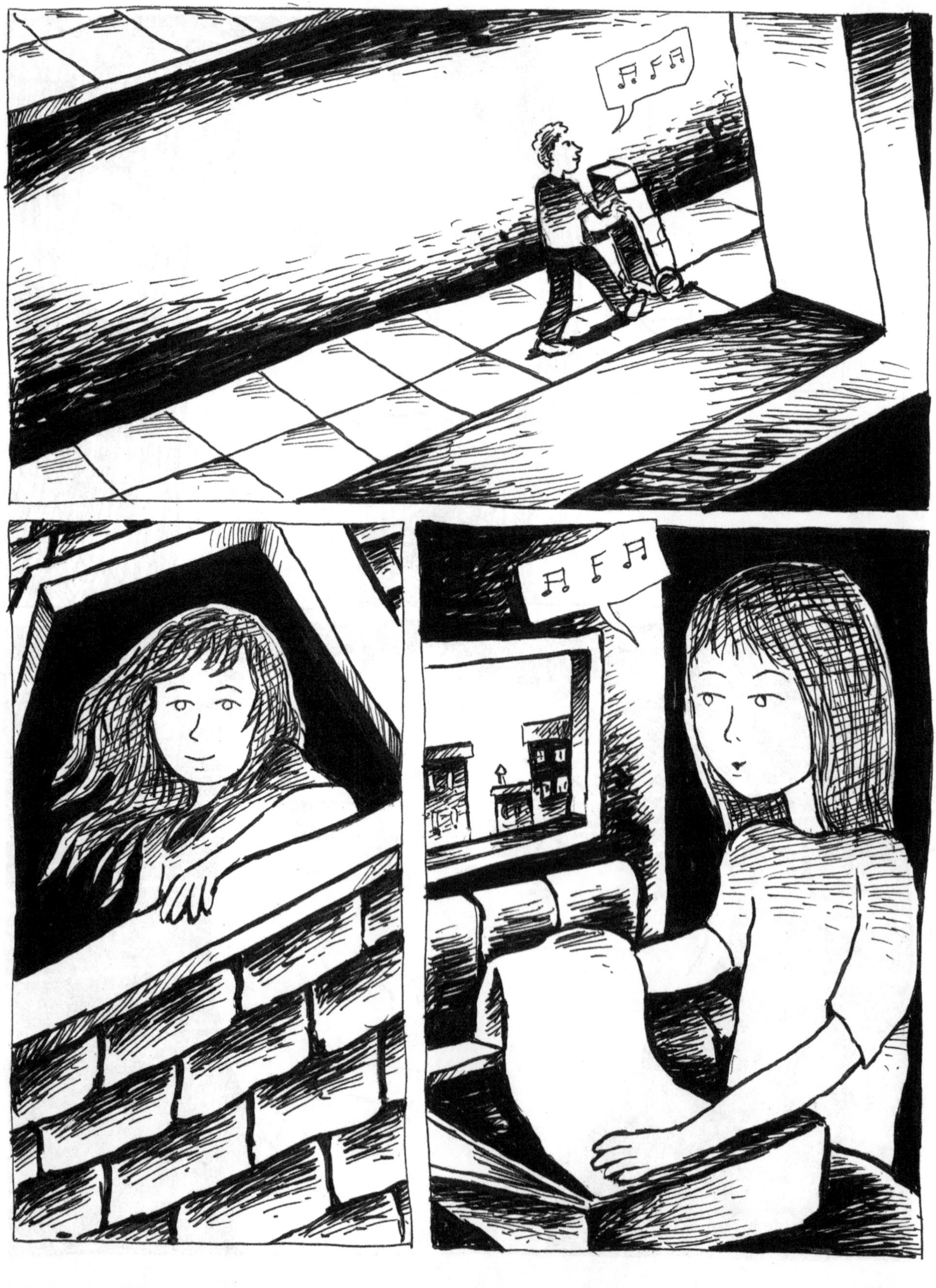

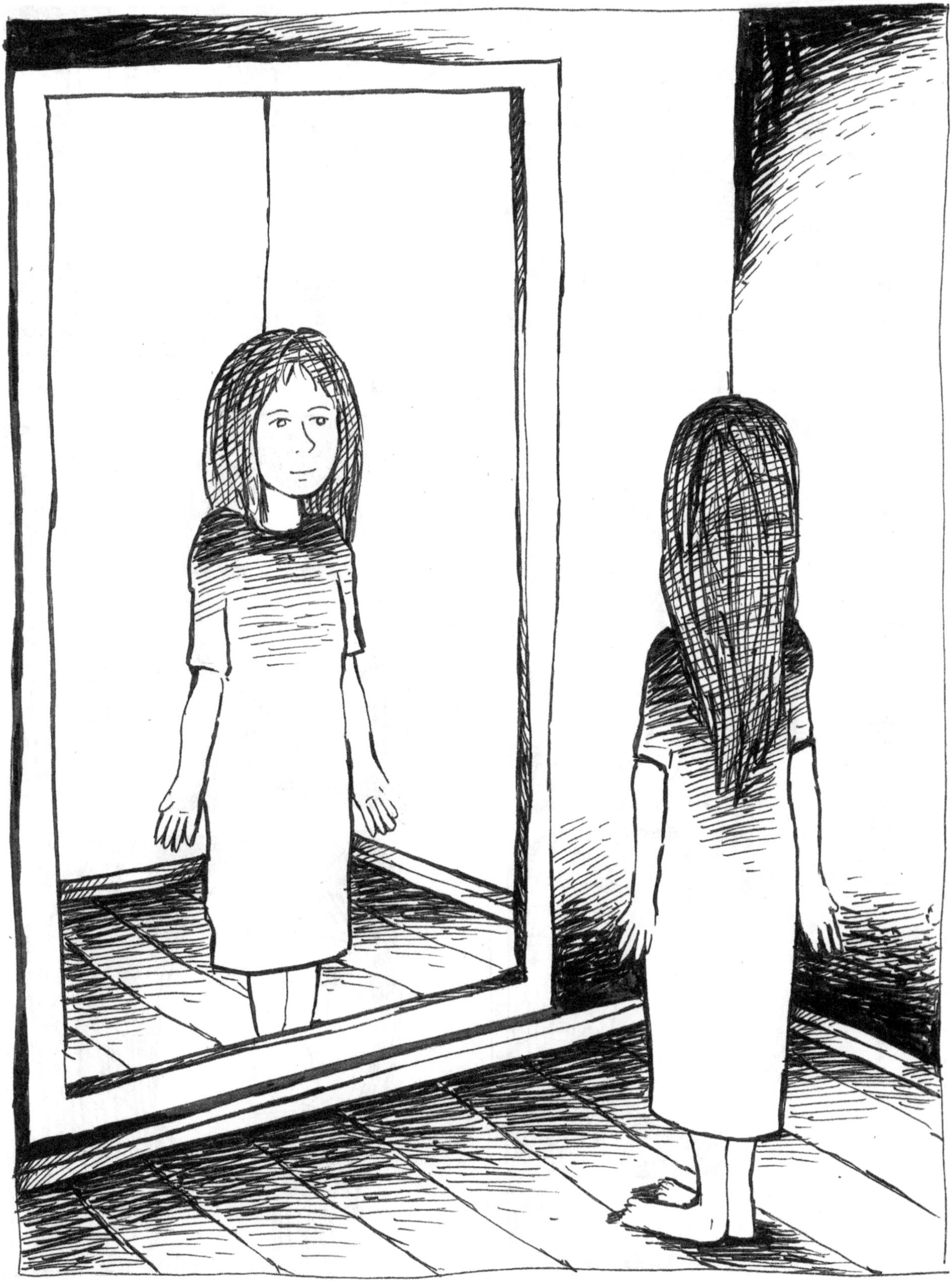

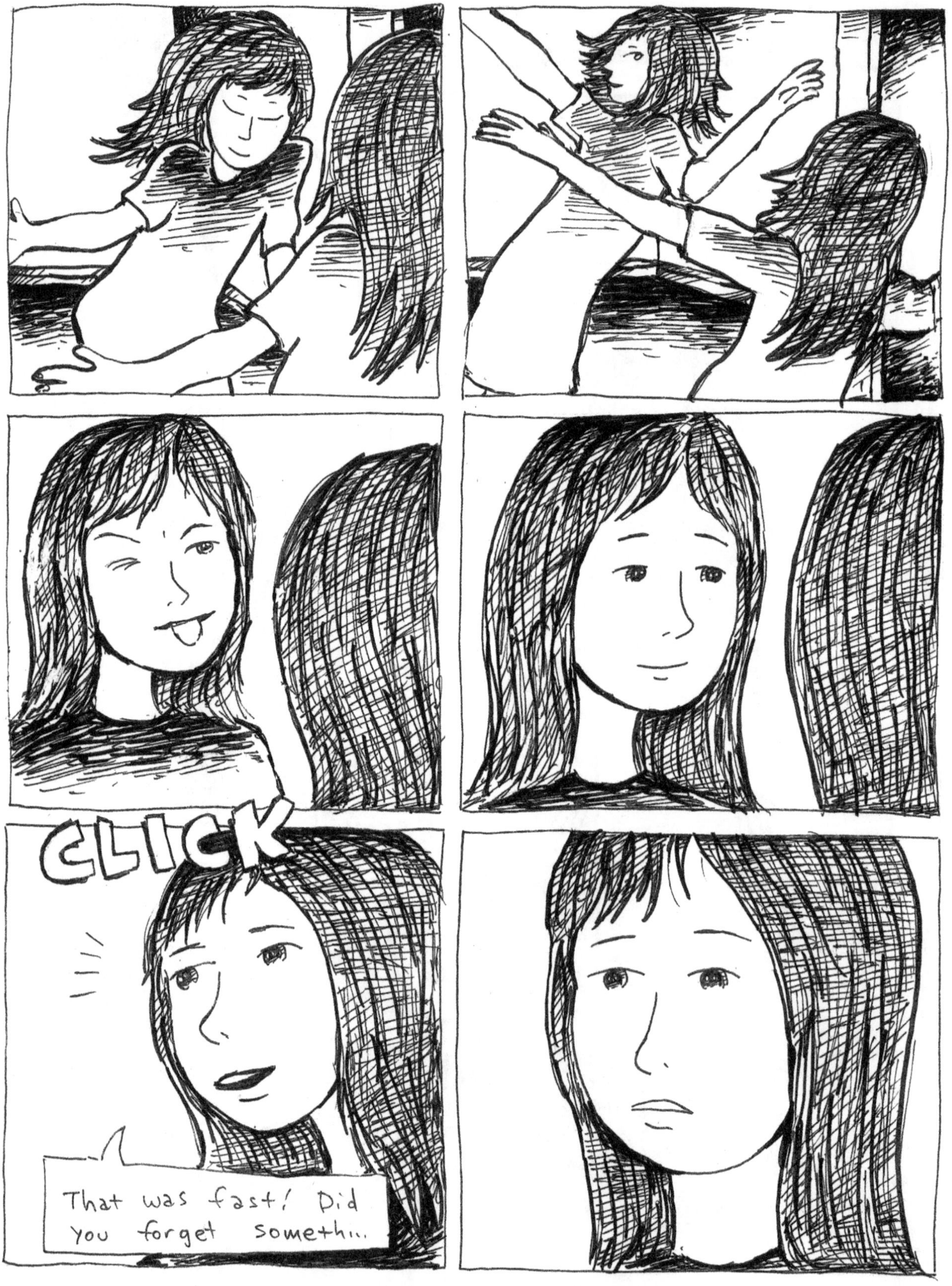
CLICK
That was fast! Did you forget someth...

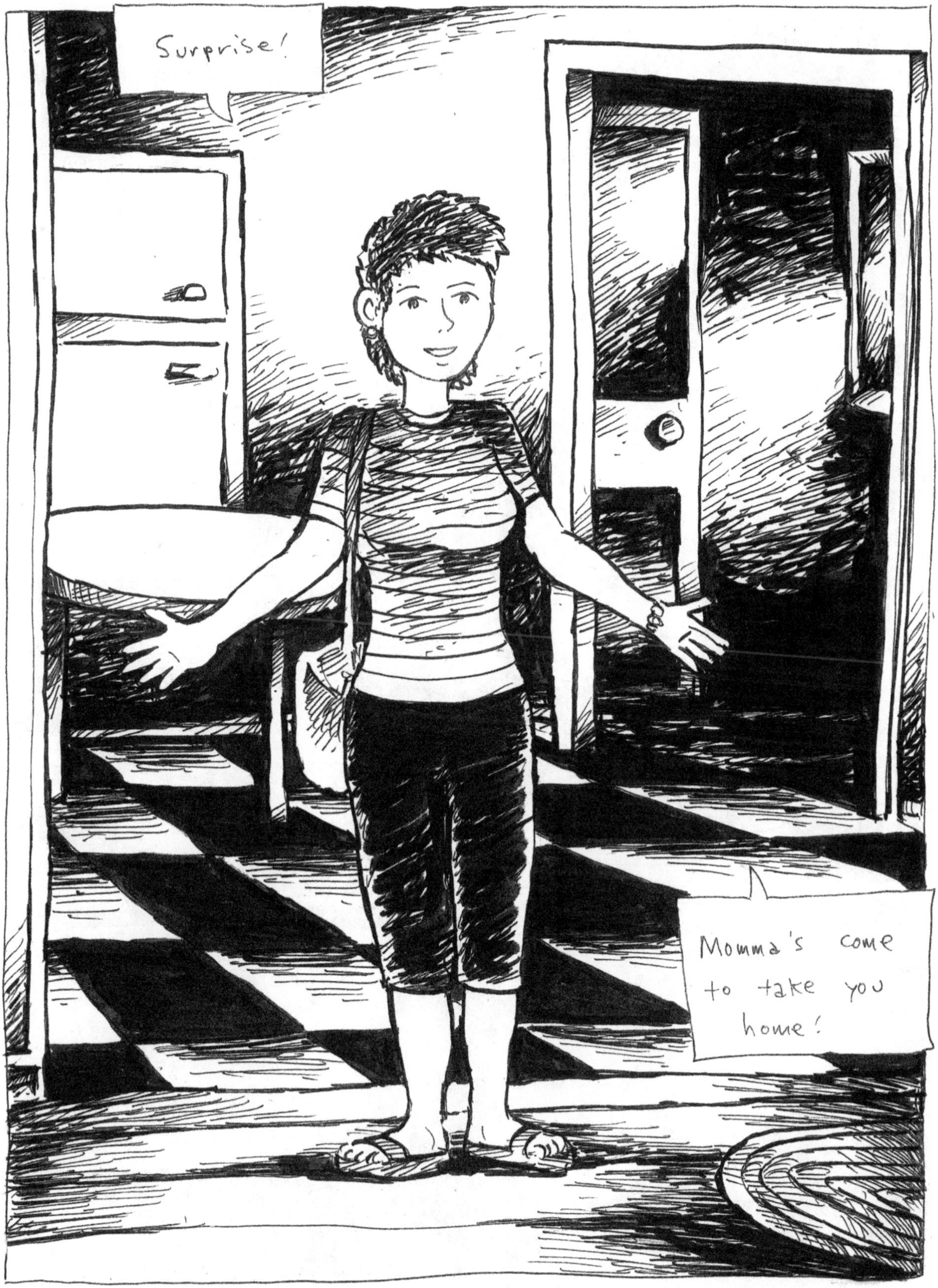
Surprise!
Momma's come to take you home!

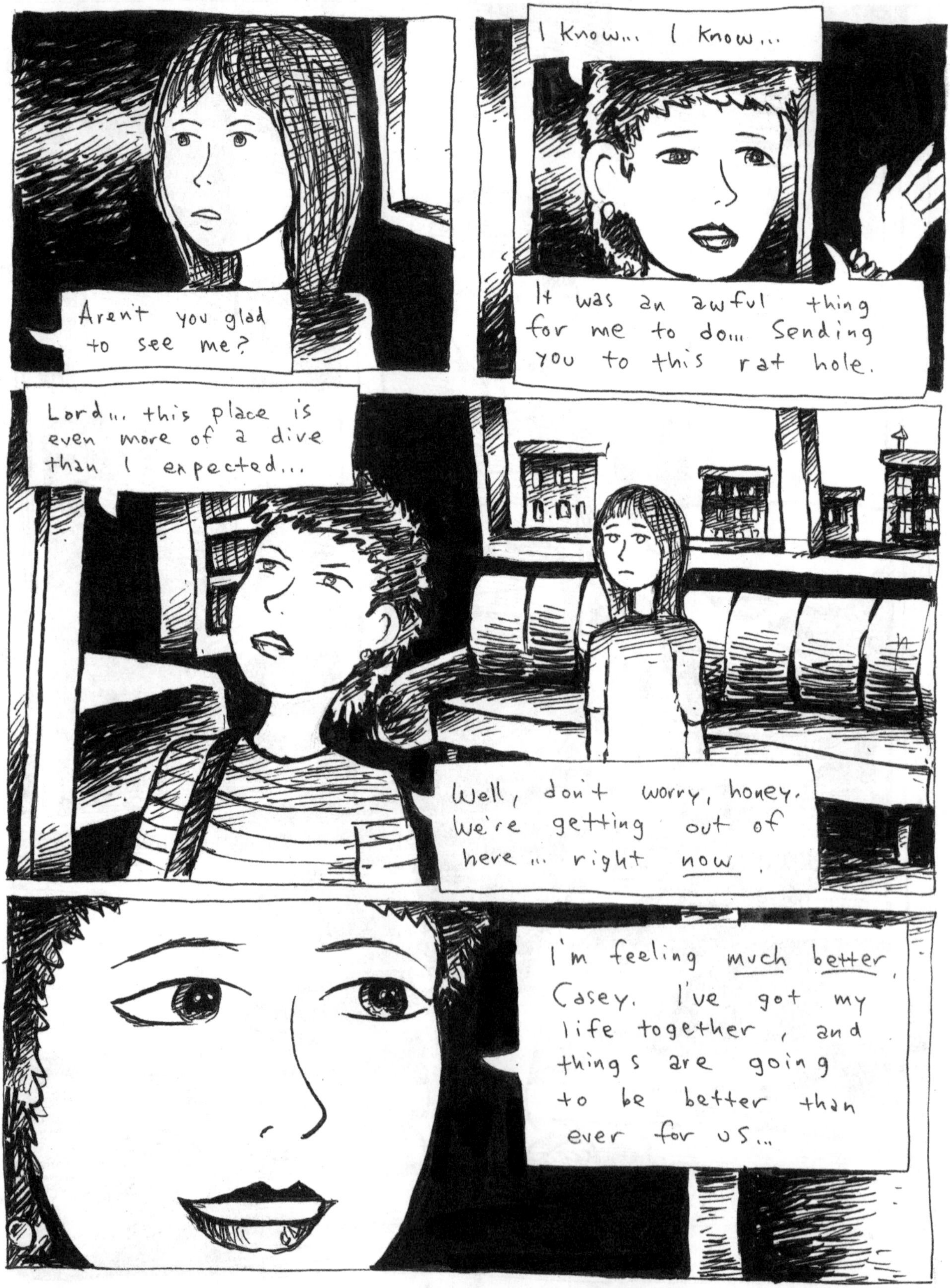
Aren't you glad to see me?
I know... I know...
It was an awful thing for me to do... Sending you to this rat hole.
Lord... this place is even more of a dive than I expected...
Well, don't worry, honey. We're getting out of here... right now.
I'm feeling much better, Casey. I've got my life together, and things are going to be better than ever for us...

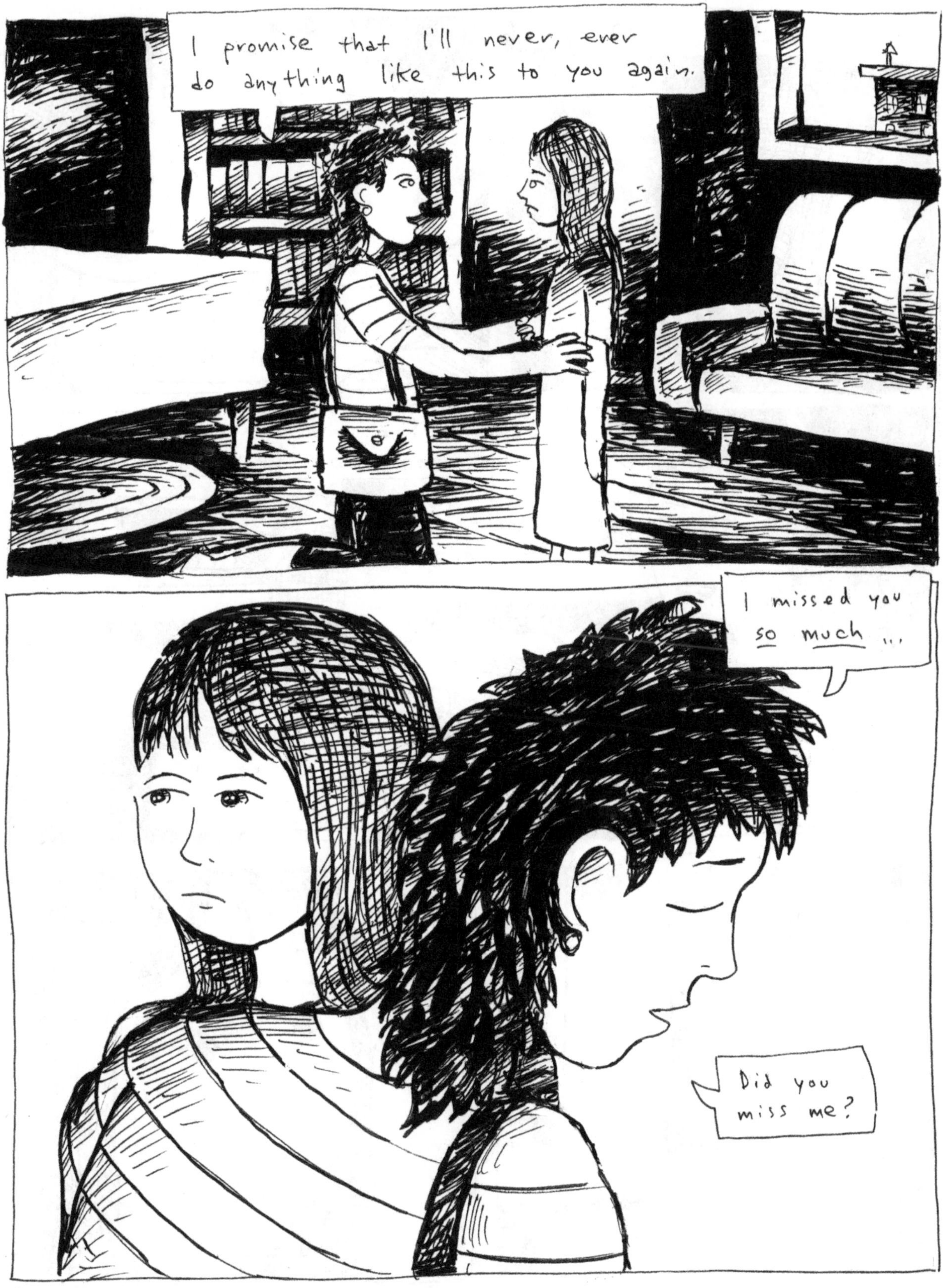
I promise that I'll never, ever do anything like this to you again.
I missed you so much ...
Did you miss me?

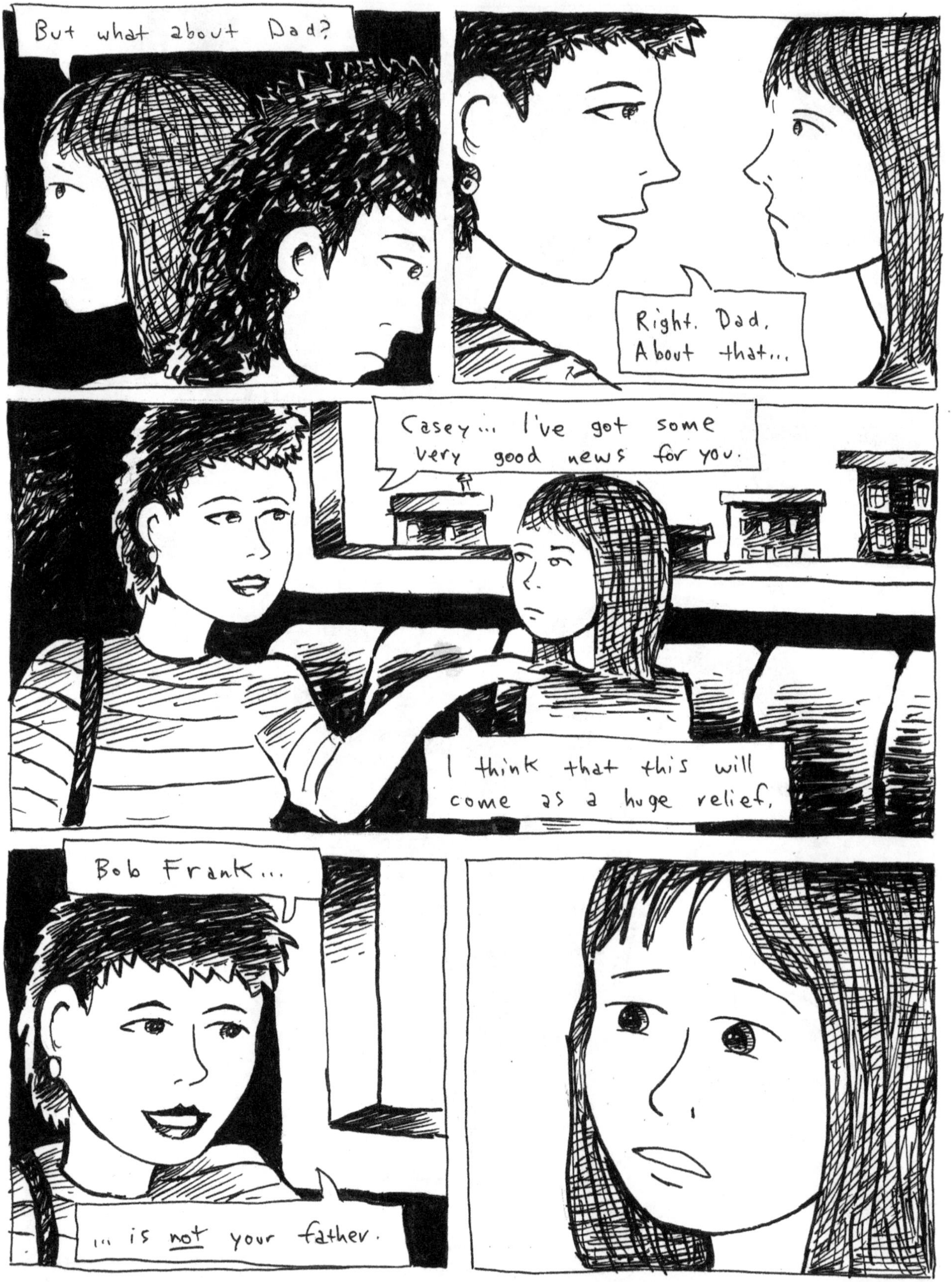
But what about Dad?
Right. Dad. About that...
Casey... I've got some very good news for you.
I think that this will come as a huge relief.
Bob Frank...
... is not your father.

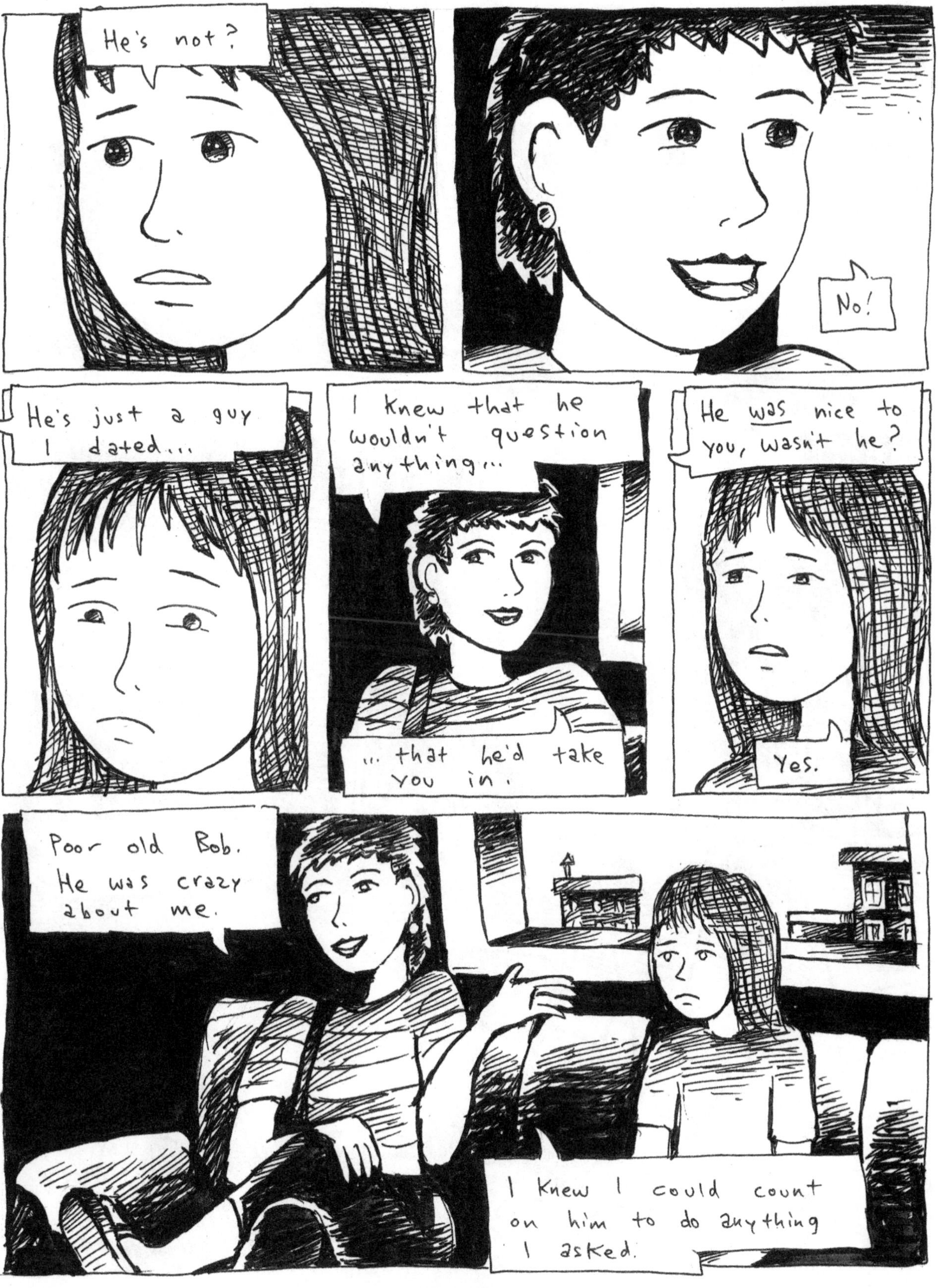
He's not?
No!
He's just a guy I dated...
I knew that he wouldn't question anything...
... that he'd take you in.
He was nice to you, wasn't he?
Yes.
Poor old Bob. He was crazy about me.
I knew I could count on him to do anything I asked.

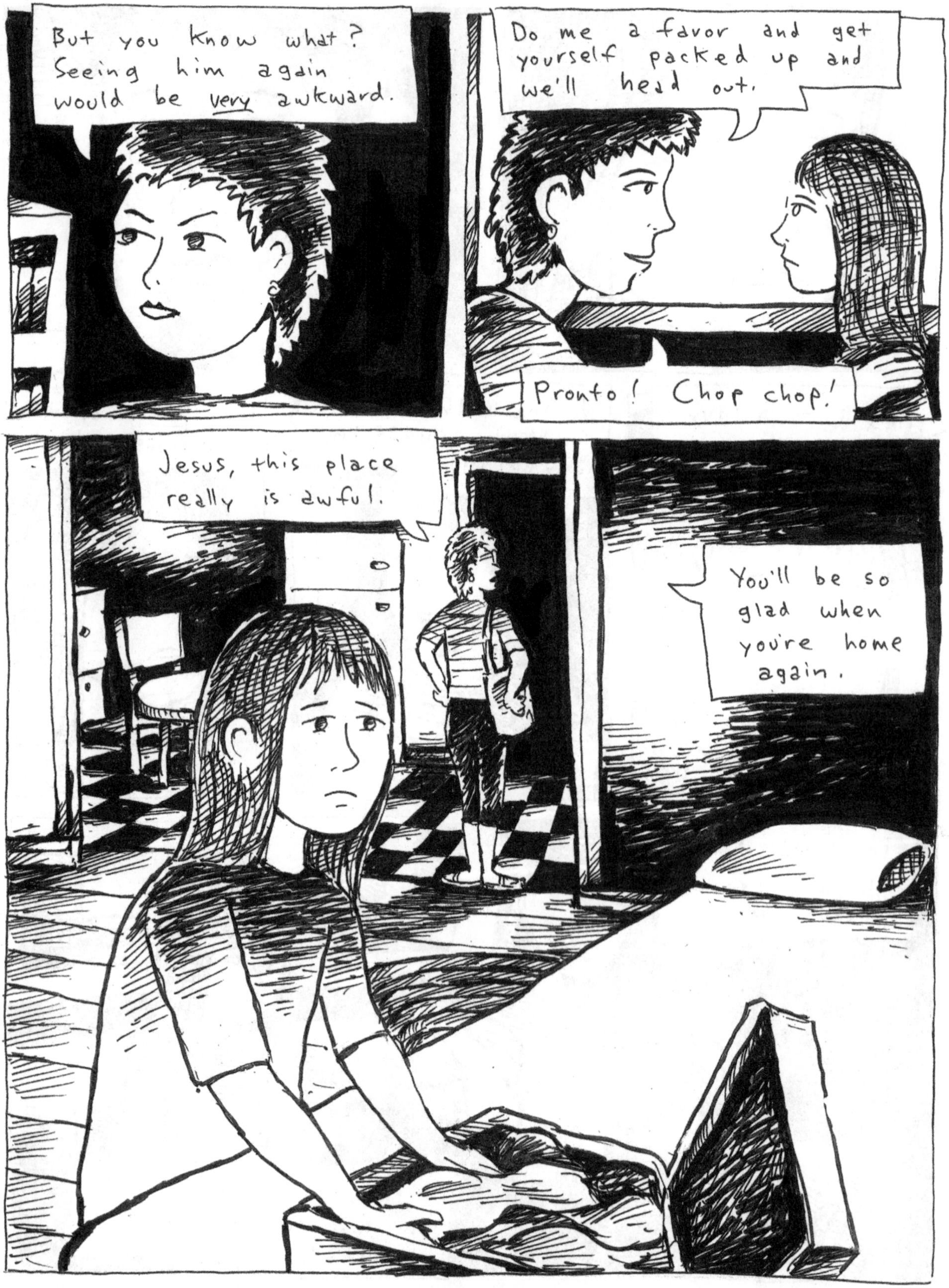
But you know what? Seeing him again would be very awkward.
Do me a favor and get yourself packed up and we'll head out.
Pronto! Chop chop!
Jesus, this place really is awful.
You'll be so glad when you're home again.

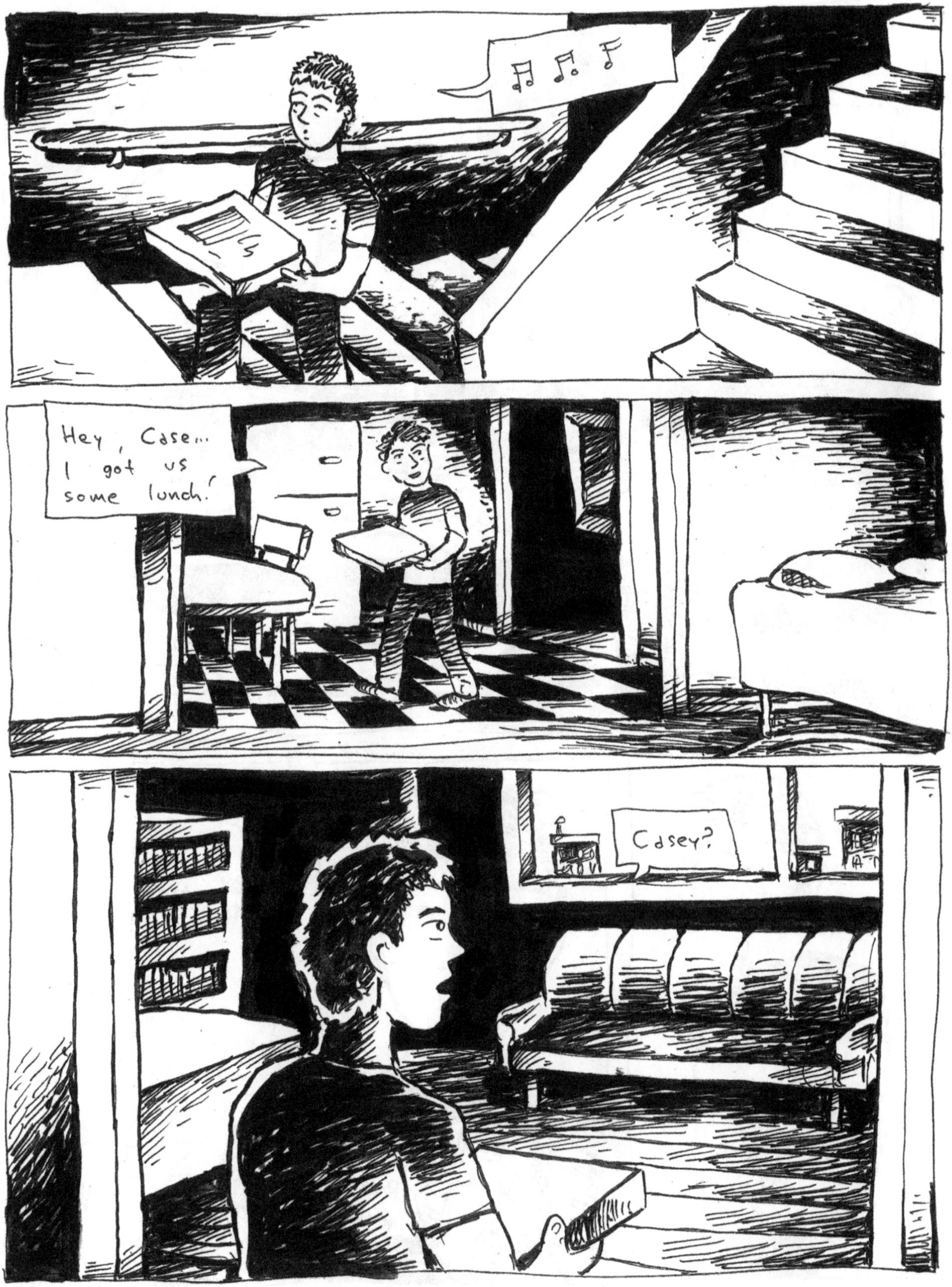
Hey, Case...
I got us
some lunch!
Casey?

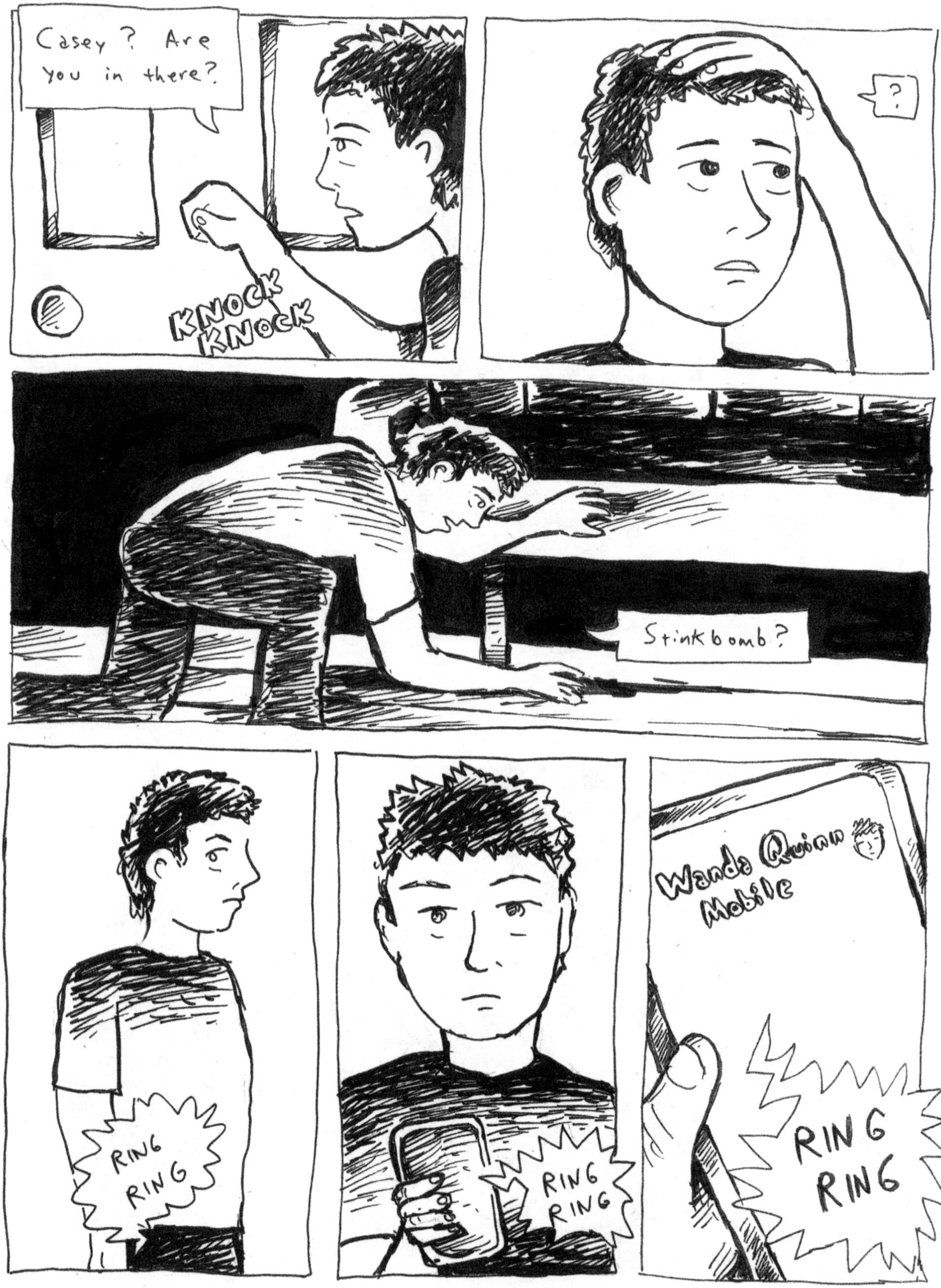
Casey? Are you in there?
KNOCK KNOCK
?
Stinkbomb?
RING RING
RING RING
Wanda Quinn Mobile
RING RING

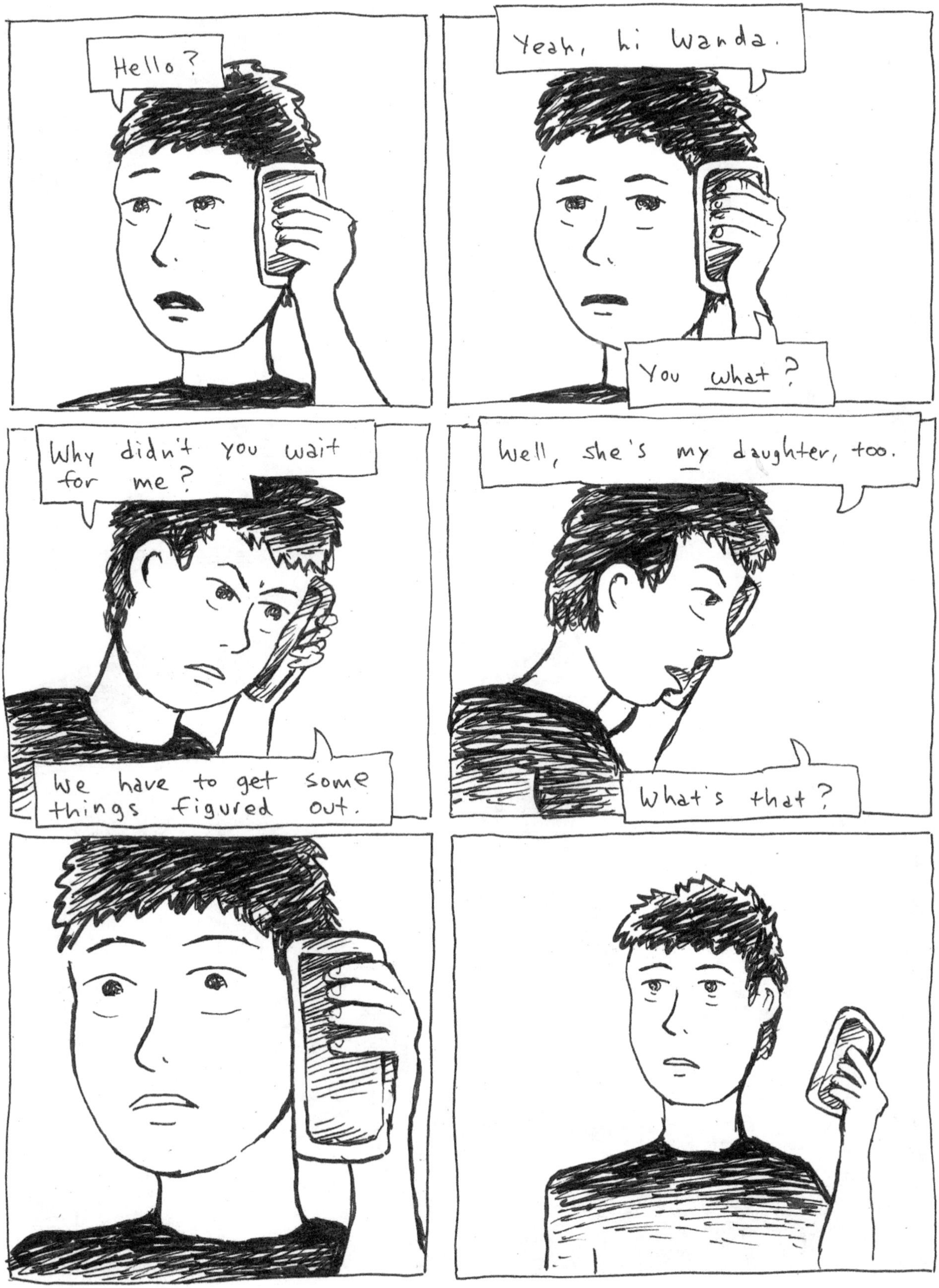
Hello?
Yeah, hi Wanda.
You what?
Why didn't you wait for me?
We have to get some things figured out.
Well, she's my daughter, too.
What's that?

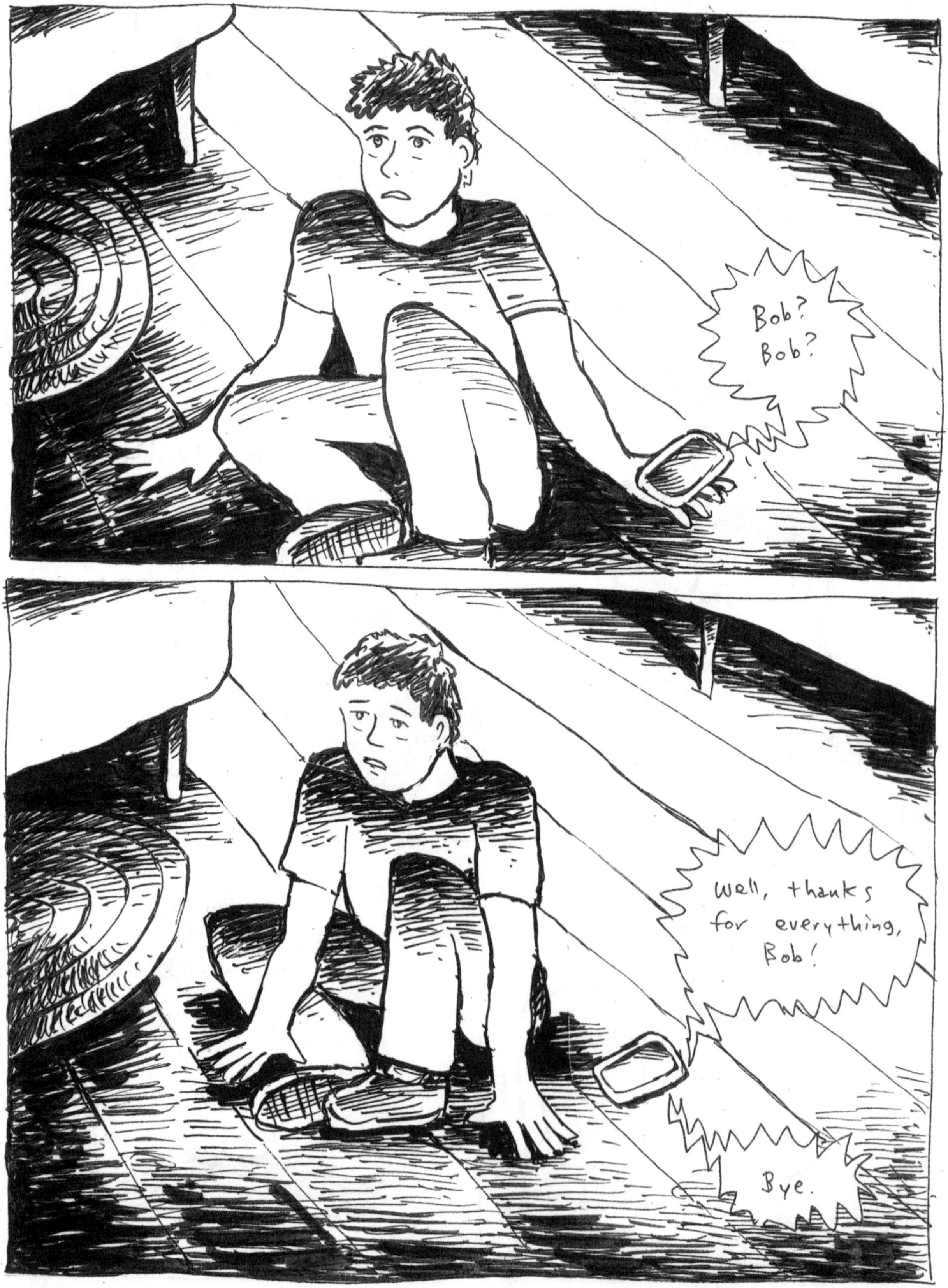
Bob? Bob?
Well, thanks for everything, Bob!
Bye.

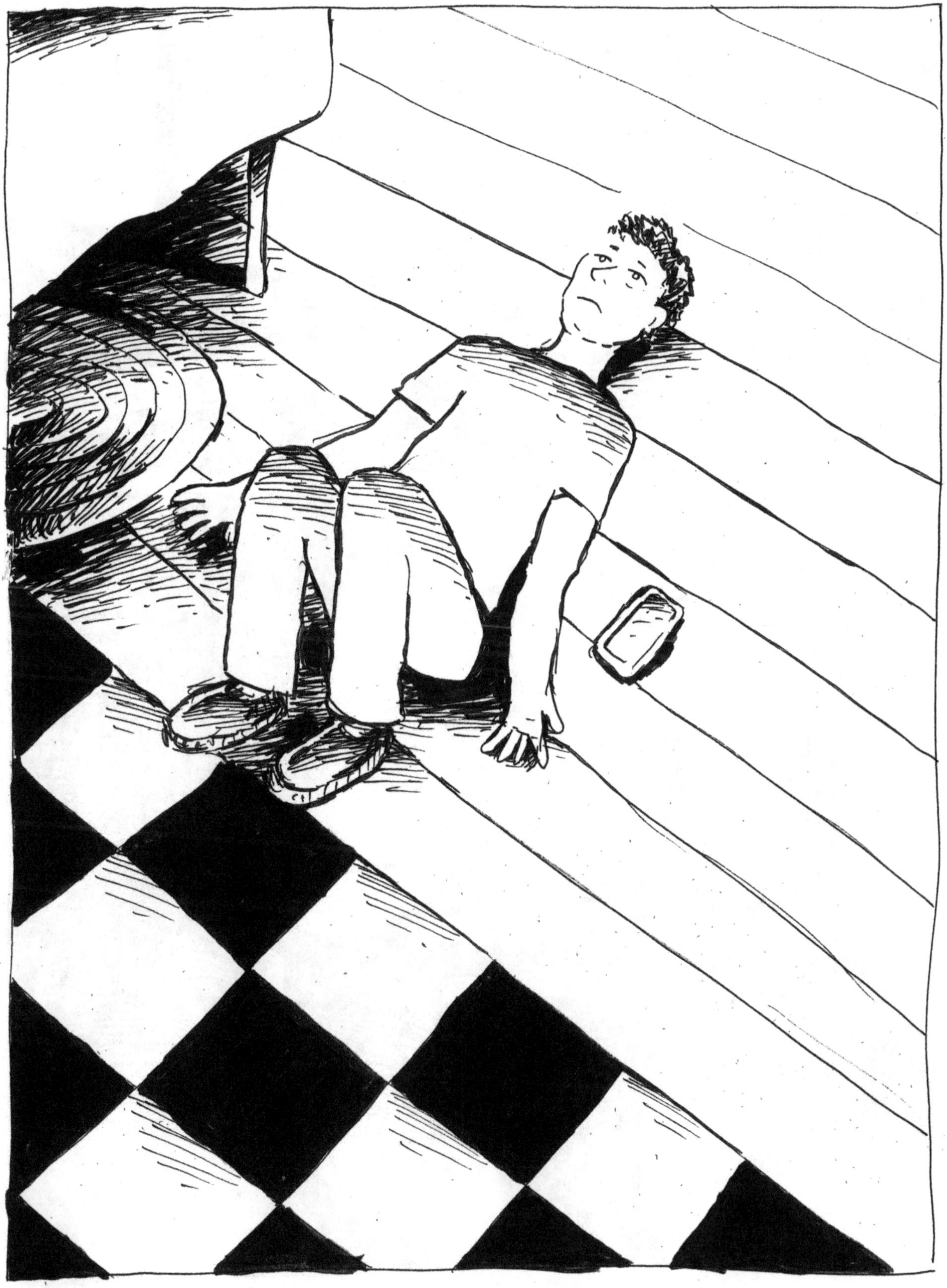

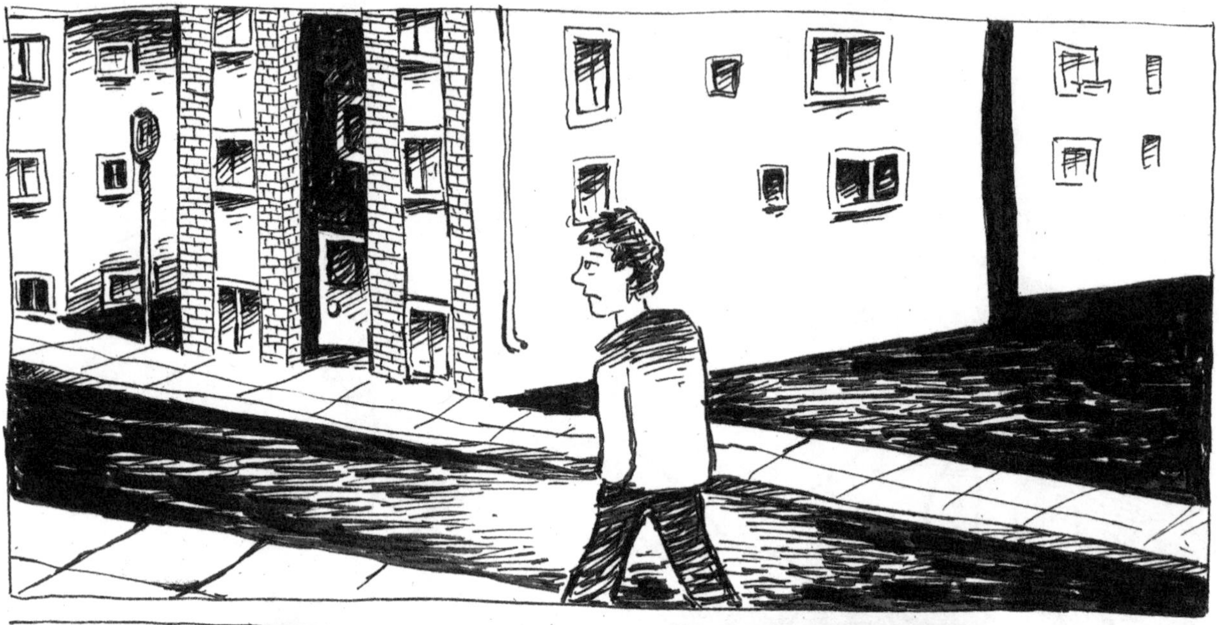

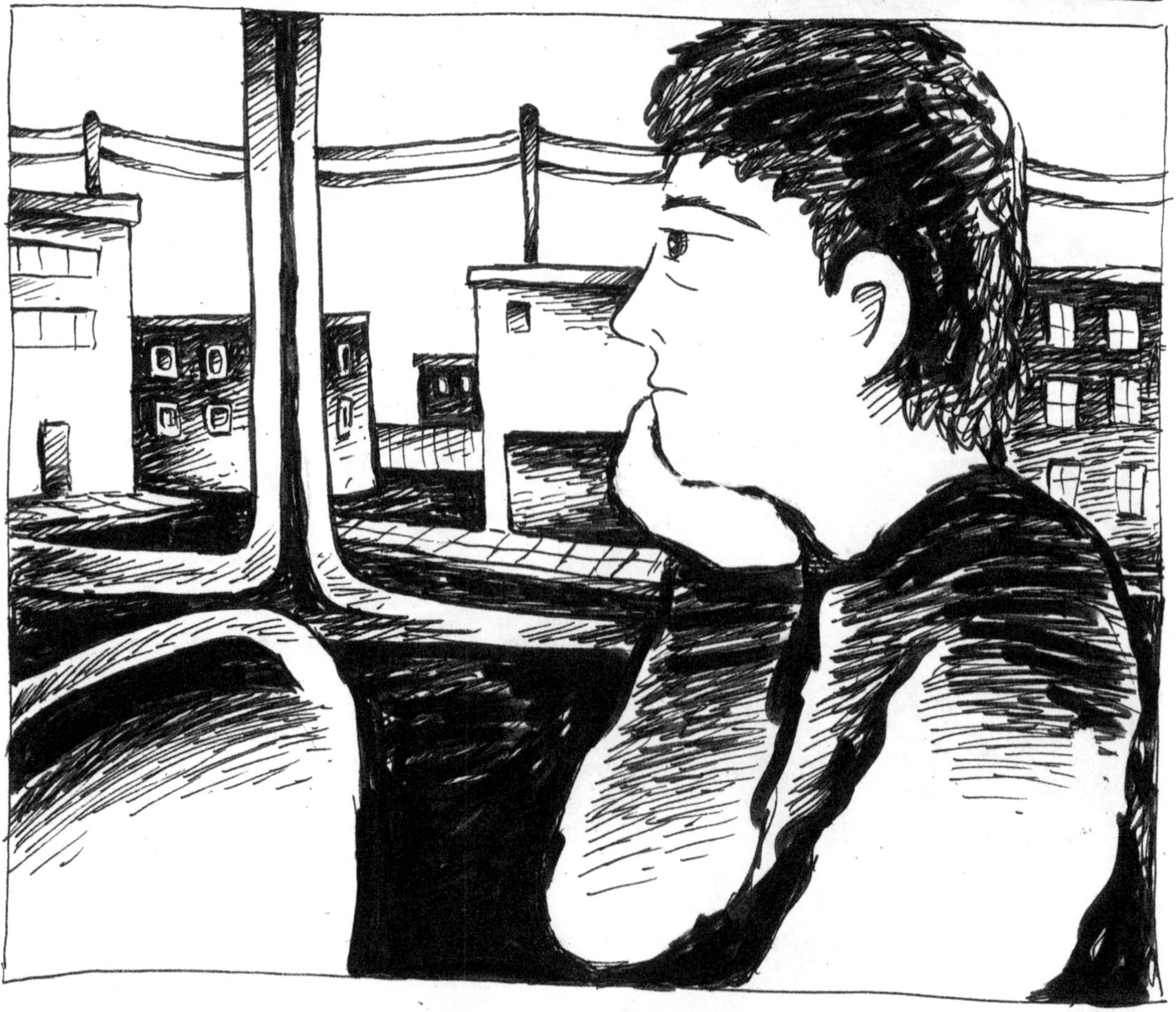

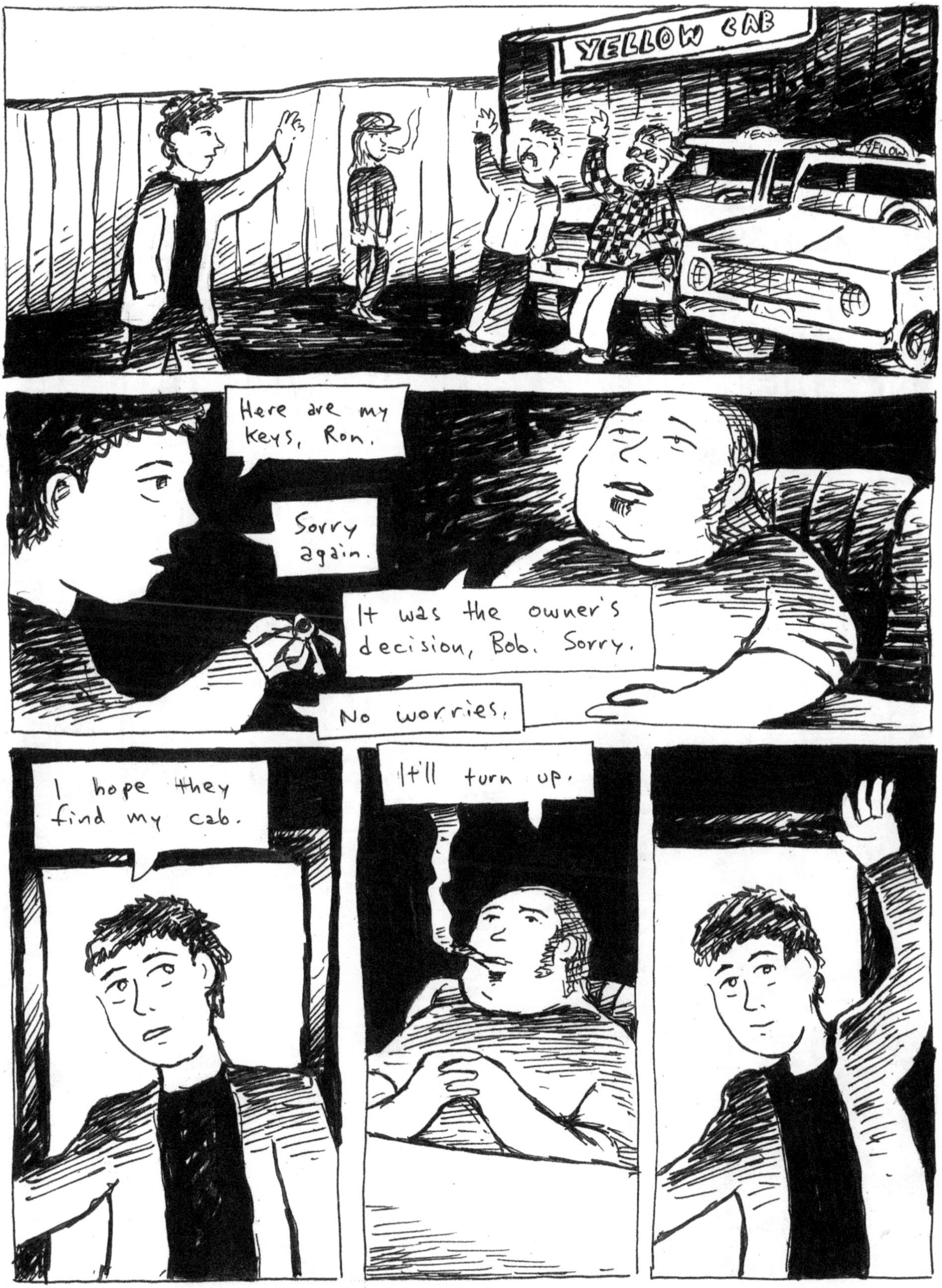
YELLOW CAB
Here are my keys, Ron.
Sorry again.
It was the owner's decision, Bob. Sorry.
No worries.
I hope they find my cab.
It'll turn up.

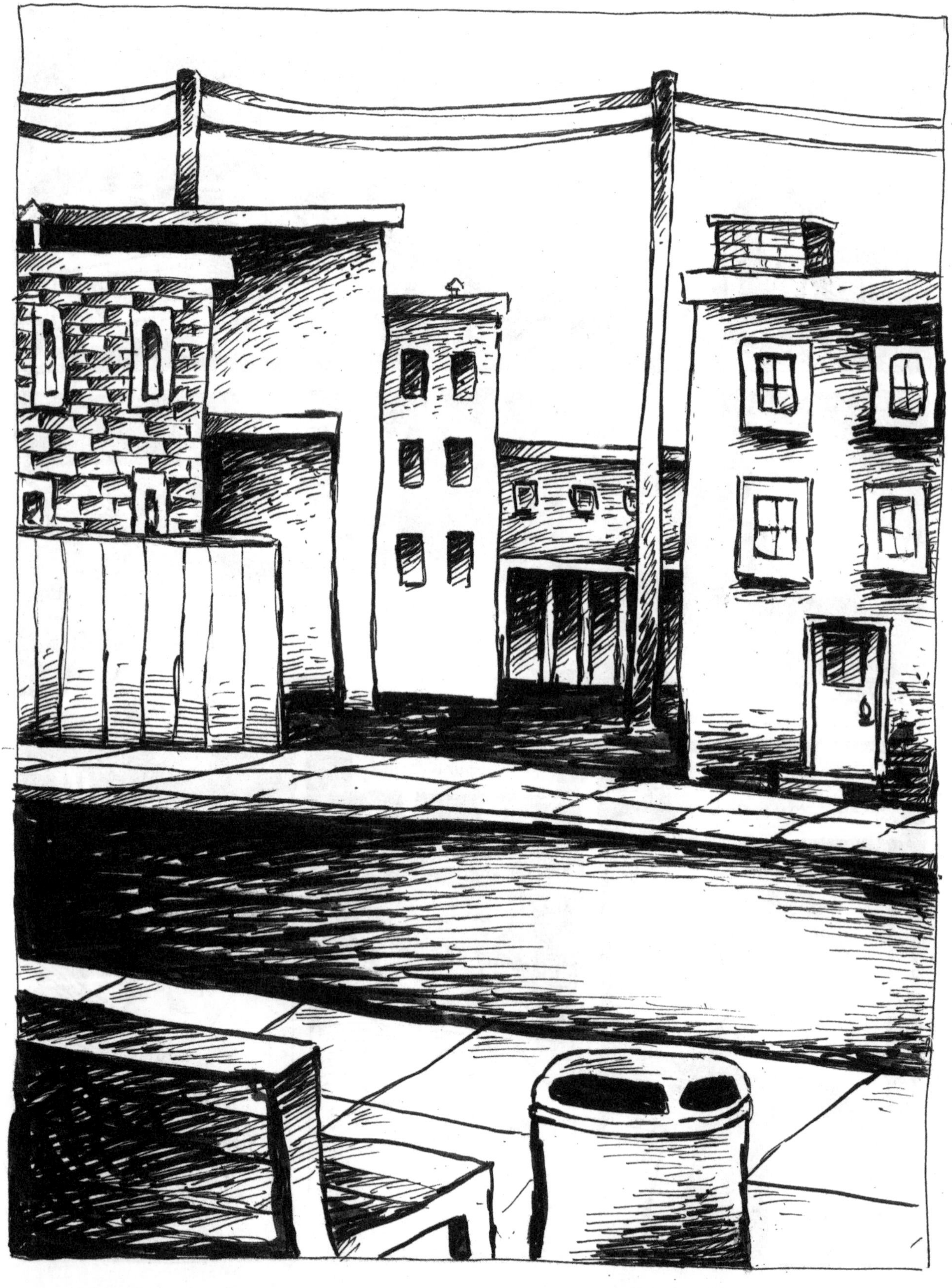

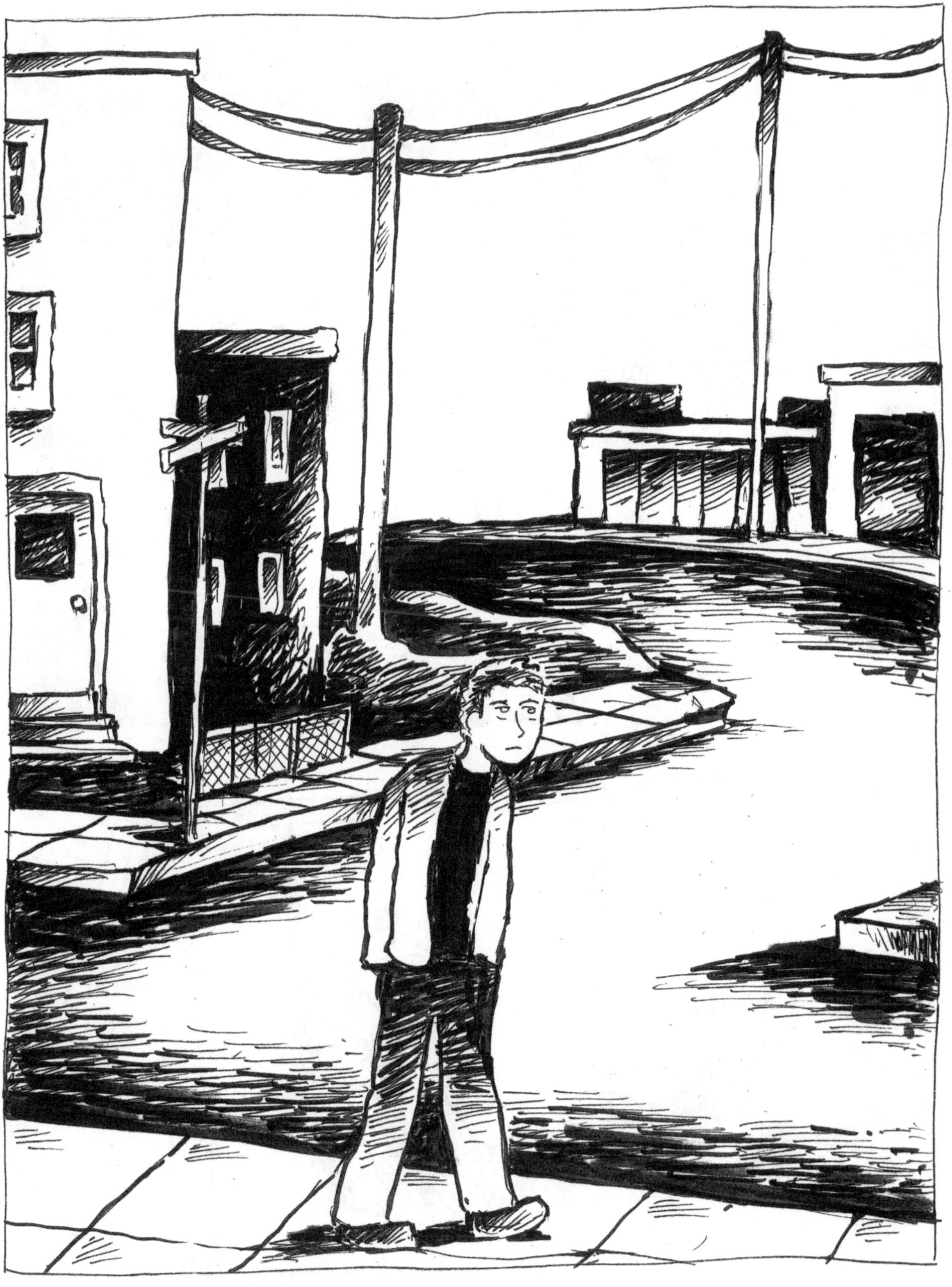

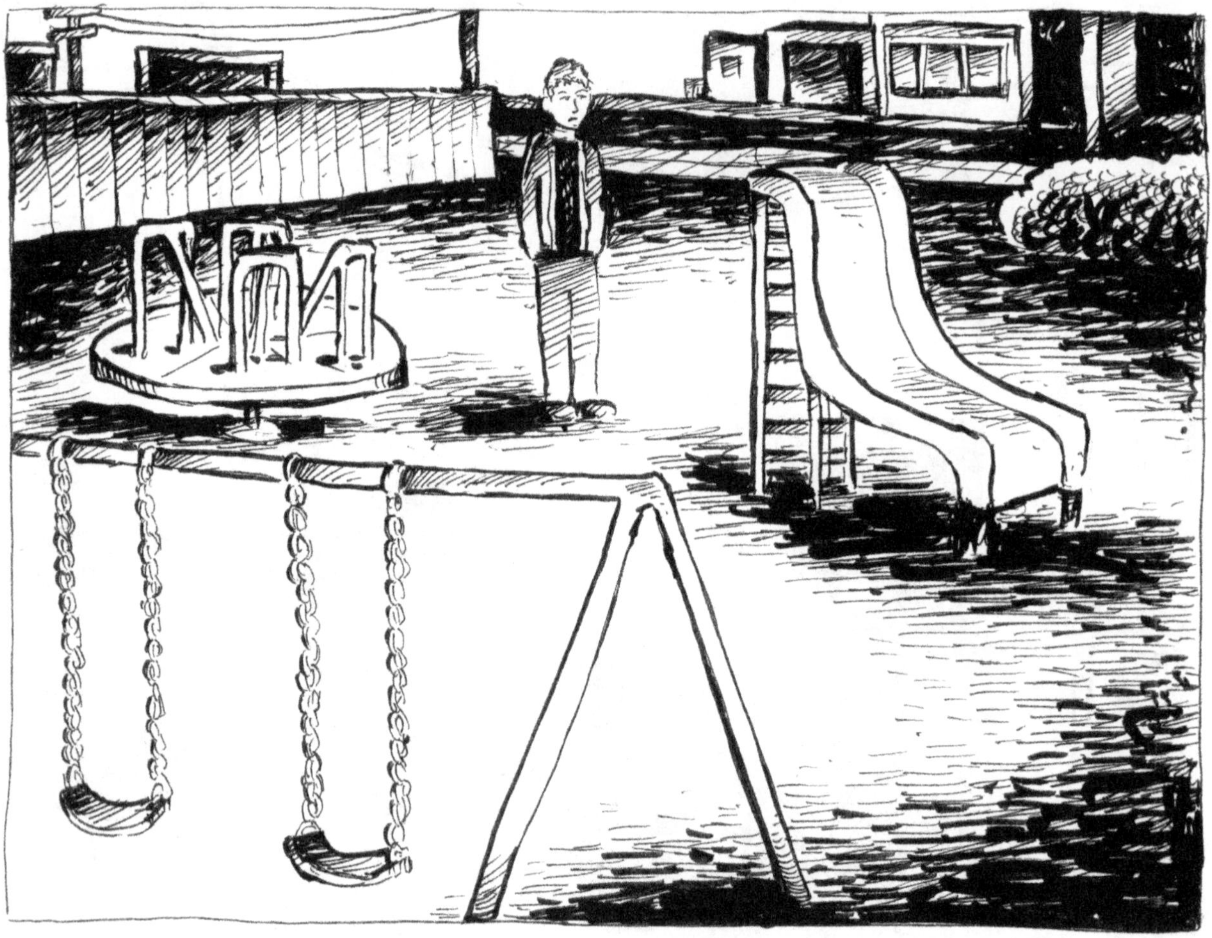

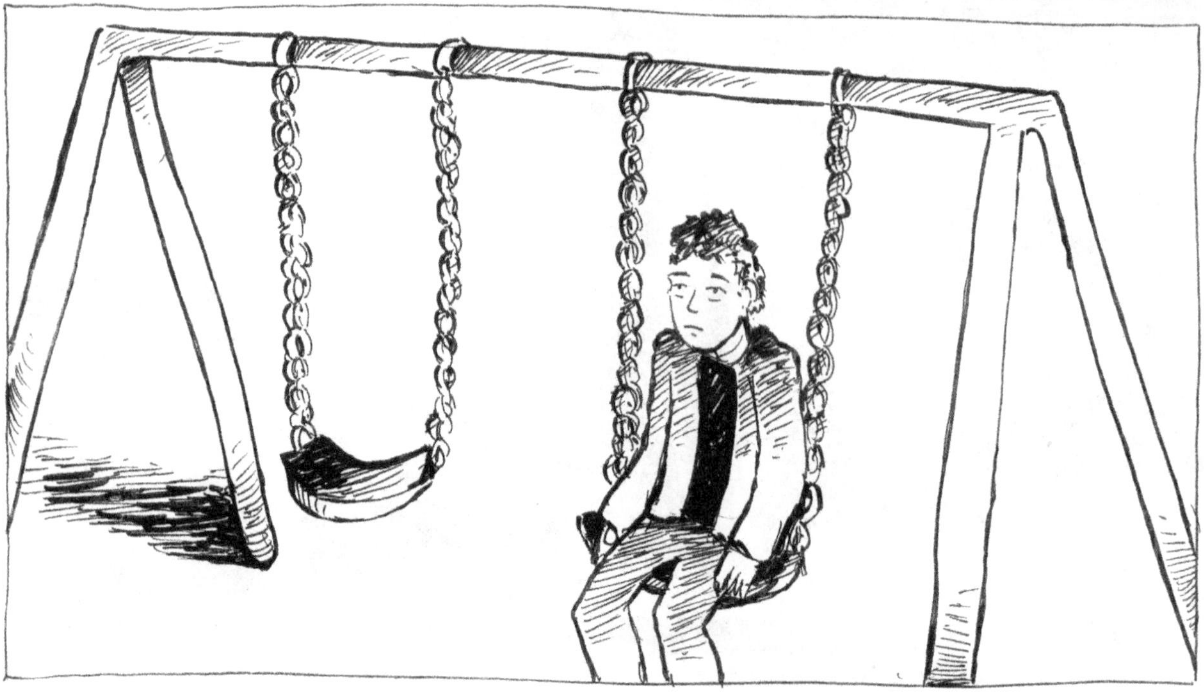

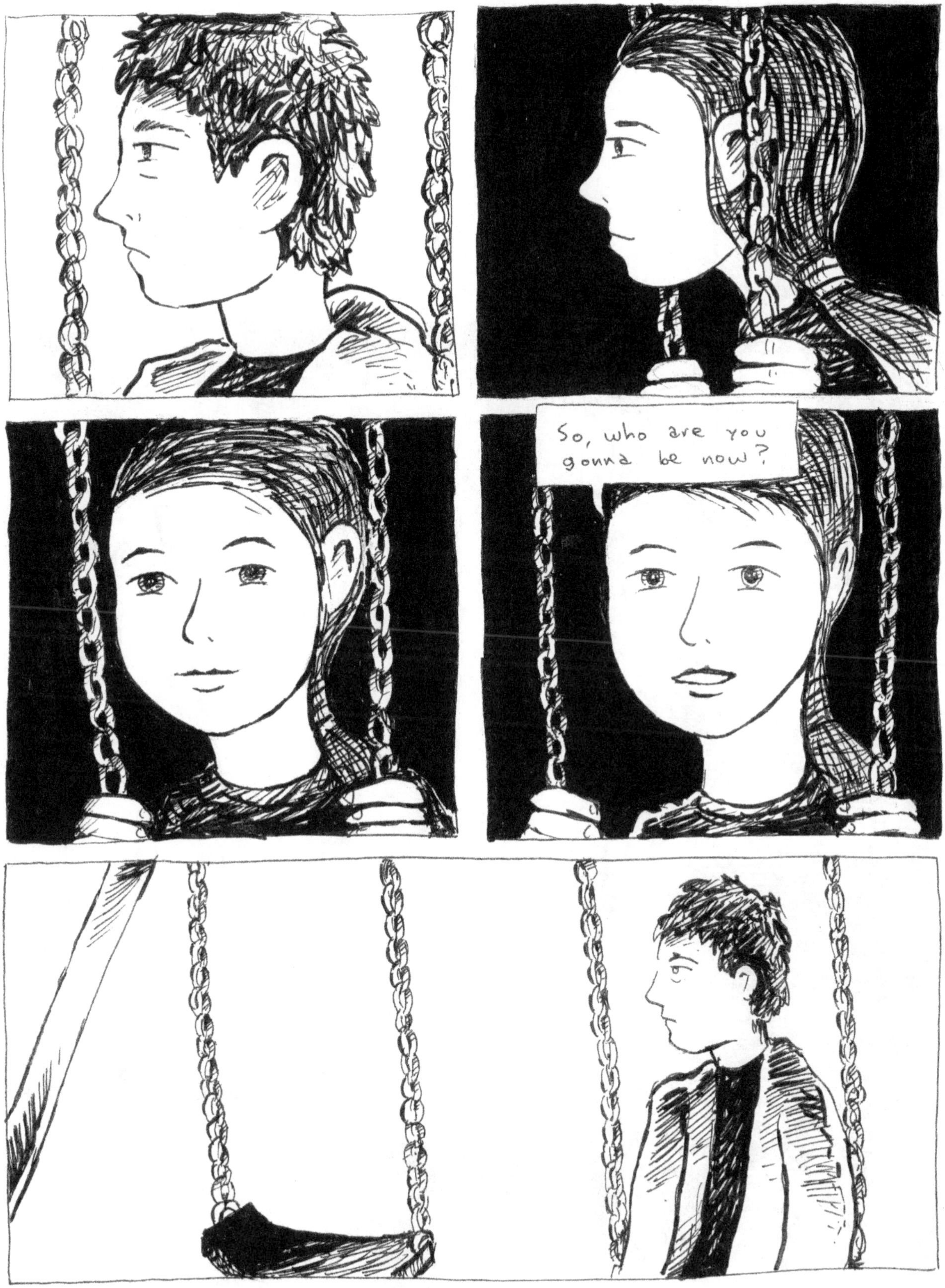
So, who are you gonna be now?

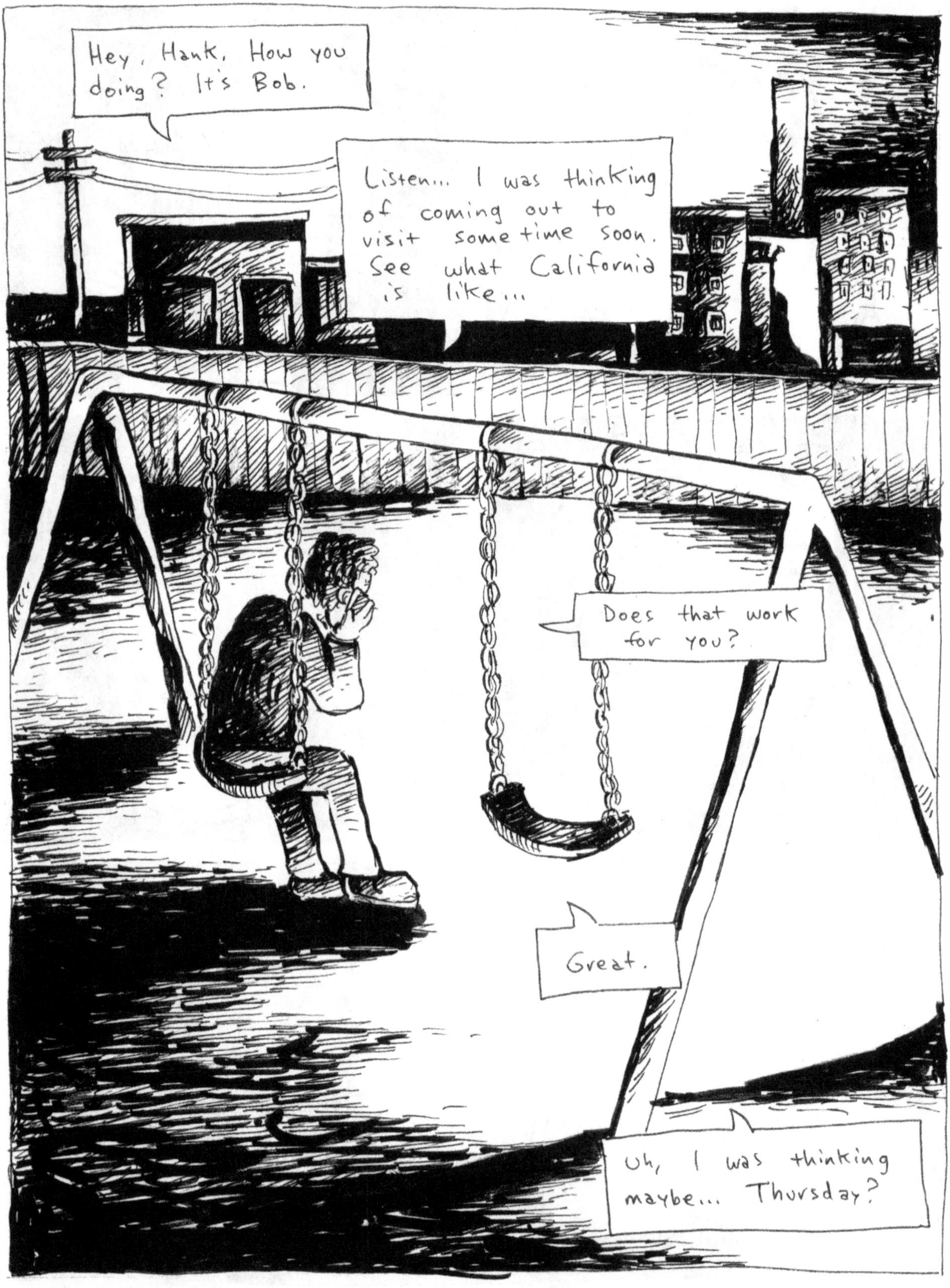
Hey, Hank, How you doing? It's Bob.
Listen... I was thinking of coming out to visit some time soon. See what California is like...
Does that work for you?
Great.
Uh, I was thinking maybe... Thursday?

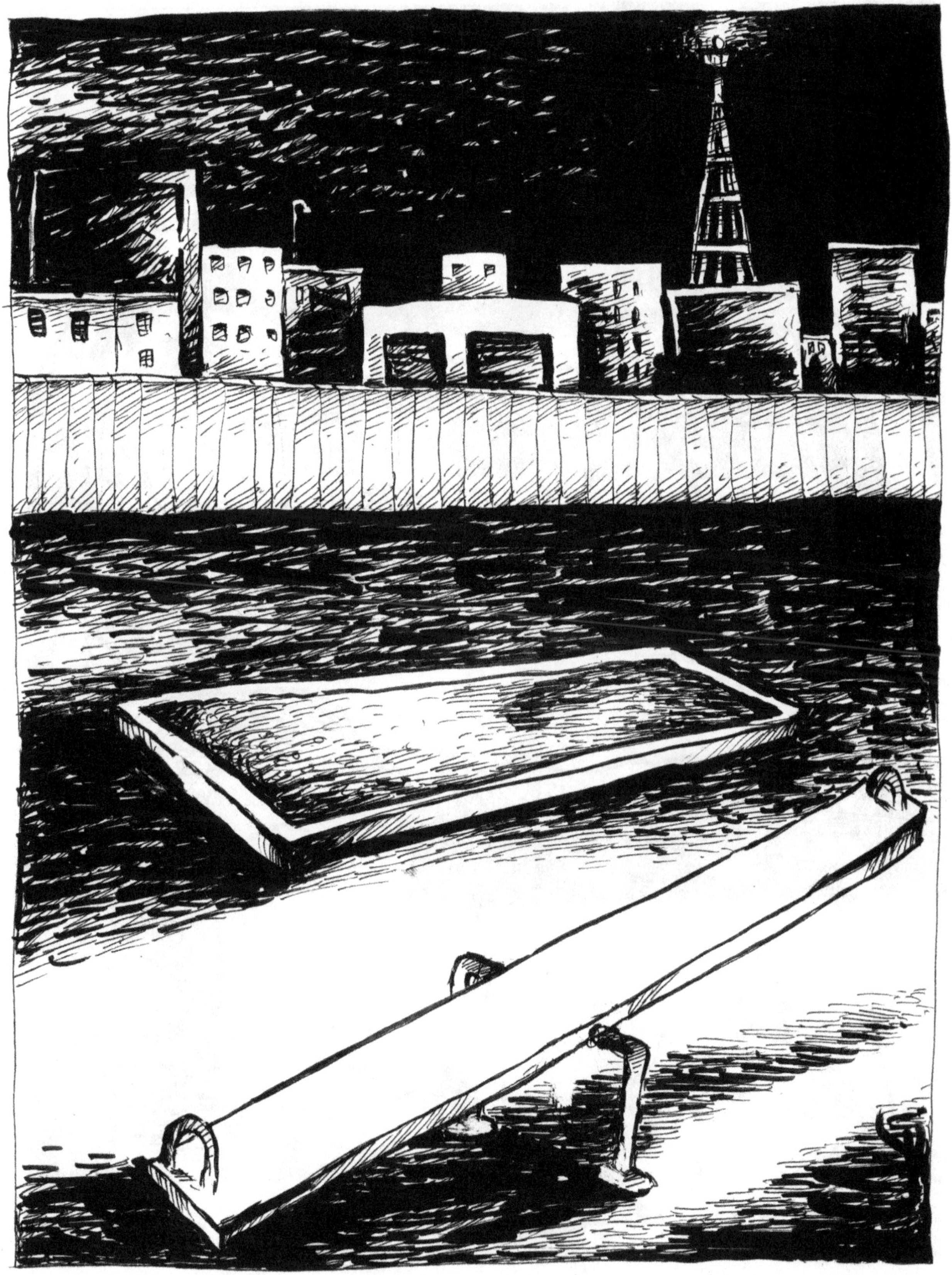

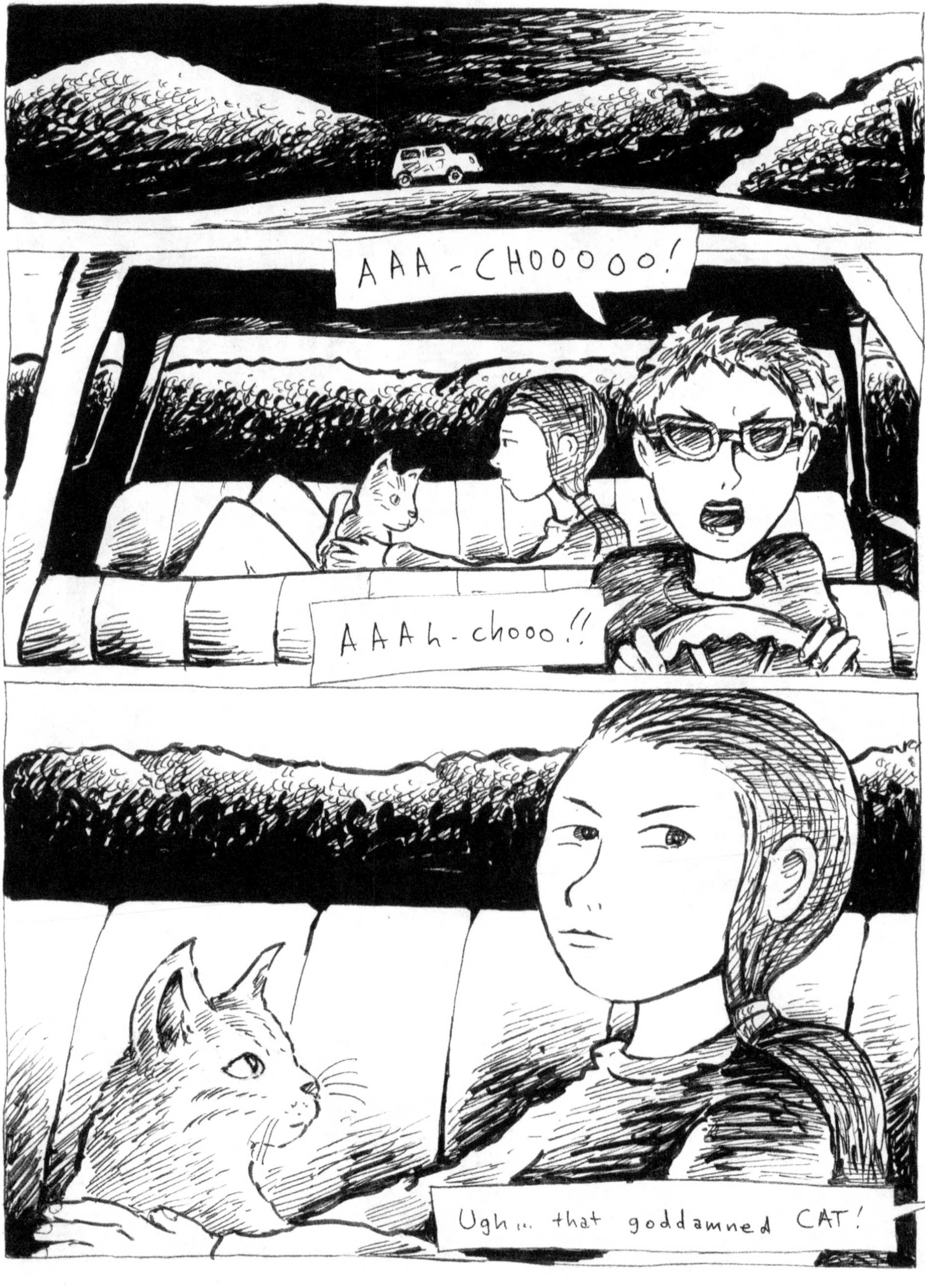
AAA-CHOOOOO!
AAAh-chooo!!
Ugh... that goddamned CAT!

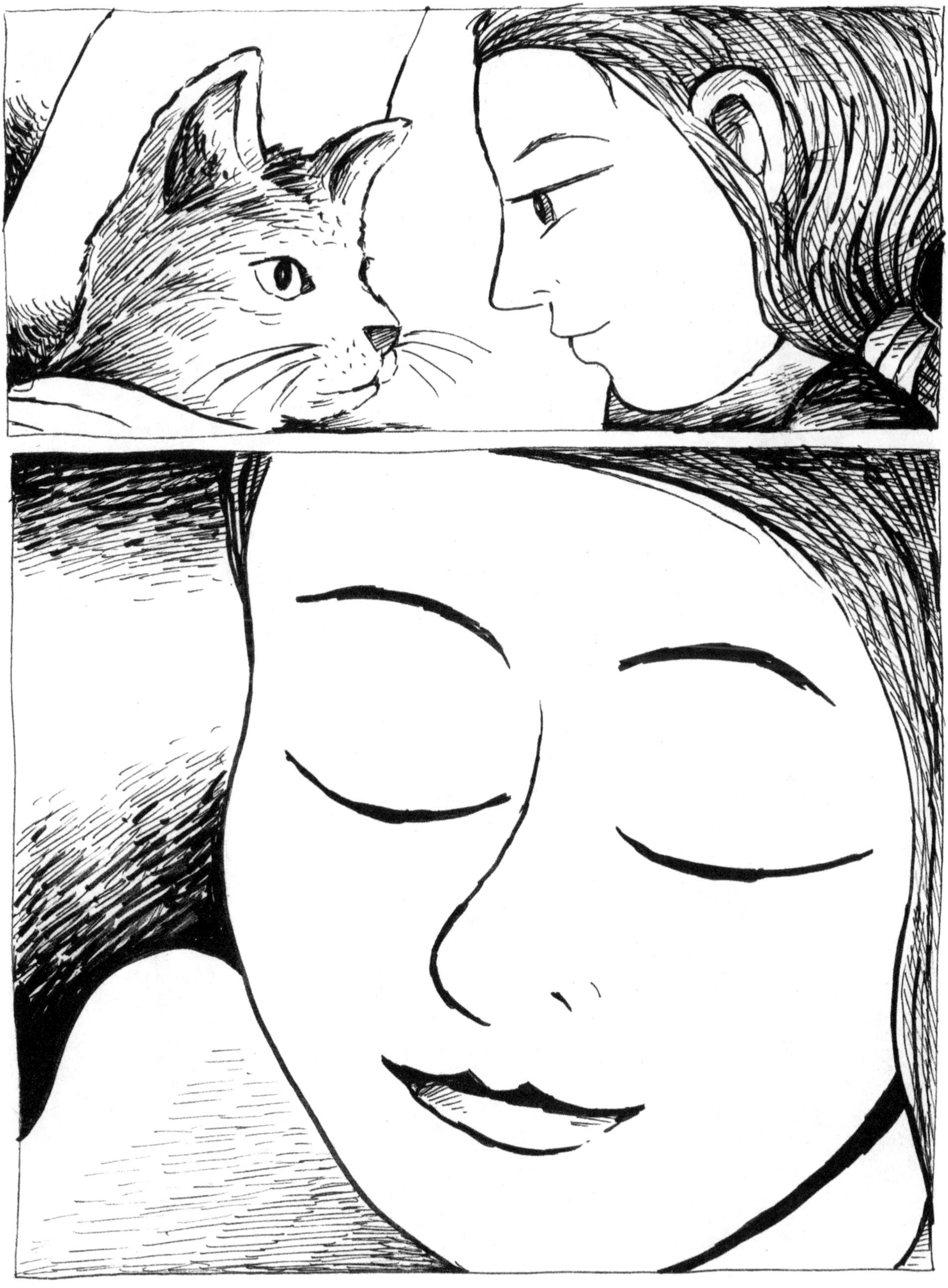

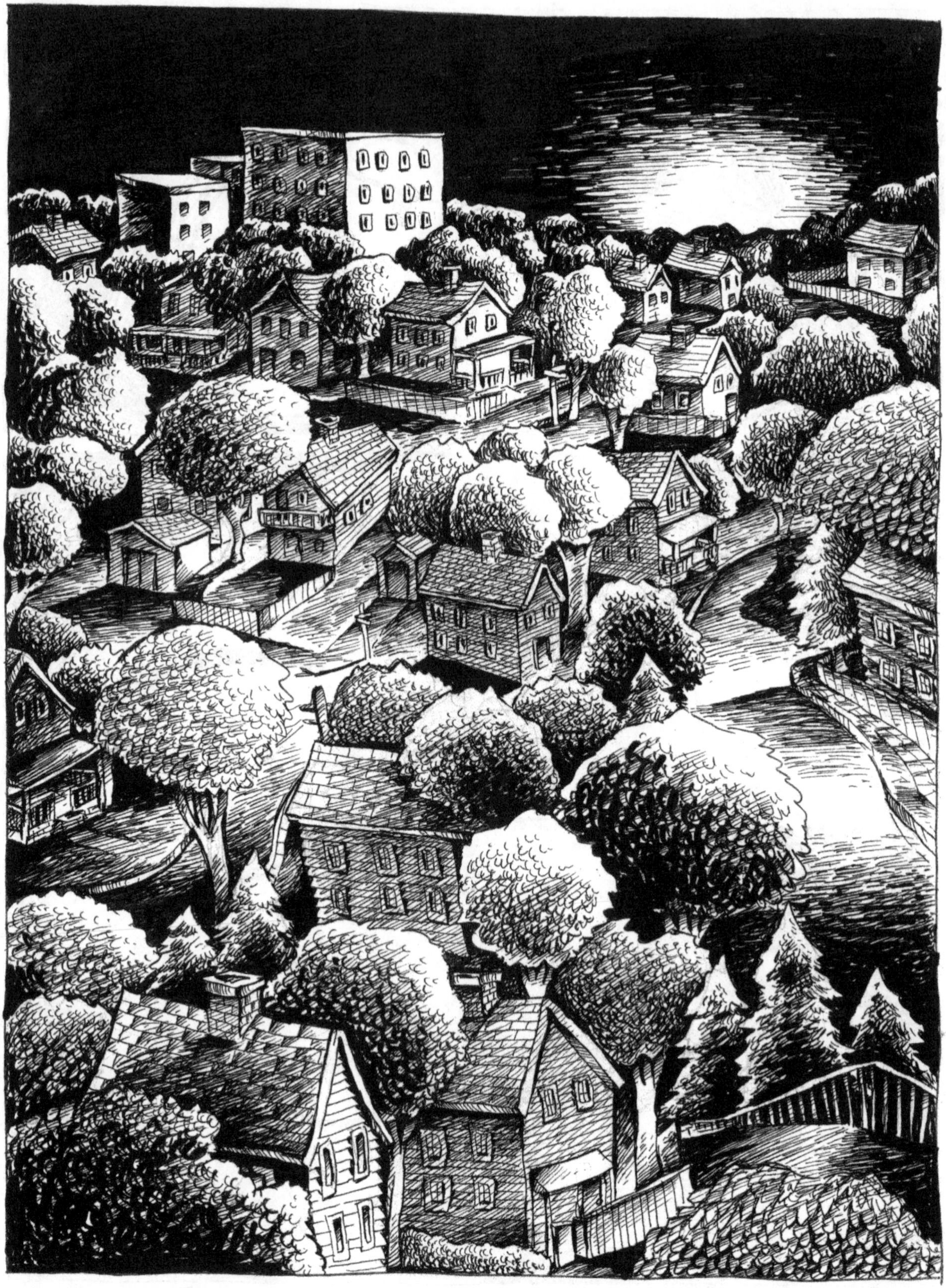

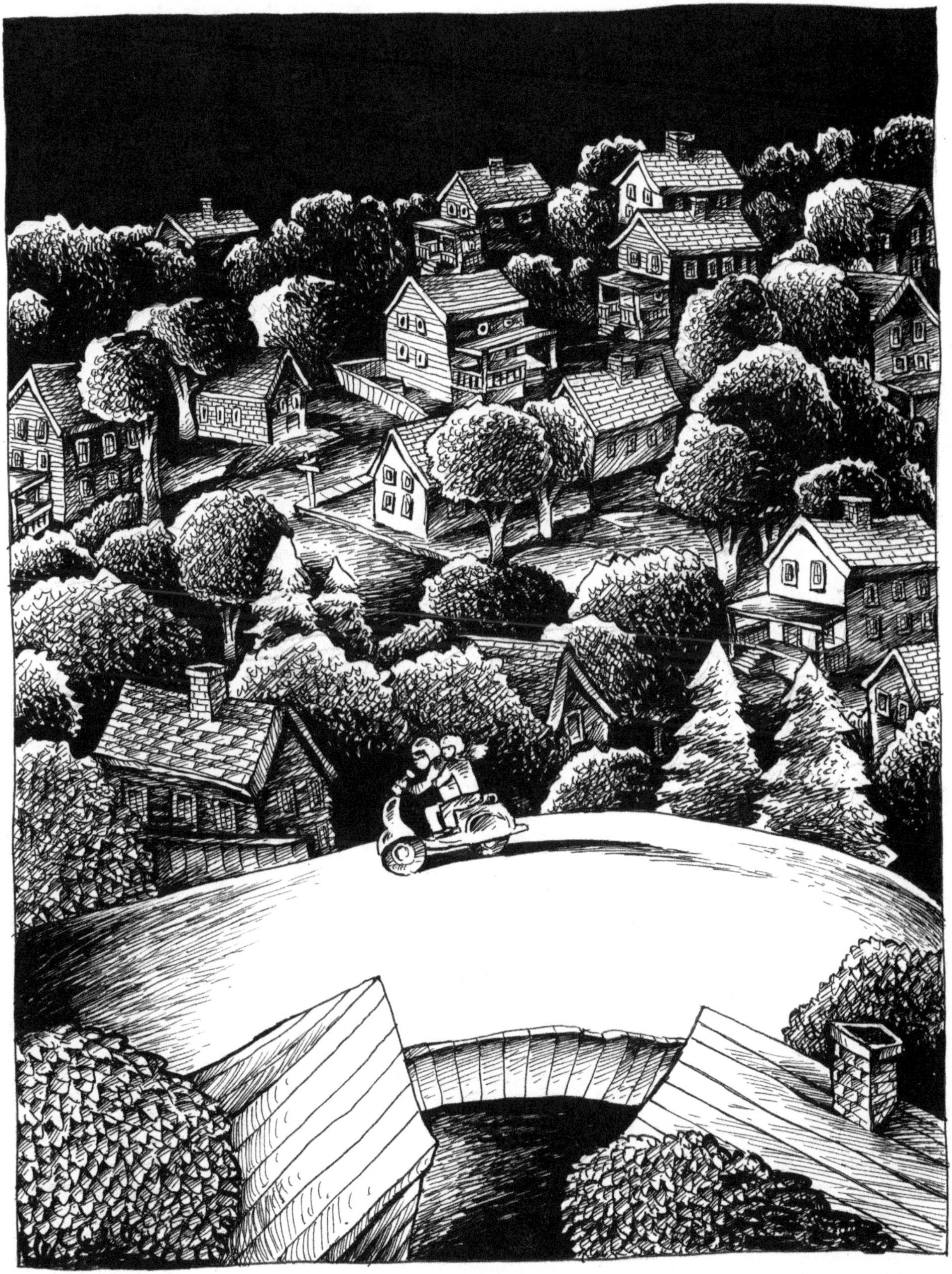

CPSIA information can be obtained
at www.ICGtesting.com
Printed in the USA
JSHW020657070819
1049JS00002BA/2

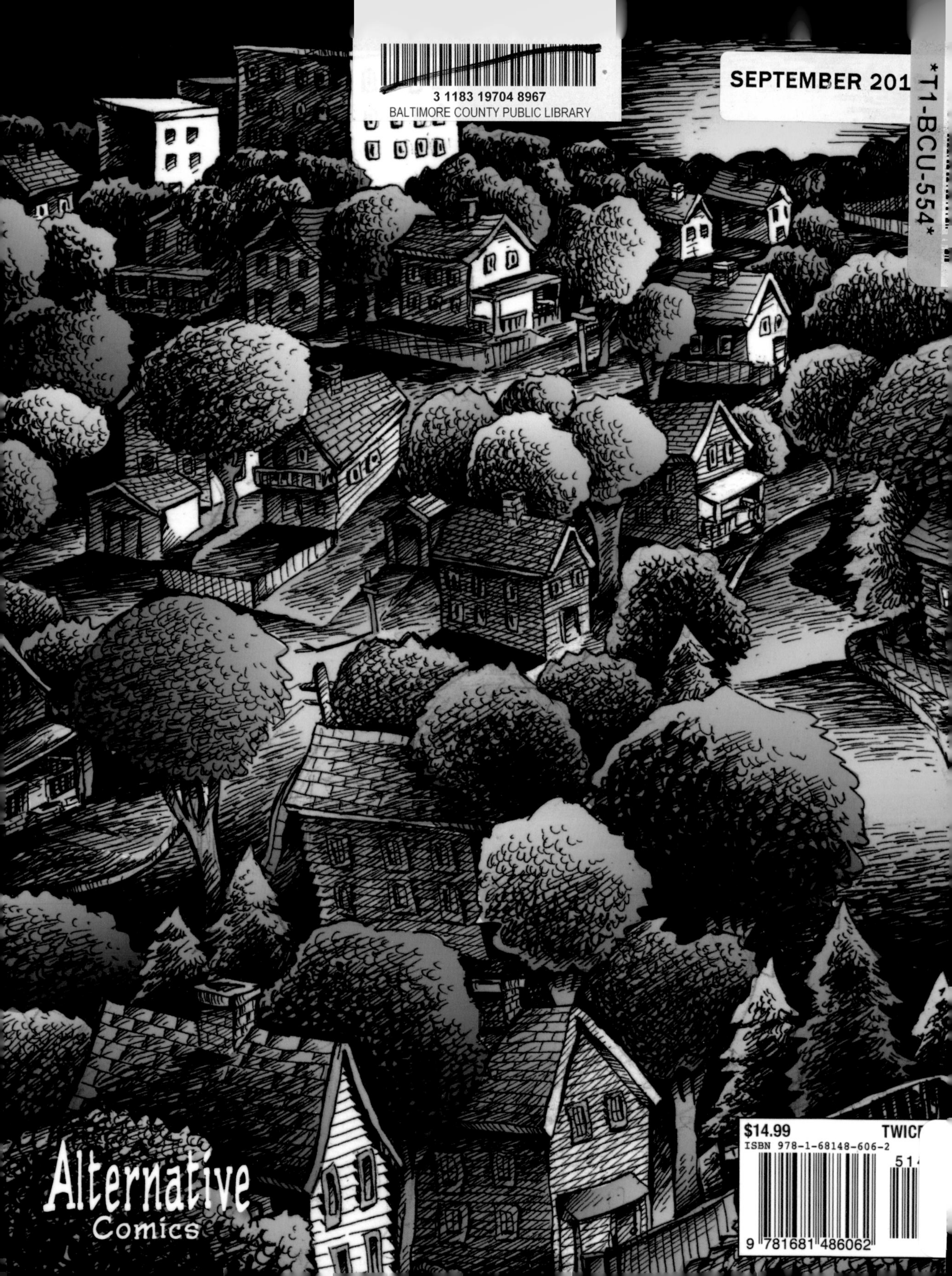

$14.99 TWICf
ISBN 978-1-68148-606-2
51
9 781681 486062

Alternative
Comics